Ruby Programming

JONES AND BARTLETT SERIES IN BIOMEDICAL INFORMATICS
SERIES EDITOR JULES J. BERMAN

Biomedical Informatics: A Data User's Guide
(2007, ISBN 0-7637-4135-3)
Jules J. Berman

Perl Programming for Medicine and Biology
(2007, ISBN 0-7637-4333-X)
Jules J. Berman

Ruby Programming for Medicine and Biology
(2008, ISBN 0-7637-5090-5)
Jules J. Berman

JONES AND BARTLETT SERIES IN BIOMEDICAL INFORMATICS
SERIES EDITOR JULES J. BERMAN

Ruby Programming
for Medicine and Biology ·

Jules J. Berman

JONES AND BARTLETT PUBLISHERS

Sudbury, Massachusetts

BOSTON   TORONTO   LONDON   SINGAPORE

World Headquarters

Jones and Bartlett Publishers	Jones and Bartlett Publishers	Jones and Bartlett Publishers
40 Tall Pine Drive	Canada	International
Sudbury, MA 01776	6339 Ormindale Way	Barb House, Barb Mews
978-443-5000	Mississauga, Ontario L5V 1J2	London W6 7PA
info@jbpub.com	CANADA	UK
www.jbpub.com		

Jones and Bartlett's books and products are available through most bookstores and online book-sellers. To contact Jones and Bartlett Publishers directly, call 800-832-0034, fax 978-443-8000, or visit our website, www.jbpub.com.

> Substantial discounts on bulk quantities of Jones and Bartlett's publications are available to corporations, professional associations, and other qualified organizations. For details and specific discount information, contact the special sales department at Jones and Bartlett via the above contact information or send an email to specialsales@jbpub.com.

Nota Bene. This manuscript is a work of literature and has no purpose other than as a literary work. The Ruby scripts in this book are provided "as is," without warranty of any kind, express or implied, including but not limited to the warranties of merchantability, fitness for a particular purpose, and noninfringement. In no event shall the author or copyright holder be liable for any claim, damages, or other liability, whether in an action of contract, tort or otherwise, arising from, out of, or in connection with the software or the use or other dealings in the software. The Ruby scripts in this book were written by Jules J. Berman and are distributed under the GNU General Public License (http://www.gnu.org/copyleft/gpl.html).

Histologic photomicrographs were prepared by G. William Moore, MD, and are in the public domain. The photomicrographs were selected from glass slides available in a public slide collection, and the patients from whom the tissues were taken are anonymous.

Laboratory Digital Imaging Project (LDIP) Common Data Elements and the LDIP schema are copyrighted property of the Association for Pathology Informatics and are available for no-cost public use under the terms of the Association for Pathology Informatics LDIP Charter (www.ldip.org).

Production Credits

Executive Editor: Cathleen Sether	Manufacturing Buyer: Therese Connell
Acquisitions Editor: Shoshanna Grossman	Composition: Arlene Apone
Managing Editor: Dean W. DeChambeau	Cover Design: Anne Spencer
Associate Editor: Molly Steinbach	Cover Image: © Andrey Stratilatov/ShutterStock, Inc.
Senior Production Editor: Louis C. Bruno, Jr.	Printing and Binding: Malloy, Inc.
Production Assistant: Leah Corrigan	Cover Printing: Malloy, Inc.
Senior Marketing Manager: Andrea DeFronzo	

Library of Congress Cataloging-in-Publication Data
Berman, Jules J.
  Ruby programming for medicine and biology / Jules J. Berman. — 1st ed.
     p. ; cm.
  Includes bibliographical references and index.
  ISBN-13: 978-0-7637-5090-9 (alk. paper)
  1. Medicine—Data processing. 2. Biology—Data processing. 3. Ruby (Computer program language) I. Title.
  [DNLM: 1. Medical Informatics. 2. Programming Languages. 3. Computational Biology. W 26.55.S6 B516r 2008]
  R858.B475 2008
  610.285—dc22   2007016383
6048

Printed in the United States of America
11 10 09 08 07   10 9 8 7 6 5 4 3 2 1

Contents

Preface

0.1. BACKGROUND

Most people think of programming as an endeavor undertaken by computer-oriented engineers who know everything that there is to know about computers and who write enormous software applications that contain thousands of lines of inscrutable code. It does not need to be that way.

Today, biologists, healthcare professionals, and students can write their own software without acquiring a deep knowledge of computers. Many of us write short programs for our own use, to solve some particular computational task. More often than not, our programs have fewer than a dozen lines of code. The code lines are typically short and are composed of recognizable words. The syntax (the grammar of the programming language) and the commands (the methods available to the language) are not difficult to learn.

The purpose of this book is to demonstrate that most of the computational work in biology and medicine can be described as a collection of common tasks, and these tasks can be accomplished with short and simple Ruby scripts.

This book has particular appeal to nonprogrammers who want to quickly acquire enough self-reliance to write simple, short programs that will help them function in their professional environment. This book is also useful to professional programmers who are curious about Ruby and who must understand the computational needs of co-workers and clients who work in the field of biomedicine.

0.2. CHOOSING A PROGRAMMING LANGUAGE

> "Can't you feel the peace and contentment in this block of code? Ruby is the language Buddha would have programmed in."—comment found on the REXML home page (1).

If you are a student, researcher, or healthcare professional, your programming needs will be different than those of full-time programmers and software applications developers. You need a programming language with the following features (List 0.2.1):

LIST 0.2.1. QUALITIES OF AN IDEAL BIOMEDICAL PROGRAMMING LANGUAGE

Free

Open source

Easy to download from the Internet and install

Easy to learn

Easy to read

Capable of fulfilling every computational task within the programmer's area of interest

Fast

Active user community

Many available libraries that expand the functionality of the language

Language supports a world view that is compatible with modern biological thinking

Three programming languages actually meet all of these requirements: Perl, Python, and Ruby. In 2007, my book, *Perl Programming for Medicine and Biology*, was published. In the Preface, I wrote that Perl, among all other languages, was the most popular language among biomedical informaticians. I still believe that Perl is a fine programming language for biologists and healthcare professionals. I have come to believe, however, that Ruby provides greater functionality than either Perl or Python (see the Epilogue).

Ruby is an appealing language for programmers and nonprogrammers. Programmers may find that Ruby lets them write well-designed object-oriented software applications in less time, with less code, and with less complexity than any other programming language. Nonprogrammers looking for the best language to learn would do well to choose Ruby.

0.3. IS RUBY LIKELY TO GROW IN IMPORTANCE OVER THE NEXT FEW YEARS?

Nobody prefers to work in obscurity. Choosing a programming language requires a considerable commitment of time and effort, and wise programmers will be wary of "fad" languages.

Today there are about 6900 spoken languages, and there may be just as many computer programming languages. An estimate of the number of programming languages varies, ranging from 2500 (Bill Kinnersley of the University of Kansas) to 8500 (Diarmuid Piggott) (2). Using the conservative estimate (2500), the world has received one programming language each week since the invention of Fortran (2).

Among all of these languages, what makes Ruby special? Ruby was created in 1995 by Yukihiro Matsumoto (known as "Matz" to his devotees). Since then, it has achieved enormous popularity in its country of origin (Japan) and throughout the world. Class libraries built into the standard Ruby distribution provide the same functionality (usually with the same names) as the standard Perl modules and the standard Python library. This means that Perl programmers and Python programmers can easily migrate to Ruby.

A new (and hopefully permanent) trend in data management involves the use of metadata that encapsulates data items with descriptors in a format that can be understood by any programming language. The most general and most important metadata model is RDF (Resource Description Framework). Ruby provides methods for manipulating RDF. Among scripting languages, YAML (Yet Another Metadata Language) has emerged as a convenient way of marshaling data structures (that is, storing the data held in data objects to an external plain-text file). YAML data structures are now used by several scripting languages (including Perl, Python, and Ruby), and this means that data objects can be easily shared by scripts written in any of these languages.

In addition to classes and modules packed in the standard Ruby distribution, Ruby programmers have access to Ruby libraries located throughout the world through RubyGem, a system for downloading and installing Ruby software located on remote servers. RubyForge is a repository and development resource for groups of programmers who collaborate on new Ruby libraries. These new libraries are freely available to the entire Ruby community.

The most successful Ruby project has been Ruby on Rails, a framework for Web application development in Ruby. It is commonly held that Ruby on Rails is responsible for the emerging popularity of the Ruby language in Europe and the United States.

In the biomedical arena, the BioRuby project closely emulates the BioPerl and BioPython projects, which provide a variety of bioinformatics-related methods and tie-ins to large genomic databases.

Today, the programming language that you use does not need to be the same as the language used by your collaborators. If you choose Ruby, you will be able to import and export RDF and YAML data, share images, create client and server Internet scripts, access databases, encapsulate requests for web services in SOAP messages, write e-mail scripts, and create clever Web applications, and your collaborators may be using Perl or Python. The long-anticipated Parrot virtual machine is being designed to run source code written in either Python, Perl, or Ruby.

In the past, your choice of programming language or operating system restricted the kinds of hardware you used and limited your opportunities for sharing data and software. Those days are ending. If you are a biologist or a health care worker who is programming for your own professional needs, you should choose the language that you most enjoy.

0.4. THE COMMON COMPUTATIONAL TASKS OF BIOLOGY AND MEDICINE

In the past few decades, biology and medicine have become data-intensive fields. In the course of normal operations, large medical organizations collect terabytes of data every week. Researchers and laboratory personnel, using high-throughput techniques (for example, gene expression arrays, flow cytometry, tissue microarrays, multiplex diagnostic tests, image analysis, Doppler scanning), create vast datasets. Everyone in the biomedical field has access to large public datasets (see the Appendix).

In the past, computational tasks in biology and medicine really came down to statistical analysis of a rather modest set of measurements. Today, data analysis is much more difficult than ever before and often requires advanced methodologies (cluster analysis, Monte Carlo modeling, neural networks, advanced digital signal processing techniques). However daunting these technologies may seem, problems related to data analysis are dwarfed by problems related to data acquisition and data organization. Health care and health care research today involves merging data held in multiple institutions. Sometimes these data merges must be real-time events, reflecting momentary fluctuations of information occurring in many different locations. Often the data are collected, described, and packaged differently in different institutions, and these data must somehow be harmonized. Sometimes, completely different types of datasets (so-called heterogeneous data) must be linked and compared.

It seems hopeless at first, but these problems can be classified as tractable generic tasks (List 0.4.1).

LIST 0.4.1. THE COMMON COMPUTATIONAL TASKS IN BIOLOGY AND MEDICINE

- Extracting subsets of data from large biomedical databases (including laboratory information systems and hospital information systems)—Chapter 10
- Creating and organizing new database objects—Chapters 6, 18, and 19
- Analyzing the data contained in biomedical databases using a wide variety of statistical and computational strategies—Chapters 10 and 13
- Indexing large texts and datasets—Chapter 9
- Autocoding large texts and datasets—Chapter 12
- Transforming large datasets into standard formats or other specified formats that permit data to be easily shared —Chapter 8
- Merging heterogeneous data into useful datasets—Chapters 12 and 18
- De-identifying (scrubbing) large datasets that contain confidential data—Chapter 11
- Distributing data and computational methods through the Internet—Chapters 15 and 16
- Specifying data (describing data in a logical manner that facilitates data sharing)— Chapters 18 and 19

0.5. HOW TO READ THIS BOOK

The first two chapters of the book serve as an introduction to Ruby programming. In Chapter 1, you will learn the general syntax of Ruby scripts. In Chapter 2, you will learn something about the logic of object-oriented Ruby programming. For most readers, Chapters 1 and 2 will be the most difficult chapters because they ask the reader to synthesize a cognitive appreciation for object oriented programming using an unfamiliar syntax. Readers cannot be expected to absorb all of the principles of object-oriented programming in a single reading. You can read chapters 1 and 2 quickly to get a general idea of Ruby principles and syntax. Later chapters provide simple examples of Ruby scripts. You can always return to Chapters 1 and 2 to review basic object/method operations.

Chapters 3 to 19 describe the common computational tasks in biology and medicine and provide solutions in Ruby. The lesson conveyed in these chapters is that before any problem can be solved, the programmer must achieve a deep understanding of the problem. From that understanding, the programmer can abstract a general solution. The actual programming is, in every instance, the easiest part of the puzzle (if you use Ruby).

Chapter 20 is a summation of lessons learned, with advice on writing your own Ruby class libraries and scripts. This chapter is an "opinion piece," and you will no doubt develop your own unique approach to Ruby programming.

Every Ruby programmer has a story to tell describing his or her personal path to Ruby. Chapter 21 relates my own professional odyssey. After many years as a cancer researcher and pathologist, I have finally found Ruby. My expectation is that Ruby will allow me to organize, specify, and make sense of large tumor-related datasets. I hope that some of the experiences in my career will resonate with students, researchers, and healthcare professionals.

The Reference section contains every citation in the book. Along with each citation is a comment explaining the relevance of each citation to biomedicine. Many of the references link to useful Web resources (documents or software). These references provide a guide to some of the most important literature in biomedical informatics.

An extensive Glossary lists over 260 terms related to Ruby and to computational biomedicine. Most of the Ruby methods found in the text are explained in detail. In many cases, a Ruby snippet, appended to its Glossary entry, demonstrates the method. If you read the chapters that precede the Glossary, you will acquire sufficient Ruby programming skill to benefit from the Glossary. The Glossary provides sufficiently detailed descriptions of methods, syntax, and logic to permit you to create your own Ruby scripts. The Glossary is written in an informal style intended to sustain a reader's interest, and it can be read as a stand-alone text. I suspect that some readers, particularly experienced programmers, will dispense with the body of this book and rely almost exclusively on the Glossary to provide all of their Ruby instruction. The body of the book can be used to supplement the Glossary with analyses of biomedical use cases. Readers are advised to consult the Glossary before consulting the Index. The Glossary provides succinct explanations of Ruby terms and concepts, whereas the Index simply points to sections of text wherein the terms are encountered.

The Appendix lists many free, open-source software utilities that complement the text. The Appendix entries are restricted to products that are mature, tested, and available.

0.5.1. Typographic conventions

Many Ruby methods are common English words. To reduce confusion, method names, object names, and Ruby code appear in Courier typeface. Regular text appears in New Times Roman. Example:

"You can determine the methods available to class objects with the `method` method."

The Ruby interactive interface, irb, evaluates single lines of Ruby code and produces an enumerated prompt, as shown.

```
irb(main):001:0> "hello world"
=> "hello world"
```

Throughout the book, to save space and improve readability, the irb prompt is shortened and both input expression and return value are placed on the same line.

```
irb>"hello world" => "hello world"
```

0.6. ACKNOWLEDGMENTS

Special thanks are given to G. William Moore, MD, PhD, who has contributed hundreds of articles in the field of computational biology and pathology and who graciously served as primary reviewer for this book. The staff members at Jones and Bartlett Publishers have been extremely helpful and supportive. The credit for producing this book from draft to final form belongs to my editor, Shoshanna Grossman; associate editor, Molly Steinbach; and production editor, Lou Bruno. I am grateful to my parents, who encouraged my educational pursuits. I wish to thank my wife and my daughters, who allowed me to choose, at some personal and professional cost, a writer's life.

Author Biography

Jules Berman, PhD, MD, is a pathologist with an eclectic technical background that includes a bachelor's degree in mathematics from MIT. He was chief of Anatomic Pathology at the Baltimore Veterans Administration Medical Center before becoming Program Director for Pathology Informatics in the Cancer Diagnosis Program of the U.S. National Cancer Institute (1998–2005). He is a past President of the Association for Pathology Informatics (2006). He has first-authored more than 100 scientific articles. His two previously published books are *Biomedical Informatics* (2007) and *Perl Programming for Medicine and Biology* (2007), both published by Jones and Bartlett Publishers, Inc. Dr. Berman is currently a freelance author.

Overview of the Ruby Language (Level 1)

1.1. BACKGROUND

Ruby is a pure object-oriented language. Everything in Ruby is an object. Ruby knows the type of every object (for example, Array, Numeric, String, and Class). Classes are special objects because they contain data and methods and can create unique instances of themselves (class object instances). Ruby classes can represent the natural world (living things, diseases, and physiologic processes) and conform to the logical construction of modern data models (such as Resource Description Framework) (List 1.1.1). Ruby is so easy to learn that healthcare workers and biomedical researchers can do their own Ruby programming and still find time to fulfill their many professional obligations. You will probably find that Ruby programming saves you time and increases your work productivity.

Ruby is a language that accommodates varying levels of user sophistication. In a few hours, you can learn to program simple and useful Ruby scripts. If you have sufficient fervor, you can devote your life to pursuing a state of Ruby enlightenment. I have arbitrarily assigned seven levels of Ruby programming (List 1.1.2).

Here we show that most common biomedical computational tasks can be accomplished using only level 1 and level 2 Ruby skills. No scripts higher than level 4 appear in this book.

1.2. A QUICK PEEK AT RUBY

Before we describe Ruby and even before we tell you how your can download and install Ruby on your own computer, let us look at a few lines of Ruby code. Throughout this book, we execute our Ruby scripts

LIST 1.1.1. THE BASIC APPROACH TO OBJECT-ORIENTED PROGRAMMING

A script written in an object-oriented language has access to all of the methods and associated data that belong to any of the classes that are built into the language. New classes can also be created by the programmer and used in her scripts.

An object of a class is created by listing the name of a class and invoking the new method on the class. After an object is created, it has access to the instance methods contained in the class as well as the instance methods contained in the ancestors of the class.

Writing a script in an object-oriented language typically involves creating class objects and writing a succession of statements that yield a desired output. The basic syntax of a Ruby statement is as follows:

```
<receiving object>.<sending method>(<arguments>){block}
```

LIST 1.1.2. THE DIFFERENT LEVELS OF RUBY PROGRAMMING

Level 1. Scripts use the built-in Ruby data structures, iterators, and classes.

Level 2. Level 1 plus scripts use extensions that come with the standard Ruby installation, including the Standard Libraries and Ruby GEMS. Level 2 programming makes use of Reflection techniques.

Level 3. Level 2 plus users create their own class libraries. Some of your classes have Mixins, and your Mixins include modules that you have written. Level 3 programmers use RDoc to prepare well-documented class libraries.

Level 4. Level 3 plus creating web applications with Ruby on Rails, CGI, or Network protocols.

Level 5. Level 4 plus using advanced class-oriented techniques such as delegation, and polymorphism, developing Graphic User Interfaces and using disciplined programming techniques such as error trapping and unit testing.

Level 6. Level 5 plus extending and embedding Ruby (in other programming languages).

Level 7. Level 6 plus preparing commercial-grade Ruby software applications.

at the DOS prompt (if your computer uses the Windows operating system) or through the shell command line (if using Linux or Unix). Command-line scripts are absolutely the simplest way of programming and avoid the need of writing graphic user interfaces.

Figure 1-1 is a screen-captured image from a short session with irb, the interactive Ruby (irb) interface. In Ruby, every line of code yields a value, and the irb interface permits you to try out your Ruby code line by line as you prepare your scripts. This is an excellent way of testing newly encountered methods (and Ruby has many methods).

After Ruby is installed in your computer, you can invoke the irb utility from the command prompt. When you type irb followed by the return key, you are provided with a new prompt listing the line number in the irb session.

Type in "Hello World".

The irb utility evaluates the string object as "Hello World".

Everything in Ruby is a member of a class. Ruby knows the class assignment of every class object, and the name of the class can be called by sending the "class" method to the object. In Ruby, you send a method to an object by placing a dot after the object followed by the method.

"Hello World".class

This yields String, the name of the class for which "Hello World" is an instance.

This tells you that "Hello World" is an object of class String and can use any of the methods that belong to the String class or to any ancestor class of the String class. Later here, we see how you can find all of the methods available to an object.

```
C:\>irb
irb(main):001:0> "Hello World"
=> "Hello World"
irb(main):002:0> "Hello World".class
=> String
irb(main):003:0> "Hello World".downcase
=> "hello world"
irb(main):004:0> "Hello World".length
=> 11
irb(main):005:0> "Hello World".split
=> ["Hello", "World"]
irb(main):006:0> exit
```

Figure 1-1 A few lines of evaluated Ruby code from the irb **(interactive Ruby) tool.**

One of the built-in methods of the `String` class is `downcase`, which converts uppercase characters to their lowercase equivalents.

`"Hello World".downcase`

This yields `"hello world"`

Another `String` method is `length`, which yields the number of characters in a `String` object.

`"Hello World".length`

This yields `11`.

The last method shown in Figure 1-1 is `split`, which breaks a string into parts and stores the parts in an `Array` object. An array is an ordered list.

`"Hello World".split`

This yields `["Hello", "World"]`

The `split` method will split a string at a specified delimiter. The delimiter can be any pattern. We will learn about patterns later. If no pattern is provided, the split function will split on the space character.

The resulting array (in this case, `["Hello", "World"]`) is an object that can receive any of the `Array` class object methods.

1.3. GETTING SCREEN INPUT

Your Ruby script can retrieve a line of input using the `gets` method. The `gets` method of class IO (Input/Output) reads a line of keyboarded text from the computer screen (List 1.3.1).

LIST 1.3.1. RUBY SCRIPT `GETINPUT.RB` RETRIEVES A LINE OF KEYBOARDED TEXT

```
#!/usr/bin/ruby
puts "Enter anything and press the return key"
input = STDIN.gets.chomp!
puts "You just entered \"#{input}\""
exit
```

The script is launched by invoking the script name from the prompt line.

```
C:\ftp\rb>ruby getinput.rb
```

A line of text appears on your computer screen.

```
Enter anything and press the return-key
```

You enter some text (hello world in this example) and press the return key.

```
hello world
```

Ruby collects your input and returns it as a quotation within a sentence.

```
You just entered "hello world"
```

The most important script line is as follows:

```
input = STDIN.gets.chomp!
```

This line tells Ruby to wait until a line of text is entered in the standard input. The standard input is your computer monitor, and the name Ruby uses for this input device is STDIN.

The last character key you entered was the return key. The return key sends your entered text followed by a newline character to the standard input. It is customary to remove the newline character from the input line with class String's chomp! command. The chomp! command removes the newline character (or any designated line separator) if it is present at the end of a line and returns the shortened line. In Ruby, methods sent to an object, such as get and chomp!, can be concatenated.

1.4. A SIMPLE RUBY SCRIPT

Our second Ruby script computes six generations of growth from a colony of 1000 cells that increases its size by 5% per generation (List 1.4.1).

LIST 1.4.1. RUBY SCRIPT GROW.RB SIMULATES SIX GENERATIONS OF BACTERIAL GROWTH

```
#!/usr/local/bin/ruby
principle = 1000
(1..6).each do
    |x|
    principle = principle*(1.05)
    print(x, " ", principle, "\n")
end
exit
```

The output of `grow.rb` is a list of values, with each element displayed on a separate line (List 1.4.2).

LIST 1.4.2. OUTPUT OF RUBY SCRIPT `grow.rb`

```
C:\ftp\rb>ruby grow.rb
1 1050.0
2 1102.5
3 1157.625
4 1215.50625
5 1276.2815625
6 1340.095640625
```

We review the `grow.rb` script line by line because it contains many of the elements that are found in all Ruby scripts.

The first line is as follows:

```
#!/usr/local/bin/ruby
```

This line tells the Ruby interpreter that the file is a ruby script. The first two characters are always `#!`, the so-called shebang. The shebang gets its name from the pound sign (recognized by musicians as the sharp sign) followed by the exclamation point (the bang). By tradition, the shebang is the first two characters of all scripting languages (Perl, Python, Ruby, Awk). Following the shebang is the path to the Ruby interpreter. For Windows users, this part of the shebang line has no meaning. The path to Ruby is automatically registered into the Windows operating system during Ruby installation. For some Unix/Linux users, this path statement should be written to contain their system path to the Ruby interpreter. The next line is as follows:

```
principle = 1000
```

Here we assign the number 1000 to the `principle` object. In Ruby, everything is an object. This means that, unlike other languages, `principle` is not a variable whose value is 1000. `principle` is an object that can be assigned a number to which it refers. This subtle difference has many consequences in an object-oriented language. The most important difference is that as an object, `principle` has access to object methods appropriate for its class. If `principle` were just another way of saying "1000," it would have no facility to receive methods designed for its class.

Just for fun, let us go into `irb` and see the methods that `principle` may receive.

```
C:\ftp\rb>irb irb>principle = 1000
=> 1000

irb>principle.methods
=> ["methods", "%", "to_r", "<<", "rdiv", "instance_eval",
">", "prec_f", "modulo", "&", "dup", "zero?", "to_int",
"size", "instance_variables", "instance_of?", "extend",
"eql?", "to_bn", "*", "next", "+", "hash", "step", "id",
"gcd", "singleton_methods", "rpower", "-", "remainder",
"nonzero?", "id2name", "/", "taint", "denominator",
"frozen?", "instance_variable_get", "kind_of?", "floor", "|",
"to_a", "quo", "type", "~", "downto", "protected_methods",
"abs", "to_sym", "instance_variable_set", "coerce",
"method", "is_a?", "^", "+@", "ceil", "respond_to?",
"between?", "to_s", "-@", "lcm", "upto", "prec", "**",
"div", "power!", "singleton_method_added", "class", "<=>",
"times", "require_gem", "<", "tainted?", "private_methods",
"==", "===", "__id__", ">", "numerator", "succ", "nil?",
"untaint", ">=", "gem", "round", "to_i", "<=", "send",
"display", "inspect", "gcdlcm", "prec_i", "divmod", "chr",
"clone", "=~", "integer?", "object_id", "require",
"public_methods", "__send__", "equal?", "freeze", "[]",
"truncate", "to_f"]
```

Sending the methods method to principle yields the many methods available to the principle object. Within this book, only a small portion of the methods that are available to objects will be used.

Let us look at the next five lines as a group.

```
(1..6).each do

    |x|

    principle = principle*(1.05)

    print(x, " ", principle, "\n")

end
```

The first line is an iterator for a block of code.

(1..6) specifies a range of numbers from 1 to 6. In Ruby, Range is a class with its own methods. One of the methods of the Range class is the each method. The each method iterates over the elements of the range, passing each element to the block. Each element is assigned to the object surrounded by straight brackets (|x|) with each loop of the block.

The statements of the block are executed in each loop.

```
principle = principle*(1.05)
```

The asterisk is the multiplication operator in Ruby. The value assigned to the principle object is recalculated and reassigned with each loop.

```
print(x, " ", principle, "\n")
```

The `print` method sends a string to the standard output (the computer monitor). The string consists of the character values of the concatenated objects within the parentheses. We will be seeing a lot of the \n character. Scripting languages interpret \n as the newline character.

```
end
```

This signifies the end of the block.

```
exit
```

This signifies the end of the script.

A sharp reader may have noticed that there are some inconsistencies between the way that the program was written and our fundamental principles of Ruby programming.

First, we have forgotten to declare a class for the principle object. Second, we twice used methods without using Ruby syntax:

```
<receiving object name>.<sent method>(parenthesized arguments)
principle = principle*(1.05)
```

In this Ruby statement, `principle` receives the "`*`" method and a parenthesized argument, 1.05. Should not there be a dot relating the method to the receiving object?

```
print(x, " ", principle, "\n")
```

In this Ruby statement, `print` is a method followed by a parenthesized list of arguments. What is the object that receives the `print` method?

Ruby, like many languages, has sacrificed consistency for efficiency. Ruby "knows" that when an object is assigned a number, it must be a member of the Numeric class. Ruby "knows" that the "`*`" multiplier operates on the preceding object. Ruby "knows" that `print` methods are sent by default to the standard output object.

Many of the shortcuts around standard Ruby syntax are built into the Ruby Kernel module included in every Ruby object (more about modules later). Purists can, if they prefer, use explicit Ruby statements in their scripts (List 1.4.3).

This script should look familiar. The `grow2.rb` script is essentially the same script as `grow.rb` with several subtle changes. First, we explicitly

LIST 1.4.3. RUBY SCRIPT grow2.rb USES EXPLICIT RUBY OBJECTS AND STATEMENTS

```
#!/usr/local/bin/ruby
principle = Numeric.new
principle = 1000
(1...6).each do
    |x|
    principle = principle.*(1.05)
    STDOUT.print(x, " ")
    STDOUT.printf "%.3f \n", principle
end
exit
```

create `principle` as an object by sending the `new` method to class Numeric. All classes have access to a `new` method that creates instances of themselves. A specific `new` method exists for most classes. Classes that do not have their own `new` method can inherit `new` from class `Class`. Each class's `new` method might be different from the `new` method found in other classes. The `new` method for the `File` class creates a `File` object, sets the object for reading and writing, and creates a file name, according to the parameters provided inside the parentheses following the method call.

```
File.new("myfile.txt", "w")
```

The `new` method sent to a `Numeric` object will behave differently from the `new` method sent to a `File` object. Polymorphism in object orientation occurs when a method behaves differently depending on the object that receives the method.

```
principle = principle.*(1.05)
```

In the `grow2.rb` script, the multiplication method "*" is preceded by a dot operator that binds the method to the receiver. Because multiplication and the other arithmetic operators are used so commonly, the creators of Ruby made use of the dot operator (in these settings) optional.

```
STDOUT.print(x, " ")
```

The print method, in the absence of an explicit receiver, returns a character string to the standard output. Here, we provide Ruby's special name for the standard output (STDOUT) as part of a fully specified Ruby statement (List 1.4.4).

LIST 1.4.4. OUTPUT OF grow2.rb

Let us look at the output of the grow2.rb script.

```
C:\ftp\rb>ruby grow2.rb
1  1050.000
2  1102.500
3  1157.625
4  1215.506
5  1276.282
```

There are two things different in this output compared to the output of grow.rb. First, the computed colony size is provided for only five generations (not six). Second, the colony size is truncated to the third decimal place, providing a neatly aligned column of numbers.

How was this accomplished?

In grow.rb, the range iterator was as follows:

```
(1..6).each do
```

In grow2.rb, the range iterator was as follows:

```
(1...6).each do
```

There are two dots between the 1 and 6 in grow.rb and three dots in grow2.rb. Ruby interprets a two-dot range to include the first number, all intervening numbers, and the last listed number in the range. Ruby interprets a three-dot range to include the first number and the intervening numbers in the range. The last number is omitted.

```
STDOUT.printf "%.3f \n", principle
```

In grow2.rb, we used printf, a formatting method common to Perl, C, Python, and other languages. The printf method is described in detail in the glossary. Here, printf tells Ruby to print a floating point number with three digits after the decimal point, followed by a newline.

1.5. A RUBY SCRIPT WITH CLASS DEFINITION

Thus far, we have used built-in Ruby classes. Let us create our own class in a Ruby script (List 1.5.1).

This simple script prints the lowercase version of a class variable (List 1.5.2).

LIST 1.5.1. RUBY SCRIPT `lowclass.rb` PROVIDES SYNTAX FOR USER-CREATED CLASSES

```
#!/usr/local/bin/ruby
class Person < String
   @@name = "JULES J. BERMAN"
   def print_downcase
      puts "let's use lowercase characters"
      puts(@@name.downcase)
   end
end
me = Person.new
me.print_downcase
exit
```

LIST 1.5.2. OUTPUT OF RUBY SCRIPT `lowclass.rb`

```
C:\ftp\rb>ruby lowclass.rb
let's use lowercase characters

jules j. berman
```

Let us review the script line by line.

```
class Person < String
```

The first line of the script declares a new class, `Person`, specifying that the `Person` class is a subclass of the `String` class (accomplished with the `<` operator).

The next line creates a class variable named `@@name` and assigns it the string `"JULES J. BERMAN"`. Until now, we have used only local variables in our scripts. It is time to discuss the different types of Ruby variables: temporary or local variables, instance variables, class variables, and global variables.

In Ruby, variables are local (also called temporary) unless designated otherwise. A local variable is an object that ceases to exist after its script scope expires. A temporary variable inside a block ceases to exist when the block ends. A temporary variable declared in a script outside of a block ceases to exist when the script exits. Script variables of a limited scope can be made available to out-of-scope objects, such as classes, subroutines, and blocks, by passing them as method arguments.

In Ruby, you can create several types of variables. By prefixing an "@" to a variable name, the variable becomes an instance variable, accessible to the instance object for the duration of the instance object's life within the script. You can also create class variables by adding a double @ sign to the variable. Class variables are available to all objects of the class and are declared as a class statement outside of any method definition.

Global variables persist through the life of a script and are available to all components of the script (that is, they can be accessed within methods without being passed as method arguments). Global variables are created by adding a "$" sign to the variable name. Although you can create your own global variables, there is never a good reason to do so. Ruby creates a set of global variables to hold operating system information (so-called environment variables) and variables that collect event information that occurs during the execution of a script. Occasionally, you may need to access or even modify Ruby's global variables, but you will never have a good reason to create global variables with your scripts.

A Ruby programmer who exclusively uses pre-existing class libraries will never need to create instance variables, class variables, or global variables. All of her programming can and should be accomplished exclusively with temporary variables. The reason for this is that in an object-oriented language, persistence is accomplished through object creation. The new and initialize methods, invoked when a new object is created, automatically create for the programmer any persistent variables that will be needed by the object. Also, within the class definition are the class variables that will be needed by the class methods and by the object instances. If you are writing a Ruby script and you find it necessary to include an instance or class variable outside of a class definition, you probably are doing something wrong and should consider inserting your persistent variables into a new class or expanding an existing class to accommodate new class methods.

In the lowclass.rb script (see List 1.5.1), the class definition occupied the top of the script. Underneath the class definitions were the lines of code that performed a task by calling on a class instance method.

One of the great features of Ruby is that it permits you to separate class libraries into external files that can be "required" into Ruby scripts whenever they are needed. In List 1.5.3, we exclude the class definition from the script and simply refer to another Ruby script that contains the class definition (see List 1.5.4). In Ruby, this is called "requiring" a class. The require statement looks like this.

```
require "person_class_file"
```

The external file containing the class definition is person_class_file.rb. The require statement consists of the word "require" followed by the

LIST 1.5.3. RUBY SCRIPT noclass.rb REQUIRES AN EXTERNAL PERSON CLASS DEFINITION

```
#!/usr/local/bin/ruby
require "person_class_file"
me = Person.new
me.print_downcase
exit
```

LIST 1.5.4. RUBY SCRIPT person_class_file.rb, A CLASS LIBRARY FOR SCRIPT no_class.rb

```
#!/usr/local/bin/ruby
class Person < String
  @@name = "JULES J. BERMAN"
  def print_downcase
    puts "let's use lowercase characters"
    puts(@@name.downcase)
  end
end
```

name of a Ruby script file (you can omit the .rb extension from the file name). When encountering a "require" statement, Ruby pulls in and evaluates the code from the external file. Use path information in the file name to ensure that Ruby can find the required file and that Ruby does not open another file (of the same name) when it looks through its list of searchable directories and subdirectories (stored in the global variable, $:). Ruby will raise a LoadError exception if it cannot find the required file. The require method will try to pull in extension files that you list, even if these files are not Ruby scripts. If you are only interested in requiring Ruby scripts, you may prefer to use the closely related "load" statement (see glossary).

A Ruby script can include many require statements.

1.6. CONCLUSION

Most programming languages provide a relatively small number of commands, a language syntax (the grammar in which the commands are conveyed), and a programming paradigm (the logic by which commands can be assembled to perform a desired task). Object-oriented programming languages are different from other languages because they come with a library of predefined classes, and each class is like a minilanguage with its own sets of commands (class and instance methods) and its own paradigm for achieving some computational goal. The names of the methods used by one class may be identical to the names of methods in other classes, and the methods may have completely different functions and respond to different sets of arguments. Consequently, many Ruby books are devoted to enumerating the classes, modules, and methods in the built-in Ruby class library. There are several excellent books that list and explain the standard classes, modules, methods, and libraries distributed with Ruby.

This book is focused on biologists, health care workers, and students, *not* professional programmers. The purpose of this book is to teach basic Ruby skills and to describe how Ruby elegantly models biomedical knowledge domains. In the next few chapters, you will acquire the skills to write short scripts that solve your common programming tasks. In later chapters, you will learn to use Ruby to structure and model biomedical data.

Survey of Ruby Classes and the Ruby Standard Library (Level 1)

2.1. BACKGROUND

Ruby is free and easy to install. After you have installed Ruby, you may find yourself at a loss for how to begin programming. All object-oriented programming languages have a steep learning curve because users must learn three things (List 2.1.1):

LIST 2.1.1. LEARNING OBSTACLES FOR OBJECT-ORIENTED PROGRAMMERS

You must master the object paradigm. This may be more difficult for experienced programmers than for newbies. If you have spent the prior decade programming in a procedural style, you may find it hard to make sense of Ruby.

You must master a new syntax. Although Ruby has many of the syntactical structures as Perl, some Ruby fundamentals (such as `Proc` objects) will be foreign to Perl programmers.

You need to acquire at least a superficial knowledge of the built-in Classes and Modules in Ruby, along with their methods, to write short, efficient Ruby scripts. Knowledge of the Standard Library (extensions bundled with the Ruby language installation files) is also important. This means that anyone who wishes to have moderate proficiency in Ruby must devote a large chunk of time to memorizing methods.

The purpose of this chapter is to provide a brief review of the Ruby Class libraries, describing methods and techniques that will be used in scripts appearing in later chapters. After you gain a general understanding of Ruby objects and methods, you will find it very easy to read and understand Ruby scripts written by other people. When you begin to write your own Ruby scripts, you can simply modify and build on scripts from this book, all of which use standard Ruby classes and methods.

2.2. DOWNLOADING AND INSTALLING RUBY

You now know something about Ruby, and you are ready to start writing your first script. You will need to install Ruby on your own computer.

Ruby is available for almost every popular operating system. Windows users can download one-click install package at

http://rubyinstaller.rubyforge.org/wiki/wiki.pl

or at

http://rubyforge.org/frs/?group_id=167

Unix/Linux users can download Ruby at

http://www2.ruby-lang.org/en/20020102.html

The latest instructions for installing Unix/Linux versions of Ruby are available from the distribution web sites.

2.3. OBJECTS AND RUBY SCRIPTS

The purpose of a Ruby class is to create instances of the class and to provide methods and data to instance objects of the class and its subclasses.

In a ruby script, new instance objects are created with the class method `"new"`.

Let us use Ruby's command-line interface to create an instance object of class Array and to send a message to the newly created instance.

```
irb>instance_of_array = Array.new([2,5,18]) => [2, 5, 18]
```

The `irb` interpreter takes your input, `"instance_of_array = Array.new([2,5,18])"` and yields `"=> [2, 5, 18]"`. Throughout this book, we will include the input statement and the `irb` interpreter's output statement on the same line. After a new instance object is created, it has access to all the methods of its class and of its class ancestors.

```
irb>instance_of_array.first => 2
```

Here, the "first" method is sent to the instance_of_array instance object and yields the value "2."

The "new" method is an example of a class method (not an instance method) because it is sent to the class itself (Array in this case), not to an instance of the class. Why is "new" a class method and not an instance method? It would be impossible to send the new method to a class instance that cannot exist until after the new method is dispatched.

What is involved in writing a Ruby script? Most Ruby scripts involve creating one or more instance objects and then applying class instance methods to the created objects with the overall goal of providing a desired script output.

In Ruby, everything is an object. Instances, classes, modules, and code are all objects. Programmers often mistakenly reserve the word object to mean an instance object (that is, an instance of a class that was created with the new method). This is inaccurate because in Ruby, an object can be many different things. Sometimes programmers will use the terms class objects and instance objects synonymously. This is correct but confusing (because classes themselves are class objects). In this book, we refer to instance objects as instances or as instance objects and never as class objects.

2.4. INSTANCE METHODS AND CLASS METHODS

In Ruby, methods in a class are either class methods or instance methods. The purpose of an instance method is to send some defined subroutine to an instantiated object of a class. The purpose of a class method is to send some subroutine to the class itself. In most cases, methods sent to a class (that is, class methods) will create a new instance of the class.

Inside a class, class methods are defined differently from instance methods. Here is an example of a class method's definition.

```
#!/usr/local/bin/ruby
class Person
     def Person.name
       return "Person"
     end
end
puts Person.name
exit
```

This simple script yields the word "Person" as its output. To define a class method, the name of the class must precede the name of the method (i.e., Person.name) in a "def" block, as shown. The class method (in this case, name) can be sent only to the class Person.

Here is an example of an instance method's definition.

```
#!/usr/local/bin/ruby
class Person
     def name
        return "Jules"
     end
end
me = Person.new
puts me.name
exit
```

This simple script yields the word "Jules" as its output. To define an instance method, simply define the method name in a def block, as shown. In this case, the instance method, name, can be sent to any instance object of the class Person. The script defines the class Person, with its one instance method, name. After the class is defined, the script creates a new instance, me, of class Person with the new method. Although a new method was not defined in class Person, it inherited a new method from class Class, an ancestor for all Ruby classes. The instance method, name, is sent to the instance object, me, and the returned value, "Jules" is sent to the standard output.

2.5. RUBY CLASSES

Ruby has classes for the standard data types contained in other programming languages (such as Perl and Python)

   String

   Array

   Hash

   File, IO (input/output) and Dir (directory)

   Numeric

   Regex (regular expressions)

These are the most commonly used classes in Ruby. Most of the computational tasks in biology and medicine can be accomplished using only these built-in Ruby classes without creating any new class definitions.

Let us look at some of the methods in String, Array, Hash, File, Numeric, and their common direct ancestor, Object.

2.6. CLASS STRING

Ruby strings are sequences of bytes that represent ASCII characters.

Strings are flanked by quotation marks.

```
"hello world"
```

Strings can be assigned to Class String instance objects. The value referenced by a class String instance object can be de-referenced by the #{} notation.

```
irb>string_object = "hello world" => "hello world"
irb>"I am shouting #{string_object}" => "I am shouting
    hello world"
```

What actually happened here? In Ruby, when you assign a value to a variable, you are actually creating an object that refers to the data. The #{} notation tells ruby to fetch the value referred to by the object name and use that value in the string expression. Ruby spares the programmer from many object-oriented mind games by providing a familiar syntax for most script operations.

Strings can be concatenated to other strings with the + operator or the << operator. Both are used in scripts within this book.

```
irb>"hello " << "world" => "hello world"
irb>"hello " + "world"  => "hello world"
```

Why does Ruby have two different methods that perform the same operation (concatenation of two strings)? The answer holds a cautionary tale.

```
irb>my_string = String.new("hello") => "hello"
irb>my_string + " world" => "hello world"
irb>my_string => "hello"
irb>my_string << " world" => "hello world"
irb>my_string => "hello world"
```

The statement

```
my_string + " world"
```

is equivalent to the statement

```
my_string.+(" world")
```

The "+" method is sent to my_string, and " world" is the passed argument. The "+" method does not change the value of the receiving object.

The statement

```
my_string << " world"
```

is equivalent to

```
my_string.<<(" world")
```

The "<<" method appends its argument to the receiving object and changes the value of the receiving object.

Ruby has many examples of methods that may return identical values but that have different behavior regarding the state of objects. When learning Ruby, it is very important to understand fully the syntax and the function of the methods you use in your scripts.

2.7. CLASS ARRAY

The class of arrays consists of ordered and indexed lists of items. The items in an array can be any data structure, including strings, numbers, hashes, or other arrays. Array indices start counting at zero.

```
irb>this_array = [43,22,18,190]   => [43, 22, 18, 190]
```

Notice that Ruby automatically adds a space character between each element.

Array values can be retrieved by invoking their index.

```
irb> this_array[1] => 22
```

You can always determine the number of elements in an array with the `size` method.

```
irb> this_array.size => 4
```

As in many programming languages, the `shift` method yields the first element of an array while deleting the element from the array contents.

```
irb> this_array.shift => 43
irb> this_array => [22, 18, 190]
```

You can add a new element (or replace the shifted element) to the front of the array with the `unshift` method.

```
irb> this_array.unshift(43) => [43, 22, 18, 190]
```

You can add an array to your array with "+" operator. But wait. In the prior section, we learned that the "+" operator was a method belonging to class String. How can it also be a method of class Array? In Ruby, any class can have methods of the same name as methods in other classes.

For that matter, any class can have methods of the same name as its ancestor classes or of its descendant classes. All of these methods may have completely different behaviors. How does Ruby know which method should be used if they all have the same name? Ruby knows the class of every created object. When a method is sent to an object, Ruby checks an internal list of method definitions that belong to instances of the object's class. If the list of instance methods for the object's class includes the called method, Ruby will implement the included method. If the list of instance methods for the object's class does not contain the called method, Ruby checks instance methods for the superclass of the object. Ruby implements the first matching method in the superclass hierarchy. If no matching method is found, Ruby sends a `NoMethodError` to the computer screen.

Here is the format for adding two arrays with the "+" Array method.

```
irb> this_array + [190,190,190,56] =>
[43, 22, 18, 190, 190, 190, 190, 56]
```

Now, let us look at the new value of the array.

```
irb> this_array => [43, 22, 18, 190]
```

Surprise! You probably were expecting to see the array with all of the elements that had been added on the prior line. What happened?

The "+" operation is a nondestructive method that yields a new array without replacing the original array that received the method. If we had wanted to save the array resulting from the "+" method sent to this_array, we should have assigned the new array to a named variable.

```
new_array = this_array + [190,190,190,56]
```

Then new_array would yield

```
new_array => [43, 22, 18, 190, 190, 190, 190, 56]
```

Let us return to the irb session. The "<<" operator appends an array object to the end of an array and is called the `append` method.

```
irb> this_array << [190,190,190,56] =>
[43, 22, 18, 190, [190, 190, 190, 56]]
```

Following the append operation, we get two surprises.

```
irb> this_array => [43, 22, 18, 190, [190, 190, 190, 56]]
```

First, unlike the "+" operation, the append operation actually modified this_array. We did not need to create a new array to refer to the value of the original array appended to [190,190,190,56]. Also, unlike the "+" operation, the added array appears in this_array as a single element (enclosed by straight brackets) consisting of an array object. In Ruby, any data structure can be an element of an array, including another array. Sometimes it is useful to create arrays of arrays or arrays of hashes or any manner of mixed data; however, often we would just as soon push the individual elements of the array object into our array.

The `flatten` method accomplishes this.

```
irb>this_array.flatten => [43, 22, 18, 190, 190, 190, 190, 56]
```

Now, let us re-evaluate this_array.

```
irb>this_array => [43, 22, 18, 190, [190, 190, 190, 56]]
```

The `flatten` method did not modify the original array. Just as we had seen when we used the "+" method, the `flatten` method returns a new array without modifying the original array. Had we wanted to preserve the value of the flattened array, we should have created a variable to hold the results. We can reuse the original variable name to refer to the new array created with the `flatten` method.

```
irb>this_array = this_array.flatten =>

[43, 22, 18, 190,190, 190, 190, 56]
```

Now we have an array with duplicate array elements. We can eliminate duplicate elements of an array with the `uniq` method. This time, we will plan ahead and create a variable name to refer to the value produced by sending the `uniq` method to this_array.

```
irb>this_array = this_array.uniq => [43, 22, 18, 190, 56]
```

There are dozens of instance methods in the Array class, and we use more of them throughout this book.

We close this section with a short Ruby script that uses Arrays (List 2.7.1). The `combo.rb` script takes a string of words and produces every ordered fragment of words from the string (List 2.7.2). For instance, "I am here" would yield:

I

am

here

I am

am here

I am here

LIST 2.7.1. RUBY SCRIPT `combo.rb` **PARSES AN ARRAY INTO ALL POSSIBLE ORDERED SUBARRAYS**

```ruby
#!/usr/bin/ruby
sentence = "refractory anemia with excess blasts in"
sentence_array = sentence.split
length = sentence_array.size
length.times do
    (1..sentence_array.size).each do
      |place_length|
      puts sentence_array.slice(0,place_length).join(" ")
    end
    sentence_array.shift
end
exit
```

LIST 2.7.2. OUTPUT OF `combo.rb`

```
C:\ftp\rb>combo.rb
refractory
refractory anemia
refractory anemia with
refractory anemia with excess
refractory anemia with excess blasts
refractory anemia with excess blasts in
anemia
anemia with
anemia with excess
anemia with excess blasts
anemia with excess blasts in
with
with excess
with excess blasts
with excess blasts in
excess
excess blasts
excess blasts in
blasts
blasts in
in
```

Let us review the script line by line.

```
#!/usr/bin/ruby
sentence = "refractory anemia with excess blasts in"
sentence_array = sentence.split
length = sentence_array.size
```

We begin with a sentence, and we transform the sentence into an array with the split method. Class String's split method is used in virtually every script that parses strings of words. The split method breaks a string at locations that match a regular expression. If no regular expression is provided, split will break the sentence at the space character.

Examples are as follows:

```
irb>my_string = String.new("calcifying epithelioma of Malherbe")
=> "calcifying epithelioma of Malherbe"

irb>my_string.split
=> ["calcifying", "epithelioma", "of", "Malherbe"]
```

We need to know the number of words in the array, and this is accomplished with class Array's size method.

```
length = sentence_array.size
```

The next lines of the script describe an iteration block within an iteration block.

```
length.times do
    (1..sentence_array.size).each do
      |place_length|
      puts sentence_array.slice(0,place_length).join(" ")
    end
    sentence_array.shift
end
```

This short snippet of code does the bulk of the work of the script. The outer block has this form:

```
length.times do
    .
    .
    .
end
```

The block tells Ruby to iterate over the code between the do....end for a number of times determined by the value of length. In this case, length is the number of words in the phrase "refractory anemia with excess blasts in" or 6.

Inside the block is another block

```
(1..sentence_array.size).each do
  |place_length|]
   puts sentence_array.slice(0,place_length).join(" ")
end
```

This inside block has the following form:

```
(1..n).each do
  |  .  |
     .

end
```

This block will iterate in a range from 1 to n. The each method applied to a range assigns each iterated number from the range to a variable specified between the vertical bars.

```
(1..sentence_array.size).each do
  |place_length|
```

In this case, each loop of the inside block will iterate over a range that extends to the size of the array sentence_array and will pass the range value for each iteration to the variable place_length.

At each iteration, the slice method is sent to sentence_array. The slice method cuts out an array from sentence_array, consisting of the array elements specified by the parenthesized arguments. In this case, the arguments to slice are 0 and place_length. This means that the slice of the sentence_array will consist of the elements from element zero (the first element) to element place_length (the range number passed by the each method in the current loop). The join(" ") method sent to the result of the sentence_array.slice(0,place_length) statement will transform the sliced array to a string with each element from the array joined by a space. Finally, the puts method sends the resulting string to the monitor.

```
puts sentence_array.slice(0,place_length).join(" ")
```

The inside iteration loop is followed by another Ruby statement.

```
(1..sentence_array.size).each do
  |place_length|
   puts sentence_array.slice(0,place_length).join(" ")
end
sentence_array.shift
```

After each iteration of the inner loop, the `sentence_array` instance object is sent the `shift` method. The `shift` method removes the first element from the array and returns an array that is shorter (by one element) from the original array. This means that after each range of iterations of the inner loop, `sentence_array` will be reduced in length by one element and returned for another turn of the outer loop.

Okay. This explains the mechanics of the nested loop structure. But what does it accomplish? The nested loop takes a string of words and produces a slice that consists of the first word, then the first word plus second word, then the first word plus second word plus third word, etc. until the full list of words is produced. Then it knocks off the first word and repeats the process producing the second word, then the second word plus the third word, etc. List 2.7.2 shows the output from each iteration through the nested iterators.

Nested iterations are incredibly powerful tools that are much less complex than their written explanation would suggest. After you start writing your own programs, you will find it very easy to write nested iterators.

In Ruby, there are two equivalent syntactic representations of iteration blocks.

In our example script, we used the following syntax:

```
object.method(arguments) do |iteration_variable| code end
```

An equivalent syntax is this:

```
object.method(arguments){|iteration_variable| code}
```

The `first` syntax is preferred if the code contains multiple statements. In Ruby, multiple statements can appear on a single line (or in a single-lined block) by placing a semicolon between each statement.

```
object.method(arguments){|iteration_variable|statement1;
statement2}
```

This exercise with Arrays is used again in Chapter 12 when we need to parse all of the possible terms from a character string to find matches between text and an external terminology. For this example, we have learned many new Ruby methods and operators, all of which are described in detail in the glossary.

2.8. CLASS HASH

A hash is an unordered list of key/value pairs. Associative array and dictionary are synonyms for hash. In Ruby, hash objects are instances of class `Hash` and have a variety of powerful methods at their disposal. We use hashes in most of the Ruby scripts provided in this book.

A key/value hash element can be created by providing a key as shown in List 2.8.1.

LIST 2.8.1. RUBY SCRIPT `hash.rb` **CREATES AND DISPLAYS KEY/VALUE PAIRS FOR A HASH INSTANCE OBJECT**

```
#!/usr/local/bin/ruby
my_hash = Hash.new
my_hash["C0000005"] = "(131)I-Macroaggregated Albumin"
my_hash["C0000039"] = "1,2-Dipalmitoylphosphatidylcholine"
my_hash["C0000052"] = "1,4-alpha-Glucan Branching Enzyme"
my_hash["C0000074"] = "1-Alkyl-2-Acylphosphatidates"
my_hash["C0000084"] = "1-Carboxyglutamic Acid"
my_hash.each {|key,value| STDOUT.print(key, " --- ", value, "\n")}
exit
```

In the statement that follows, "C0000005" is the key, and "(131)I-Macroaggregated Albumin" is the hash value. Together they comprise a key/value hash element.

```
my_hash["C0000005"] = "(131)I-Macroaggregated Albumin"
```

The last line of the Ruby script uses the `Hash#each` method. The `each` method iteratively submits hash elements (that is, key/value pairs) to a block of code. The code block prints to the monitor each key and value for each iteration, including a " --- " string between the two variables and ending each string with a newline character.

```
my_hash.each {|key,value| STDOUT.print(key, " --- ", value,"\n")}
```

The output is shown in List 2.8.2. The output order of the key/value pairs does not correspond to the order in which the hash elements were created in List 2.8.1. Remember that a hash is an unordered collection of key/value pairs. Ruby stores the hash values internally to facilitate retrieval of pairs based on a lookup indexed to the key. Although the internal order makes sense to Ruby, the printed output of key/value pairs appears random to humans (List 2.8.2).

When should you use hashes? Hashes have particular utility when you have lists of data elements, each of which is intimately bound to another element. For instance, in a biomedical nomenclature, a term may be bound to a code number (that uniquely identifies the term) or to a definition (that

LIST 2.8.2. OUTPUT OF hash.rb

```
C:\ftp\rb>ruby hash.rb
C0000005 -- (131)I-Macroaggregated Albumin
C0000039 -- 1,2-Dipalmitoylphosphatidylcholine
C0000084 -- 1-Carboxyglutamic Acid
C0000074 -- 1-Alkyl-2-Acylphosphatidates
C0000052 -- 1,4-alpha-Glucan Branching Enzyme
```

explains the term) or to a byte location (that tells you the precise spot in the nomenclature that holds the term) or to a specific web site (where the term is used). In all of these cases, there is a term, and there is a value associated with the term.

The other advantage of the hash data structures relates to the speed with which Ruby can access key/value pairs. When you provide Ruby with the key for any key/value pair, Ruby can quickly access the associated value. Ruby accomplishes this without actually traversing all of the key/value pairs in the hash. Ruby has an internal structure for key/value pairs that supports quick access.

We now describe a script that performs several hashing tasks related to parsing biomedical text (List 2.8.4). Our Ruby script, neohash.rb, creates two hash instance objects that we will use again in the fastcode.rb script (List 12.3.1).

Here is the computational task. We have a neoplasm nomenclature that contains about 145,000 names of neoplasms. It is called the Developmental Lineage Classification and Taxonomy of Neoplasms, or Neoplasm Classification for short (3). The entire classification is provided as an XML document. We learn more about XML and the Neoplasm Classification in Chapter 5. For now, all we need to know is that terms are arranged in a consistent format throughout the file.

We would like to tease apart the Neoplasm Classification into two hash instance objects. The first hash will consist of the multiword terms in the classification followed by their code. The key/value pairs for the terms in List 2.8.3 are as follows:

```
mixed embryonal carcinoma and teratoma => C3756000
ovary with dermoid cyst => C3856000
dermoid cyst arising in ovary => C3856000
teratocarcinoma => C3756000
```

Finally, we would like to make a hash consisting of all of the two-word phrases that can be extracted from the term. The phrases will be the

LIST 2.8.3. EXCERPT FROM THE NEOPLASM CLASSIFICATION
`neocl.xml`

```
<name nci-code = "C3756000">mixed embryonal carcinoma and
teratoma</name>
<name nci-code = "C3756000">teratocarcinoma</name>
<name nci-code = "C3856000">ovary with dermoid cyst</name>
<name nci-code = "C3856000">dermoid cyst arising in ovary</name>
```

hash keys. All of the hash keys will be assigned the empty string, `""`, as their values. The two-word key/hash pairs from List 2.8.3 are as follows:

```
mixed embryonal => ""
embyronal carcinoma => ""
carcinoma and => ""
and teratoma => ""
ovary with => ""
with dermoid => ""
dermoid cyst => ""
cyst arising => ""
arising in => ""
in ovary => ""
```

Why would we want to make these hashes? In Chapter 12, we build an autocoder script that parses through text, extracting phrases that match terms from a nomenclature and assigning unique concept codes to the phrases. We build the autocoder from class methods that we develop. One of the advantages of object-oriented programming is that we can add short, abstract methods to a class library that can be called by a variety of Ruby scripts, as needed.

Here is the Ruby script (List 2.8.4) that creates our hashes (Lists 2.8.5 and 2.8.6) from the full Neoplasm Classification.

Let us review the `neohash.rb` script line by line.

```
#!/usr/local/bin/ruby
begin_time = (Time.new).to_f
```

I like to begin my parsing scripts by creating an instance object for class Time. The value returned is the number of seconds transpired since January 1, 1970.

```
irb>Time.new.to_f => 1168431440.25
```

LIST 2.8.4. RUBY SCRIPT neohash.rb **CREATES TWO HASH INSTANCES FOR THE NEOPLASM CLASSIFICATION**

```ruby
#!/usr/local/bin/ruby
begin_time = (Time.new).to_f
text = File.open("c:\\ftp\\neocl.xml", "r")
literalhash = Hash.new; doubhash = Hash.new
text.each do
  |line|
  next if (line !~ /\"(C[0-9]{7})\"/)
  line =~ /\"(C[0-9]{7})\"/
  code = $1
  line =~ /\"\> ?(.+) ?\<\//
  phrase = $1
  if (phrase !~ / /)
     literalhash[phrase] = code
     next
  end
  literalhash[phrase] = code
  hoparray = phrase.split
  (0..hoparray.length).each do
      |i|
      doublet = "#{hoparray[i]} #{hoparray[i+1]}"
next if !(doublet =~ /[a-z]+[a-z0-9\-]* [a-z]+[a-z0-9\-]*/)
      doubhash[doublet] = ""
  end
end
text.close
f = File.open("hashes.txt", "w")
puts "The number of vocabulary terms is#{literalhash.length}"
puts "The number of doublets is #{doubhash.length}"
doubhash.each{|key,value| f.print "#{key} #{value}\n"}
literalhash.each{|key,value| f.print "#{key} #{value}\n"}
end_time = (Time.new).to_f
puts "Script time to execute is #{end_time - begin_time}
   seconds"
exit
```

LIST 2.8.5. SCREEN OUTPUT OF neohash.rb

```
C:\ftp\rb>ruby neohash.rb
The number of vocabulary terms is 140710
The number of doublets is 29200
Script time to execute is 37.125 seconds
```

LIST 2.8.6. SAMPLE OF FILE, HASHES.TXT, OUTPUT OF `neohash.rb`

adenocarcinoma endometrial

dolorosa adiposis

melanot freckle

haemangiopericytoma of

malignant laryngeal

of hand

from pericardium

neoplasms hypothalamic

.

.

.

.

dukes a ca of the colon C9358000

stage ii adenocarcinoma of pharynx C8769000

noninfiltrating cystic hypersecretory duct adenoca involving breast C7443000

plat—paraganglioma-like adenoma of thyroid C6846000

carcinoma involving the paranasal sinus C6014000

stage i carcinoma arising from urinary bladder C7896000

ehe—epithelioid haemangioendothelioma of the soft tissues C3800100

At the end of the script, we create a new time object. By subtracting the first class Time instance object from the second instance object, we recover the script's execution length (in seconds).

```
text = File.open("c\:\\ftp\\neocl.xml", "r")
```

`File.open()` sends the class method, open, to class File. The `open` method serves two functions. It substitutes as the `new` method for class File (creating a new object), and it opens a file (supplied as the parenthesized argument) for reading or writing. The second argument, `"r"`, tells Ruby that the file will be read from and not written to. The file we want to open is neocl.xml, and it is located in the c:\ftp subdirectory. We "escape" the colon and the slashes with a slash to tell Ruby that the nonalphanumeric characters that follow the slash should be interpreted as characters and not as special programming symbols.

```
literalhash = Hash.new; doubhash = Hash.new
```

We create two new Hash instance objects. Ruby expects one statement per line of code; however, Ruby allows you to put multiple statements on a single line if each statement is separated by a semicolon. Some programmers prefer to create their script objects on a single line that they can find and review with one glance.

```
text.each do
  |line|
  next if (line !~ /\"(C[0-9]{7})\"/)
```

These lines set up and begin the loop. The each method, when sent to a File object, instructs Ruby to parse the file one line at a time, assigning each line to the iterator variable (named line in this loop). The next statement tells Ruby to abandon the remaining code in the loop and start the loop again, with the next iterated line, if the specified condition does not evaluate to true. The condition is described in a Regex (pattern) expression.

```
line !~ /\"(C[0-9]{7})\"/)
```

We learn Ruby Regex in detail in Chapter 7. For now, you only need to know that the Regex expression in this example describes a string pattern where the uppercase letter C is followed by seven consecutive characters that are 0, 1, 2, 3, 4, 5, 6, 7, 8, or 9. This pattern corresponds to a nomenclature code, as found in the following example. The !~ expression tests for the absence of a match. The =~ expression tests for the presence of a match. We use both later in this script.

```
<name nci-code = "C3756000">mixed embryonal carcinoma and
teratoma</name>
```

If there is no fragment of the line that matches the Regex expression, we can infer that the line does not contain a coded term and can be skipped.

If the line matches the Regex expression, then we can extract the matching code number. In Ruby, when a string contains a substring that matches a Regex expression, the matching substring is put into a special global variable, called $&. If the expression contains parenthesized parts, Ruby assigns $1, $2, $3, etc. for each succeeding parenthesized pattern. In this case, there is one parenthesized subpattern, (C[0-9]{7}). The substring from each line that matches this expression is assigned the global variable $1, and we reassign the global variable to the temporary variable "code".

```
line =~ /\"(C[0-9]{7})\"/
code = $1
```

We repeat this trick in the next two lines. This time, we want to capture the neoplasm term contained in the same line. The neoplasm term is blocked by angle brackets.

```
<name nci-code = "C3756000">mixed embryonal carcinoma and
teratoma</name>
```

We write a Regular expression that matches against the text between the angle brackets and assigns the matched substring, to the temporary variable "phrase".

```
line =~ /\"\> ?(.+) ?\<\//
phrase = $1;
```

The next few lines may puzzle you, but they make sense if you anticipated all of the intended purposes of the script.

An if expression determines whether the phrase does not contain a space character. Remember that !~ tests for the absence of a match. If the phrase contains no space character, we assign a new key/value pair to literalhash, the class Hash instance object. The neoplasm phrase is the key, and the code is the value. The subsequent line tells Ruby that the current iteration loop is finished and that the next iteration loop should begin. The last line indicates that the if block has ended. Every block must have a beginning and an end. The most common error for nubies (Ruby newbies) is omission of balanced end remarks for blocks.

```
if (phrase !~ / /)
    literalhash[phrase] = code
    next
end
```

What is so special about terms that have no space character? Why did we create a special if block to capture these terms? In the next portion of the script, we create a hash of the doublets (two-word phrases) found within the neoplasm terms. If a term lacks the space character, it must be a single-word neoplasm term (for example, lipoma, rhabdomyosarcoma, and nephroblastoma) and cannot be further reduced to a set of two-word components. By assigning these one-word terms to the literalhash Hash object and ending the current loop block at this point, we save the time and effort of trying to find doublets in single word terms (in the next portion of the script).

As we proceed through the remaining portion of the script, we deal with multi-word phrases. We create a new `literalhash` key/value pair with our multi-word phrase as our key.

```
literalhash[phrase] = code
```

Then we take the phrase and split it into an array consisting of the words in the array, using the `split` method.

```
hoparray = phrase.split
```

We create a range consisting of numbers from 0 to the length of `hoparray`. Using the `each` method, we iterate over these number, assigning each successive number to the variable "`i`".

```
(0..hoparray.length).each do
     |i|
```

Each doublet of the phrase consists of the array element of index i followed by a space followed by the array element of index i+1.

For example, for the array `["adenocarcinoma", "of", "prostate"]`

`adenocarcinoma` is the 0 index element

`of` is the 1 index element

`prostate` is the 2 index element

The doublets are as follows:

`adenocarcinoma of`

and

`of prostate`

```
doublet = "#{hoparray[i]} #{hoparray[i+1]}"
```

We are only interested in doublets that begin with an alphabetic letter. We would accept "`p53 adenocarcinoma`" as a doublet, but not "`53 tumors`" as a doublet. The regular expression rejects doublets that do not conform to this requirement.

```
next if !(doublet =~ /[a-z]+[a-z0-9\-]* [a-z]+[a-z0-9\-]*/)
```

Finally, we add doublets to the `doubhash` Hash object. In this case, the doublet is the key. The value is the empty string. At this point, we do not require an informative variable for our `doubhash` value. The end remark closes the block.

```
doubhash[doublet] = ""
end
```

Another end remark closes the main block.

```
end
```

We have finished with the File object, and, thus, we send it a `close` method.

```
text.close
```

The script has finished its job of creating a hash of term/code pairs and a hash of doublets from the nomenclature. The remaining lines simply document what we have done.

We open a new File object. This time, we set its parameter as `"w"` to indicate that we will be writing to the file.

```
f = File.open("hashes.txt", "w")
```

We print a message to the screen stating the number of terms collected in the literalhash Hash object.

```
puts "The number of vocabulary terms is #{literalhash.length}"
```

We print a message to the screen stating the number of terms collected in the doubhash Hash object.

```
puts "The number of doublets is #{doubhash.length}"
```

We iterate over each key/value pair in the `doubhash` Hash object, and we print each key/value pair to the file object that we have just created.

```
doubhash.each{|key,value| f.print "#{key} #{value}\n"}
```

We do the same for the `literalhash` Hash object.

```
literalhash.each{|key,value| f.print "#{key} #{value}\n"}
```

We determine the time now, at the end of the script.

```
end_time = (Time.new).to_f
```

We compute the script execution time (end_time − begin_time) and announce the interval in a sentence printed to the computer screen.

```
puts "Script time to execute is #{end_time - begin_time} seconds"
```

At last, we exit the script.

```
exit
```

Although long and (admittedly) tedious, this line-by-line review of the `neohash.rb` script has prepared you with most of the Ruby scripting techniques that you will ever need.

2.9. CLASSES FILE AND IO

In Ruby, methods that would normally be considered file operations are assigned to class IO (Input and Output). IO is the superclass for class File. IO includes files and all types of data streams, including those received by network ports. Useful methods such as `seek`, `tell`, `print`, `printf`, `pos`, and `read` are all IO instance methods.

The methods from Class File that you will be using in almost every script are `open` and `each`. We have just seen example of these methods (List 2.8.4) when we opened a file for reading (with `open`) and parsed it one line at a time (with `each`).

Let us look at one example of the succinct power of IO methods.

We can count the number of words in any text file with a short, one-line command.

```
irb>(IO.read("c\:\\ftp\\rb\\haystack.rb")).split.size => 113
```

This line of code file determines the number of words in the `haystack.rb` file (List 10.2.1). You may skip ahead and count the number of words in the file if you would like to verify that there are 113 words in the listing. How does this work? The class IO instance method, `read()`, opens the file specified in the argument and puts it into a string object.

The syntax for IO#read is as follows:

```
read(filename, length to read, offset)
```

For example, if we wanted to retrieve byte 100 to byte 300 of the 775-megabyte MRCONSO file (see Chapter 5), we could do it with the following Ruby code.

```
irb>puts IO.read("c\:\\entrez\\MRCONSO",200,100)
```

Ruby can directly access any byte of any file; it takes virtually no time to return the text chunk.

```
ted Albumin|0|N||
C0000005|ENG|S|L0270109|PF|S0007491|Y|A0016458||M0019694|
D012711|MSH|EN|D012711|(131)I-MAA|0|N||
C0000039|CZE|P|L3180523|PF|S3708014|Y|A3909890|||D015060|
MSHCZE|MH|D015060|1,2-DIPALM
```

When no size or offset is provided in the IO, `read` argument, the entire file is returned as a string. After we have the returned string (representing the entire file), we can chain two string methods together to determine the number of words in the file.

```
irb>(IO.read("c\:\\ftp\\rb\\haystack.rb")).split.size => 113
```

Class String's `split` method splits a character string into an array. When the `split` method is provided with no arguments, it splits the string on white space (for example, the space character). This effectively produces an array consisting of every word in the file. Class Array's `size` method returns the number of elements in the array. Together, these methods produce the number of words in the file `haystack.rb` (seen in List 10.2.1).

2.10. CLASS DIR

As we see again and again throughout this book, computational bio-medicine almost always involves parsing input streams, and often the input consists of groups of files organized in a local or remote computer's directory. Ruby provides a class Dir to list directories, with their locations and contents.

Here is a one-line script that lists all of the text files in the current sur-directory (that is, the directory in which the system prompt is currently located) (List 2.10.1).

LIST 2.10.1. RUBY SCRIPT `glob.rb` **DEMONSTRATES THE DIR CLASS** `glob` **METHOD**

```
#!/usr/local/bin/ruby
print(Dir.glob("*.txt").sort.join("\n"))
exit
```

The script uses the venerable `glob` method, which is available to many scripting languages and is often referred to in its verb form ("I globbed the files") (List 2.10.2).

LIST 2.10.2. SAMPLE OUTPUT OF `glob.rb`

```
C:\ftp\rb>glob.rb
altmail.txt
anatomy.txt
email.txt
rubyhead.txt
rubyind.txt
rubylist.txt
rubyref.txt
tax_names.txt
taxnames.txt
zipfomim.txt
```

An alternate to `glob` is `Dir.each`. Class Dir's `each` method is a pure Ruby method, using Ruby syntax (List 2.10.3). The `glob` method is a concession to Unix/Linux programmers and uses a non-Ruby syntax (that is, the `"*"` wild-card character).

LIST 2.10.3. RUBY SCRIPT `dirlist.rb` LISTS THE FILES IN THE CURRENT DIRECTORY

```
#!/usr/local/bin/ruby
filearray = Array.new
Dir.foreach(".") do #"." is the current directory
  |filename|
  filearray << filename if (filename =~ /.txt/)
end
puts(filearray.sort)
exit
```

Another useful class Dir method is `getwd`, which yields the path to the current directory. An example from my personal computer is as follows:

```
irb>Dir.getwd  => "C:/ftp/rb"
```

2.11. CLASS NUMERIC

In Ruby, there are five numeric classes: `Numeric`, `Float`, `Integer`, `Bignum`, and `Fixnum`. Subclasses of `Numeric` are `Float` and `Integer`. Subclasses of `Integer` are `Bignum` and `Fixnum`. Each class is entitled to implement mathematical methods as they see fit, and, thus, an operation as simple as division ("/") can produce surprising results (List 2.11.1).

LIST 2.11.1. SURPRISING DIVISION OUTCOMES IN RUBY

```
irb>5/6 => 0
irb>5.div(6) => 0
irb>5.to_f/6.to_f => 0.833333333333333
irb>5.to_f/6 => 0.833333333333333
irb>5.0/6 => 0.833333333333333
irb> 5/6.0 => 0.833333333333333
```

In Ruby, every object has a class, and every class can have its own set of methods, even when those methods have the same name as methods appearing in other classes. When Ruby encounters the number 5, it assigns it to class `Fixnum` (a subclass of Integer) and sends Integer methods to the object. Integer division is completely different from float division. If you want to divide 5 by 6 and get something other than 0, you must coerce Ruby into thinking the numbers are floats by assigning a decimal value to one of the integers (for example, 5.0), or you must use the to_f method to convert the object of class Integer to an object of class Float.

The Mathn library (see Chapter 13) eliminates much of the fussiness engendered by the Numeric class.

2.12. CLASS TIME

Time is the Ruby class that provides the time in a standard format. It is often useful and necessary to identify the time that script events occur. Sometimes an object can be identified with a specified time. The time can be invoked with the new method.

```
irb>Time.new => Fri Dec 29 18:07:46 Eastern Standard Time 2006
```

Time is kept in an internal format as the number of seconds since epoch, defined as midnight, January 1, 1970.

```
irb>Time.new.to_f => 1167433761.992
```

By subtracting Time at the beginning of the script from Time at the end of a script, the execution time of a script is determined (Lists 2.12.1 and 2.12.2).

LIST 2.12.1. RUBY SCRIPT time.rb MEASURES THE LENGTH OF TIME FOR ANY PROCESS

```
#!/usr/local/bin/ruby
begin_time = (Time.new).to_f
puts "Script began at #{begin_time}"
sleep 2
end_time = (Time.new).to_f
puts "Script ended at #{end_time}"
puts "Total time is " << ((end_time - begin_time).to_s)
exit
```

LIST 2.12.2. OUPUT OF time.rb

```
C:\ftp\rb>ruby time.rb
Script began at 1167569825.078
Script ended at 1167569827.078
Total time is 2.0
```

Object Orientation in Ruby (Level 2)

3.1. BACKGROUND

Children learn to play chess in a single teaching session. The teacher explains how each piece moves and how pieces are captured. The student learns that players take turns moving their pieces until the opposing king's capture is inevitable (checkmate). The teaching process takes about 20 minutes, but mastering the game of chess takes more than a lifetime.

In the prior two chapters, you received all of the instruction necessary to write Ruby scripts. The purpose of this chapter is to describe the conceptual underpinnings of Ruby. I would have preferred to place this chapter somewhere closer to the end of the book; however, you will find that discussing these topics is necessary to justify the time and effort needed to master object-oriented programming.

If you would rather skip this chapter and move immediately into programming examples, feel free to do so. You can return to this chapter when you are overcome by existential angst.

3.2. RUBY UPPER LEVEL HIERARCHY

All Ruby classes are subclasses of class `Object` and inherit the class methods of class `Object`. All classes in Ruby implicitly become instances of class `Class` and inherit the instance methods of class `Class`. Ruby's class `Class` inherits from class `Module`, which inherits from class `Object`. This paragraph is irreducibly complex, but readers will be relieved to know that they can write useful scripts without understanding the underlying structure of the Ruby class system. You can return to this paragraph if you need to understand upper-level inheritance, or you can use Reflection (see Section 3.6) to yield the structure of Ruby's class system, as needed.

3.3. INHERITANCE, POLYMORPHISM, ENCAPSULATION, AND ABSTRACTION

Object-oriented languages all come with a set of properties that enhance the general programming experience and that permit part-time programmers to benefit from class libraries that more experienced programmers have donated to the Ruby community.

Let us first examine two general structures of Ruby scripts (List 3.3.1 and List 3.3.2).

Here, we have a script that includes two class definitions: class `Example` and class `MathFunctions` (List 3.3.2). Presumably, each class would define a set of methods.

Here we have an equivalent script with the two classes, each located in an external file that is required into the script. Otherwise, List 3.3.1 and List 3.3.2 are equivalent.

LIST 3.3.1. GENERAL STRUCTURE OF A RUBY SCRIPT THAT DEFINES ITS OWN CLASSES

```
#!/usr/local/bin/ruby
Class Example < Goodstuff
   .
   .
   .
end
Class MathFunctions < Calculations
   .
   .
   .
end
some_object = Example.new(some_argument)
another_object = MathFunctions.new(math_argument)
some_object.a_method
another_object.a_math_method
   .
   .
   .
exit
```

LIST 3.3.2. GENERAL STRUCTURE OF A RUBY SCRIPT THAT USES EXTERNAL CLASS LIBRARIES

```
#!/usr/local/bin/ruby
require 'example'
require 'mathfunctions'
some_object = Example.new(some_argument)
another_object = MathFunctions.new(math_argument)
some_object.a_method
another_object.a_math_method
.
.
.
exit
```

Following the class definitions in List 3.3.1 or following the `require` statements in List 3.3.2 is the so-called main part of the script. The main part of the script creates instance objects of pre-existing classes, and these instance objects use any of the methods of their class. The `Example` class indicates that it has a parent class, `Goodstuff`, as expressed in this statement:

```
Class Example < Goodstuff
```

Instance objects of class `Example` can call methods from class `Goodstuff`. If class `Goodstuff` indicates that it has a parent, then every instance object of class `Example` can use any method in the parent class of class `Goodstuff`. This is inheritance. For inheritance to work, every object must have a class, and Ruby must know the class of every object. Ruby must also know every parent class of every class that has a designated parent class. Ruby must also have a way of searching through the methods available to each class through an ancestor lineage.

Methods in different classes may have the same name. Most Ruby classes have an `each` method and a `new` method and a "+" method. When a named method behaves differently depending on its class or depending on the kinds of arguments passed with the method, this is called polymorphism. Polymorphism is a double-edged sword for object-oriented programmers. It can be used to enforce object-appropriate actions, or it can be used to create hopelessly anarchic programs. We discuss this issue further in Chapter 20.

When we created the instance object, `some_object`, we passed it an argument (`some_argument`).

```
some_object = Example.new(some_argument)
```

When instance objects are created, a method named `initialize` will usually assign the passed argument to an instance object variable. This effectively binds the passed data to the newly created instance object. The data can be accessed through additional methods available to the object. This is one example of encapsulation. Encapsulation is important because it permits us to write Ruby scripts using only temporary variables. All instance variables, class variables, and global variables are encapsulated for us within instance objects or class objects. When an object is created in a script, its encapsulated data can be accessed throughout the script.

The Ruby script is divided into two parts: the class definitions and the main section. The class definitions hold methods that were designed in ignorance of the specific purposes of the main section of the script. In the main section, methods are passed arguments that provide the input for script actions that lead to a desired output. Because object methods are general and are not purposefully written with any specific input data, they are abstract. The main section of an object-oriented script can often be quite short, as its function is to send chosen methods and data to created instance objects. That does not usually require much code.

3.4. MODULES, NAMESPACES, AND MIXINS

In Ruby, a module is a section of invoked code that contains methods and constants assigned to a namespace (the declared module name) (List 3.4.1).

LIST 3.4.1. EXAMPLE OF A COMPLETE, BUT SHORT, RUBY MODULE

```
module Greetings
  def say hello
    puts "hello"
  end
end
```

A module differs from a typical class in several ways.

1. A module is invoked with the "module ModuleName" statement, (not the "class ClassName" statement), and the statement is never followed by the name of an assigned parent module.
2. Modules cannot make instances objects of themselves.

3. Module methods are added to a script by using an `include` statement. Like classes, if the module definition is part of an external file, the external file must be required into the script as well.

Let us see two examples of a Module working inside three scripts, all of which send the string "hello" to the monitor (Lists 3.4.2–4).

LIST 3.4.2. RUBY SCRIPT `mod1.rb` **DEFINES AND INCLUDES A SIMPLE MODULE**

```
#!/usr/local/bin/ruby
module HelloModule
    def say_hello
        puts "hello"
    end
end
include HelloModule
say_hello
exit
```

The module `HelloModule` has a single method (`say_hello`). After the module definition ends, the main part of the script begins. `HelloModule` is called into the main part of the script with the `include` statement. `HelloModule`'s `say_hello` method is invoked, and the word `"hello"` is sent to the monitor.

Notice that we did not create an instance object of the module. Unlike classes, modules never create instance objects. Also notice that the `say_hello` method was not sent to a specified object. In this case, the `say_hello` method was implicitly sent to `self` (the object representing the current script). A fastidious Ruby programmer would have called the `say_hello` method with the following:

```
self.say_hello
```

Ruby lets us call Module methods and constants with the `scope` operator. This assures us that even if multiple modules are included in the script and they all have a `say_hello` method, Ruby will use the method in the namespace of the scoped module (List 3.4.3).

The `scope` operator's syntax uses the name of the module (representing the namespace of the contained methods and constants) followed by a double colon followed by the method or constant name.

```
HelloModule::say_hello
```

LIST 3.4.3. RUBY SCRIPT mod2.rb **CALLS A MODULE WITH THE SCOPE OPERATOR**

```
#!/usr/local/bin/ruby
module HelloModule
    def say_hello
        puts "hello"
    end
end
include HelloModule
HelloModule::say_hello
exit
```

In most instances, Ruby modules are not called directly from scripts. Instead, modules are included in classes. By including modules within classes, the user has access to the module methods via class instance objects. The user does not need to put include statements in the script (because the module is included through the class), and the user does not need to know which class methods were created for the class and which methods were included into the class through a module. As far as the user is concerned, the Module methods included in a class are just like any other class methods.

Here is an example in which the HelloModule is included in class Container (List 3.4.4).

LIST 3.4.4. RUBY SCRIPT mod3.rb **EMBEDS A MODULE WITHIN A CLASS**

```
#!/usr/local/bin/ruby
class Container
    module HelloModule
        def say_hello
            puts "hello"
        end
    end
    include HelloModule
end
my_object = Container.new
my_object.say_hello
exit
```

In this case, the `include` statement appears within class Container's definition. To call `HelloModule's say_hello` method, you create a new instance object of class `Container`. Then you send the method name to the instance object. Nowhere in the main part of the script is `HelloModule` invoked. The work is done behind the scenes. When a module is included in a class definition, it is called a Mixin.

Despite its deceptively simple definition, modules are the heart of compositional object orientation and provide a way for classes to acquire methods that enhance the functionality of the class without changing the identity and the purpose of the class. Many of the built-in Ruby classes contain modules that are common to other Ruby classes.

Some programmers think of Mixins as a sneaky way to gain multiclass inheritance, wherein one class inherits methods from more than one direct ancestor. Although technically true, this thinking is counterproductive. You should think of modules as a way of enhancing a class without changing the intrinsic identity of the class. Module methods provided to a class should be methods that are natural extensions of features that are characteristic of the class. If you have a `Neoplasm` class, it might be reasonable to include a `Growth` module with a `doubling_time` method. Neoplasms, unfortunately, grow, and they have a calculated doubling time. A `Growth` module may be appropriate to include in classes that are unrelated (that is, not ancestors and not descendants of the `Neoplasm` class). An `Amoeba` class might appropriately include a `Growth` module. A `Bacteria` class may include the `Growth` module as well. The point here is that modules contain general methods that are not specific to any class. Classes create objects of a specific type, but these objects may need methods that dissimilar objects also need. Through the careful and disciplined use of Mixins, you can vastly expand the utility of classes without changing the identity of the class.

3.5. COMPOSITION (LAYERING, AGGREGATION, DELEGATION)

With few exceptions, people tend to associate object-oriented programming with the trinity of inheritance, polymorphism, and encapsulation. In Ruby, there is a fourth property: composition.

Composition (also called layering and aggregation) is a technique of object-oriented programming languages in which classes are provided with a set of methods that are not constitutive for the class (that is, their exclusion from the class would not change your concept of the objects contained in the class). In Ruby, as discussed in the preceding section, Mixins is an easy and powerful compositional programming technique.

Another composition technique is delegation. We will not use delegation in this book. Suffice it to say that delegation is a subtle but powerful technique that creates a "shadow" object in a specified second class when you invoke delegation during the initialization of an object. When an object with a delegate is sent a method appropriate for the delegation class, it will respond just as though it were an object from the delegated class.

3.6. WHO AM I REALLY? REFLECTION ON RUBY CLASSES AND OBJECTS

Ruby comes with a large library of classes and modules and methods. You can create classes and subclasses in Ruby, and you can add methods to new and existing classes. As a Ruby programmer, it is easy to become confused if you do not have access to information that clarify the meaning and content of classes, methods, and objects. Luckily, Ruby comes with dozens of so-called Reflection methods that shed light on the internal state of any Ruby script.

Without going deeply into the uses of each method, we provide simple demonstrations of Reflection in an `irb` session.

Ruby keeps track of the class of every object. You can determine any object's class with the `class` method.

```
irb>my_array = Array.new([1,2,3]) => [1, 2, 3]
irb>my_array.class => Array
```

Method `ancestors` provides the inherited classes and modules of an object.

```
irb> Fixnum.ancestors =>
[Fixnum, Integer, Precision, Numeric, Comparable, Object, Kernel]
```

Method `superclass` provides the immediate parent of a class.

```
irb> Fixnum.superclass => Integer
```

If you have an object that is not a class and would like to know the name of the superclass of the class that it resides within, chain the `class` and `superclass` methods.

```
irb>my_array = Array.new([1,2,3]) => [1, 2, 3]
irb>my_array.class.superclass => Object
```

After you have the name of a class, you can determine the methods available to class objects with the `methods` method.

```
irb(main):017:0> my_array = Array.new([1,2,3]) => [1, 2, 3]
irb(main):018:0> my_array.class => Array
irb(main):019:0> my_array.class.methods
=> ["methods", "instance_eval", "dup", "instance_variables",
"include?", "private_instance_methods", "autoload",
"instance_of?", "protected_method_defined?", "extend",
"const_defined?", "eql?", "name", "public_class_method",
"new", "hash", "instance_method", "id", "singleton_methods",
"taint", "constants", "frozen?", "instance_variable_get",
"kind_of?", "ancestors", "to_a", "private_class_method",
"const_missing", "type", "protected_methods",
"instance_methods", "autoload?", "superclass",
"method_defined?", "instance_variable_set", "const_get",
"method", "is_a?", "respond_to?", "to_s", "module_eval",
"class_variables", "allocate", "class", "<=>",
"require_gem", "<", "tainted?", "private_methods", "==",
"public_instance_methods", "__id__", "===",
"public_method_defined?", ">", "included_modules", "nil?",
"untaint", "const_set", ">=", "gem", "<=", "send", "display",
"inspect", "class_eval", "clone", "=~", "object_id",
"require", "protected_instance_methods", "public_methods",
"private_method_defined?", "__send__", "equal?", "freeze","[]"]
```

Similarly, methods `instance_methods`, `class_variables` and `instance_variables` yield the methods and variables for their respective objects.

Class `ObjectSpace` provides a method (`each_object`) to iterate over the permanent objects (for example, constants, environment variables) available to a class or module. Ruby allows you to extract every object in its object space.

```
irb>ObjectSpace.each_object(Numeric){|object|puts object}
2.71828182845905
3.14159265358979
2.22044604925031e-016
1.79769313486232e+308
2.2250738585072e-308
100.0
=> 6
```

For the `Numeric` class, the objects are constants, such as the values of PI and e. The `each_object` method returns the total number of objects (six in this case). If you substitute `Kernel` for `Numeric` in this example, you will see about 14,000 internal objects flash on your monitor!

Method `instance_of?` tests whether an object is an instance of a provided class.

```
irb>hash1 = Hash.new => {}
irb>hash1.instance_of?(Array) => false
irb>hash1.instance_of?(Hash) => true
```

Method `constants` yields the constants defined for a class.

```
irb>Math.constants => ["PI", "E"]
irb>Math::PI => 3.14159265358979
```

Method `is_a?` tests whether an object belongs to the provided class.

```
irb>my_string = String.new => ""
irb>my_string.is_a?Array => false
```

Ruby provides an id (identifier) number to every object. The id number can be retrieved with method `object_id`. Here, we retrieve the object id of the Array class:

```
irb>Array.object_id => 20697230
```

Whenever we create a new object, it is given an id.

```
irb>my_array = Array.new([1,2,3]) => [1, 2, 3]
irb>my_array.object_id => 20612470
```

Ruby has many more Reflection methods. Crafty programmers use Reflection to engineer dynamic control over script objects and methods. Less experienced programmers can use these same methods to find their bearings.

CHAPTER 4

Ruby Extensions and Standard Libraries (Level 2)

4.1. BACKGROUND

In addition to the built-in Ruby classes and modules, the Ruby interpreter is distributed with dozens of standard libraries and extensions. The Standard Libraries are programs written in Ruby that can be "required" into your own programs (that is, called from your own Ruby script by invoking "require" followed by the name of the library).

For example, the Date standard library could be required into a script with the following line of code:

```
require 'date'
```

Ruby is also distributed with a variety of programs called extensions. Extensions are Ruby programs that are extended by their inclusion of other resources, particularly C routines. Ruby extensions will be supported only if your operating system has access to the resources called by the extension.

The advantage of the Ruby Standard Library is that everyone using Ruby is likely to have the same libraries included in their installation (List 4.1.1). This enhances your ability to share scripts that require programs that are not actually built into the Ruby language.

The purpose of this chapter is to familiarize you with those Ruby Standard Libraries and Extensions that may benefit biologists and healthcare workers.

LIST 4.1.1. SOME EXAMPLES OF THE RUBY STANDARD LIBRARY

Base64

Benchmark and Profile

CGI

CSV

Date

DBM, GDBM, and SDBM

Delegator

Digest

Mail

Mathn

Matrix

Net::FTP, Net::HTTP, Net::POP, Net::SMTP, Net::Telnet

PStore and YAML

RDoc

REXML

SOAP and XMLRPC

Socket

Tk

Zlib

4.2. SELECTED RUBY STANDARD LIBRARIES

Base64 provides a way of converting so-called binary data into so-called 7-bit ASCII (see Chapter 8, Section 3). Some data formats, including HTML and XML, permit only ASCII text, and, thus, base64 is a popular method for transporting binary data in web documents (see List 8.2.1).

Benchmark and Profile is used by programmers to determine the speed of scripts, the frequency of subroutine calls, and the time spent in subroutines.

CGI (Common Gateway Interface) facilitates the composition of CGI Ruby scripts that reside on servers and that respond to web requests sent by clients (web browsers) to servers, through the standard HTTP communication protocol. The CGI script prepares, on the fly, a web page that often contains data collected from a database in response to a client query and sends the web page back to the client's web browser (see Chapter 15 and List 15.2.2).

CSV manipulates data prepared as comma-separated spreadsheet files.

Date manipulates date and time information through an implementation of Ruby's built-in Date and DateTime classes.

DBM, GDBM, and SDBM database management libraries tie hashes to external files that persist after your scripts have finished executing. The external files can be called for subsequent sessions of the script or from any script, yielding the key/value pairs from the persistent hash whenever needed. The DBM, GDBM, and SDBM libraries are distributed with Ruby and should always be available to Ruby users, regardless of their operating system and environment (see Lists 6.6.1 and 6.6.2). Judicious use of Ruby's database management libraries can reduce your dependence on external database applications.

Delegator assigns an object, within a class, to membership in some other class. Ruby has three strategies whereby classes can access methods not written into their class definition: inheritance, Mixins, and delegation.

Digest produces one-way hashes for strings, using MD5, SHA, or RIPEMD methods. One-way hashes are used extensively for de-identification techniques that preserve the confidentiality of medical records and are described in detail in Chapter 14 and List 14.6.2.

Mail parses e-mail messages.

Mathn extends Ruby's built-in class Math. As we saw in Chapter 2, several built-in Ruby math operators (particularly, the division operator, "/") have polymorphic behavior for the subclasses of class Numeric. This is a potential source of error in Ruby scripts. Mathn provides methods that work in an expected manner for objects of the different subclasses of class Numeric (see Chapter 13).

Matrix provides classes Matrix and Vector and methods for each class.

Net::FTP, Net::HTTP, Net::POP, Net::SMTP, Net::Telnet. Ruby supports all of the basic Internet protocols.

PStore and YAML PStore (persistent store) supports storage of Ruby objects in external files. YAML (Yet Another Metadata Language) marshals Ruby objects into a standard plain-text format that is recognized by other scripting languages, including Python. Marshalling (also called serializing) is a process wherein data objects that are typically kept in an internal, binary state are transformed into a readable format.

RDoc is bundled with Ruby (versions 1.8 and higher); the RDoc tool extracts documentation embedded in Ruby source code and creates an HTML document that lists the contained files, classes, and methods, along with any annotations that might have been embedded in your code (4).

As a simple example of the ease and power of the RDoc tool, let us create an RDoc for a `fastcode.rb` (List 12.3.1), a Ruby script that we create in Chapter 12.

After you have installed Ruby, the RDoc tool is ready to operate from your command prompt.

Just enter `rdoc` followed by a space and the name of your script.

```
C:\ftp\rb>rdoc fastcode.rb
```

RDoc outputs information as it executes.

```
fastcode.rb: c.......
Generating HTML...


Files:   1
Classes: 1
Modules: 0
Methods: 7
Elapsed: 0.516s
```

RDoc creates a new subdirectory, named \doc, and loads dozens of new files under the \doc directory.

```
01/10/2007  12:47 PM    <DIR>  classes
01/10/2007  12:47 PM           48 created.rid
01/10/2007  12:47 PM    <DIR>  files
01/10/2007  12:47 PM           684 fr_class_index.html
01/10/2007  12:47 PM           682 fr_file_index.html
01/10/2007  12:47 PM           1,171 fr_method_index.html
01/10/2007  12:47 PM           770 index.html
01/10/2007  12:47 PM           4,521 rdoc-style.css 6
       File(s) 7,876 bytes]
```

The RDoc HTML files can be reached from the index.html file (see Figure 4-1).

Programmers can supplement their scripts with documentation that will display as informative notes in the HTML files produced by RDoc. There is extensive documentation of the RDoc tool at *http://www.ruby-doc.org/stdlib/libdoc/rdoc/rdoc/index.html*

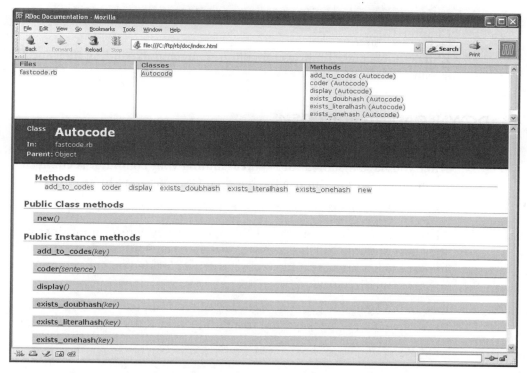

Figure 4-1 **RDoc creates a uniform interface that lists the files, classes, and methods of a Ruby script.**

REXML is a simple and fast XML processor (see Lists 18.14.2 and 19.3.1).

SOAP and XMLRPC RPC is a remote procedure calling. In a remote procedure call, a client computer invokes a computational method and calls another networked computer to execute the method. XML-RPC is an RPC call performed using XML configured commands. SOAP is a formalized protocol that establishes uniform terms and methods for describing RPC transactions in XML syntax. Ruby provides Standard Libraries to facilitate these useful protocols.

Socket is a software device that allows you to make connections to other computers that are connected to the Internet. The Ruby Socket Library is a standard library distributed with Ruby. It provides a group of classes that support socket-level communication over the Internet.

Tk is a library that allows you to create a graphic interface for your Ruby scripts. Ruby Tk works very much like Perl Tk. A Tk script begins with instructions for creating a window with embedded window objects such as buttons, text boxes, canvases, etc. Under the TK graphic instructions, the script begins a mainloop, consisting of a familiar Ruby script that uses the graphic interface for input and output.

WEBrick is a Ruby tool that implements an HTTP-based server (see Chapter 16).

Zlib contains class libraries for compressing and expanding files and IO streams.

4.3. DOWNLOADING RUBY GEMS

Ruby gems are Ruby programs that can be accessed through the Internet. After you have installed Ruby and assuming your computer is connected to the Internet, you can use the bundled GEM program to install gems.

```
C:\ruby\bin>gem list —remote >c:\ftp\rubylist.txt
```

This command line, entered at the operating system prompt, instructs the GEM program to fetch a list of available gems from remote sites and to port the list into a text file (`rubylist.txt`) located on your computer's `c:\ftp\` subdirectory.

One of the available gem packages is `rtf`. You can use the GEM program to retrieve the `rtf` package and install it in your Ruby `\bin` subdirectory.

```
C:\ruby\bin>gem install rtf —remote
```

```
remote
Attempting remote installation of "rtf" Successfully installed
rtf-0.1.0 Installing RDoc documentation for rtf-0.1.0...
```

One of the most popular Ruby gems is Ruby on Rails (Figure 4-2). We use this gem in Chapter 16. Ruby on Rails can be easily downloaded and installed with a single command-line expression.

4.4. CONVERTING RUBY SCRIPTS TO EXECUTABLE (EXE) FILES

The `rubyscript2exe` package compiles Ruby scripts as executable files. This means that people who do not have Ruby installed on their computers can use your Ruby scripts if they are distributed as .exe files. To get the rubyscript2exe package,

```
C:\ruby\bin>gem install rubyscript2exe —remote
```

```
C:\ruby\bin>"c:\ruby\bin\ruby.exe" "c:\ruby\bin\gem" install
rubyscript2exe —remote
```

```
Attempting remote installation of 'rubyscript2exe'
Successfully installed rubyscript2exe-0.4.2
```

Figure 4-2 Gem installation output for Ruby on Rails.

Here is an example of a Ruby script (scrub4.rb) as it is converted to an .exe file with rubyscript2exe.

```
C:\ftp>ruby c:/ruby/bin/rubyscript2exe scrub4.rb
Tracing scrub4 ... What would you like to scrub? This is the
next version of the adenocarcinoma of the colon this is the
* * of the adenocarcinoma of the colonGathering files...
Copying files... Creating scrub4.exe ...
```

Instructions for rubyscript2exe are at *http://www.erikveen.dds.nl/ rubyscript2exe/index.html*

Biomedical Data Files Used in Later Chapters (Level I)

5.1. BACKGROUND

There is no escaping it. If you want to do any useful programming in the field of biology or medicine, you will need to master biomedical data files. Although standardization of biomedical data is a noble pursuit, biomedical data come in a variety of forms. The most common informatics tasks involve one or more of the following activities (Lists 5.1.1 and 5.1.2).

LIST 5.1.1. COMMON FORMAT-INTENSIVE BIOMEDICAL TASKS

Collecting and organizing data into one of about a dozen general formats.

Accessing data in a particular format and transforming the data into a different format.

Accessing data in a particular format and writing a utility that parses the data for the purpose of retrieving a subset of the data.

Accessing data in a particular format and adding annotations to the data.

Accessing data in a particular format and analyzing a subset of the data.

LIST 5.1.2. THE DIFFERENT TYPES OF DATA FILES IN BIOLOGY AND MEDICINE

Free-text, such as essays and books

Semistructured plain text, such as radiology reports and surgical pathology reports, with different reports separated by a standard delimiter (such as a formalized accession number preceding each report)

Quasistructured plain-text narrative, such as field-designated hospital forms

Structured plain-text narrative, such as field-designated hospital forms with entries chosen from a provided list

PubMed mixed text and data file

Byte-designated files

Flat files with bar-delimited records

Database files

Comma-delimited spreadsheet files

XML (eXtensible Markup Language) files

RDF (Resource Description Framework) data files

RDF schemas

YAML (Yet Another Markup Language) files

Image files

Word processor files

5.2. DOWNLOADING BIOMEDICAL DATA FILES

External data files are not included inside the script, but are located as separate files elsewhere on your computer or on some publicly available server.

The scripts included in this book use real-world biomedical data obtained from publicly available files. The scripts are written specifically to accommodate the way that data are organized in the files.

About a dozen file formats account for most of the data files that biomedical informaticians commonly encounter. In Chapter 18, you will learn RDF (Resource Description Framework) and RDF Schema, the two principle ideas behind the Semantic Web. In the future, RDF may become the universal format for all data exchange. Today, however, we need to settle for about a dozen popular data formats that we can parse, transform, and analyze with Ruby scripts.

Whether you are an experienced programmer, an experienced biological scientist, or a healthcare worker focused on patient care, you should be familiar with all of the file types listed and all of the individual data files described in this chapter. With these files, you can begin to use Ruby to integrate research data with medical records and retrieve all types of data with domain-specific nomenclatures.

All of the external data files used in this book are open-access documents available through the Internet at no cost.

You do not need to download all of these files to understand and benefit from the lessons in this book. If you would like to try some of the Ruby scripts, you can download files when necessary, or you may wish to modify our Ruby scripts to accommodate your own personal files (List 5.2.1).

LIST 5.2.1. FREE, AVAILABLE FILES USED IN RUBY SCRIPTS FROM THIS BOOK

OMIM (Online Mendelian Inheritance in Man) semistructured plain-text file

PubMed semistructured plain-text file

TAXONOMY.DAT structured file

UMLS (Unified Medical Language System)

MeSH (Medical Subject Headings)

MRCONSO (UMLS Metathesaurus concepts)

MRSTY (UMLS Metathesaurus relationships)

U.S. Census comma separated spreadsheet file

SEER byte-designated data file

Foundational Model of Anatomy SQL database file

Neoplasm classification XML file

Gene Ontology RDF file

Dublin Core RDF schema file

The purpose of this chapter is to describe the general types of biomedical data files and to provide specific descriptions of those publicly available files that will be used in scripts throughout this book. You may prefer to skip over this chapter now, returning when you study the scripts that call data sources included herein.

5.3. TEXT RECORDS: OMIM, THE ONLINE MENDELIAN INHERITANCE IN MAN

OMIM is a curated listing of every known inherited condition in humans. Each condition has biologic and clinical descriptions in a detailed textual narrative that includes a listing of relevant citations (List 5.3.1). There are nearly 17,000 conditions described, and the OMIM file exceeds 114 Mb. The OMIM file can be downloaded from the National Center for Bioinformatics' anonymous ftp site: *ftp://ftp.ncbi.nih.gov/repository/omim/*.

LIST 5.3.1. THE FIRST RECORD IN OMIM, SHORTENED

```
*RECORD*
*FIELD* NO
100050
*FIELD* TI
100050 AARSKOG SYNDROME
*FIELD* TX
```

Grier et al. (1983) reported father and two sons with typical Aarskog syndrome, including short stature, hypertelorism, and shawl scrotum.

.

.

.

The mother seemed less severely affected, compatible with X-linked inheritance.

```
*FIELD* RF
```

1. Grier, R. E., Farrington, F. H., Kendig, R., & Mamunes, P. Autosomal dominant inheritance of the Aarskog syndrome. *Am J Med Genet.* 15:39–46, 1983.

2. Teebi, A. S., Rucquoi, J. K., & Meyn, M. S. Aarskog syndrome: report of a family with review and discussion of nosology. *Am J Med Genet.* 46:501–509, 1993.

3. Welch, J. P. Elucidation of a "new" pleiotropic connective tissue disorder. *Birth Defects Orig Art Ser.* 10:138–146, 1974.

FIELD CS

Growth:

    Mild to moderate short stature

Head:

    Normocephaly

Hair:

    Widow's peak

Facies:

    Maxillary hypoplasia

    Broad nasal bridge

    Anteverted nostrils

    Long philtrum

    Broad upper lip

    Curved linear dimple below the lower lip

(continues)

```
             .

             .

             .



      *FIELD* CD
        Victor A. McKusick: 6/4/1986



      *FIELD* ED
        alopez: 06/03/1997

        .

        .

        .

      marie: 3/25/1988
```

Additional information on OMIM is available at *http://www.ncbi.nlm. nih.gov/omim/*.

5.4. TEXT RECORDS: PUBMED DOWNLOAD FILES

PubMed is the National Library of Medicine's public database of medical journal articles. PubMed is an expansion of Medline and contains journal abstracts and a set of sophisticated search routines. PubMed also links open-access journal articles to Websites from which the complete text can be downloaded.

Every biomedical professional should be adept at using PubMed. PubMed provides Ruby programmers with a great many opportunities to acquire, search, transform, and organize large text files of abstracts and other PubMed citation data.

As an exercise, go to the PubMed Website, and enter a search on the word "informatics" (see Figure 5-1). Click on the "GO" button, and the first 20 citations (from over 7500 citations) will appear on your screen. PubMed lets you change the display format for citations. From the "Display" button, pick "MEDLINE." Your screen will refresh with citations listed in longer entries that include each journal article's abstract

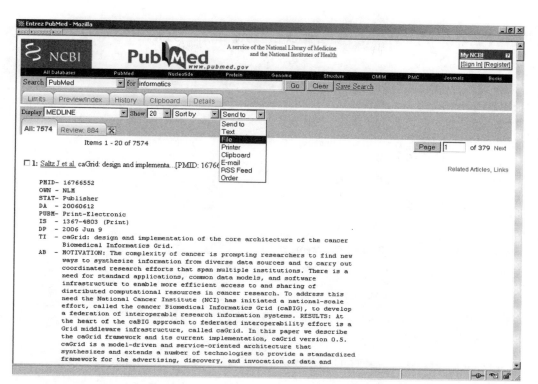

Figure 5-1 PubMed browser interface.

and a variety of annotative data in a uniform format. Then click on the "Send To" button and choose "File." PubMed will download to your hard drive a file containing 7500+ citations in MEDLINE format. The file size for this particular search should be in excess of 13 Mb.

The resultant citation file, in Medline format, is a perfect crucible for data mining projects.

Here is an example of a PubMed record in Medline format (List 5.4.1).

As an exercise, you might want to extract the names, street address, and e-mail addresses for all of the authors in the citation files for whom e-mails are listed (not all citations will contain e-mail addresses) (see List 7.7.1).

5.5. COMMA-DELIMITED DATA FILES: CENSUS DATA EXAMPLE

The U.S. Census Bureau publishes data files of its decennial census at *http://www.census.gov/*

Public datasets can be downloaded from *http://www.census.gov/popest/datasets.html*

LIST 5.4.1. A TYPICAL PUBMED ENTRY IN MEDLINE FORMAT (SHORTENED)

> PMID—15113444
>
> OWN—NLM
>
> STAT—MEDLINE
>
> DA—20040519
>
> DCOM—20040629
>
> LR—20050810
>
> PUBM—Electronic
>
> IS—1471-2407 (Electronic)
>
> VI—4
>
> DP—2004 Mar 17
>
> TI—tumor classification: molecular analysis meets Aristotle.
>
> PG—10
>
> AB—BACKGROUND: Traditionally, tumors have been classified by their morphologic appearances. Unfortunately, tumors with similar histologic
>
> .
>
> .
>
> .
>
> document that can be used by cancer researchers to relate tumor classes with heterogeneous experimental and clinical tumor databases.
>
> AD—Cancer Diagnosis Program, National Cancer Institute, Bethesda, MD. bermanj@mail.nih.gov
>
> FAU—Berman, Jules J
>
> AU—Berman JJ
>
> LA—Eng
>
> PT—Journal Article
>
> DEP—20040317

PL—England

TA—BMC Cancer

JT—BMC cancer [electronic resource]

JID—100967800

SB—IM

MH—Germinoma/classification

MH—Humans

MH—Neoplasms/*classification/genetics/pathology

MH—*Vocabulary, Controlled

EDAT—2004/04/29 05:00

MHDA—2004/06/30 05:00

PHST—2003/11/15 [received]

PHST—2004/03/17 [accepted]

PHST—2004/03/17 [aheadofprint]

AID—10.1186/1471-2407-4-10 [doi]

AID—1471-2407-4-10 [pii]

PST—epublish

SO—BMC Cancer. 2004 Mar 17;4:10.

Most of the datasets are in simple comma delimited ASCII format, with a key provided that lists the order and named data elements in each row (record) of the file.

In Chapter 10, we examine records from the 5-Mb alldata6.csv file.

http://www.census.gov/popest/states/asrh/files/sc_est2004_alldata6.csv

This file is an example of a comma-delimited data file. An external file serves as the key to the records.

The first four records of the data from file alldata6.csv U.S. Census file are shown in List 5.5.1.

At the U.S. census site, a key to the data files is provided (List 5.5.2).

After you have "deciphered" the data file with the key, comma-delimited files become easy to analyze in Ruby scripts (see List 10.5.1).

LIST 5.5.1. FIRST FOUR RECORDS FROM A U.S. CENSUS DATA FILE

040,01,3,06,1,1,01,0,19163,19164,19291,19157,18607,18511,18707

040,01,3,06,1,2,01,0,866,866,892,1019,1145,1266,1277

040,01,3,06,2,1,01,0,18034,18035,18169,18318,17736,17678,17721

040,01,3,06,2,2,01,0,869,869,895,951,1126,1202,1222

LIST 5.5.2. DICTIONARY KEY TO A U.S. CENSUS FILE

SUM

LEV,STATE,REGION,DIVISION,SEX,ORIGIN,RACE,AGE,

CENSUS2000POP,ESTIMA

TESBASE2000,POPESTIMATE2000,POPESTIMATE2001,

POPESTIMATE2002,POPESTIMATE2003,

POPESTIMATE2004

5.6. BYTE-DESIGNATED DATA FILES: SEER DATA EXAMPLE

The Surveillance, Epidemiology, and End Results (SEER) Program of the National Cancer Institute is an authoritative source of information on cancer incidence and survival in the United States.

The SEER Public-Use Data include SEER incidence and population data associated by age, gender, race, year of diagnosis and geographic areas (including SEER registry and county).

Public use Seer data are available at *http://seer.cancer.gov/publicdata/*.

Users must sign a public-use data agreement before downloading SEER public use files. The DATA Agreement is available at *http://seer.cancer.gov/publicdata/access.html*.

The public can download 113 Mb of compressed SEER data (expands to 700 Megabytes).

SEER distributes cancer records from multiple geographic sites and distributes files as byte-designated flat files (Lists 5.6.1–3). Sequences from the SEER file correspond to sequences in other data files (Lists

5.6.4–5). In Chapter 12.5, we will assign ICD terms to sequences from the SEER file and compile the occurrences of diseases in a sampled population (List 12.5.1).

LIST 5.6.1. SOME OF THE ORGAN-SPECIFIC PUBLIC DATA FROM SEER

2002	34,785,520	BREAST.TXT
2002	23,085,062	COLRECT.TXT
2002	15,104,782	DIGOTHR.TXT
2002	20,239,758	FEMGEN.TXT
2002	16,321,074	LYMYLEUK.TXT
2002	32,392,052	MALEGEN.TXT
2002	28,956,158	OTHER.TXT
2002	28,339,542	RESPIR.TXT
2002	12,987,282	URINARY.TXT

LIST 5.6.2. FIRST 4 RECORDS (TRUNCATED) OF SEER FILE "URINARY.TXT", SETS OF CHARACTERS CORRESPOND TO DATA ELEMENTS

```
020000354901100900719150770202500041993C67408120331999209800 ...
020002232202100300719230720101202091995C65928120341999300980 0 ...
020002756101100100719400540202100121994C679080103319999999800 ...
020003435501100141019280670101200121995C64928312321050609980 0 ...
```

LIST 5.6.3. CHARACTERS 45–59 OF FOUR INDIVIDUAL SEER RECORDS

Characters 45–49 of record 1 of urinary.txt 81203

Characters 45–49 of record 1 of urinary.txt 81203

Characters 45–49 of record 1 of urinary.txt 80103

Characters 45–49 of record 1 of urinary.txt 83123

LIST 5.6.4. A FEW ICD RECORDS

C0007117 I .....ICD10AM I PT I M8090/3 I Basal cell carcinoma NOS I 3 I N I I

C0007118 I .....ICD10AM I PT I M8094/3 I Basosquamous carcinoma I 3 I N I I

C0007118 I .....ICD10AM I PT I M8095/3 I Metatypical carcinoma I 3 I N I 256 I

C0007120 I .....ICD10AM I PT I M8250/3 I Bronchiolo-alveolar
     adenocarcinoma I 3 I N I I

C0007120 I .....ICD10AM I PT I M8251/3 I Alveolar adenocarcinoma I 3 I N I I

C0007124 I .....ICD10AM I PT I M8500/2 I Intraductal carcinoma,
     noninfiltrating NOS I 3 I N I I

LIST 5.6.5. ICD NAMES FOR CODES CONTAINED IN CHARACTERS 45–49 OF 4 SEER RECORDS

Record 1 of urinary.txt 81203—Transitional cell carcinoma NOS

Record 1 of urinary.txt 81203—Transitional cell carcinoma NOS

Record 1 of urinary.txt 80103—Carcinoma NOS

Record 1 of urinary.txt 83123—Renal cell carcinoma

5.7. UMLS METATHESAURUS

By far the largest medical nomenclature is the U.S. National Library of Medicine's Unified Medical Language System Metathesaurus (UMLS Metathesaurus), which contains several million terms grouped under about a million concepts (5). The UMLS is comprised of over 100 individual thesauruses (see the Glossary), many of which are contributed by efforts funded by the U.S. government. The UMLS metathesaurus can be acquired at no cost from the National Library of Medicine. UMLS users must agree to abide by the terms of the UMLS license.

Although the UMLS metathesaurus is made available at no cost, there are restrictions on the uses of the vocabularies included in the metathesaurus distribution. The UMLS metathesaurus is composed of approximately 100 different vocabularies and thesauruses. Many of these vocabularies have very few restrictions on their use (the so-called Category 0 vocabularies), whereas other included vocabularies have policies that limit their uses.

To get UMLS Metathesaurus files

1. Get the free UMLS license. Fill out your application at *http://www.nlm. nih.gov/research/umls/license.html.*

   Usually within 1 day, the National Library of Medicine will e-mail you a license number and a link to a URL in which you will complete step 2.

2. Use your login number to create a login id and a password (both of which you will need when you want to download UMLS metathesaurus files).

3. Go to *http://umlsks.nlm.nih.gov/kss/servlet/Turbine/template/admin, user,KSS_login.vm.*

4. Enter your login id and password.

5. This takes you to the UMLSKS server.

6. On left side of the Web page, go to downloads, and click on "UMLS Knowledge Sources."

7. Download the latest metathesaurus file collections. In 2006, the metathesaurus is contained in three files (see Figure 5-2):

   2006aa-1-meta.nlm, 865,654,454 bytes

   2006ac-2-meta.nlm, 631,192,874 bytes

   2006ac-3-meta.nlm, over 800 Mbytes

8. The .nlm extension is a zipped archive. Rename the files with .zip extensions, such as (Figure 5-2)

   2006ac-1-meta.nlm -> 2006ac_1.zip

   2006ac-2-meta.nlm -> 2006ac_2.zip

9. Use a zip utility, such as the freely available 7-zip (see the appendix).

   You will see that the zip-archived files are individual gzipped (.gz) files.

10. The most important file is MRCONSO.RRF.gz.,

    MRCONSO is the list of every term in the UMLS metathesaurus. Each term is assigned a CUI code (concept unique identifier).

    Expand MRCONSO.RRF.gz with gunzip.exe (see the appendix).

    The file expands to a single file that can be renamed MRCONSO. The 2006 version of the MRCONSO file is 775,041,624 bytes. Each line of MRCONSO is a unique term.

Here is an example of the first records in the MRCONSO file. The online MRCONSO record is broken here into two lines to fit the printed page (List 5.7.1).

The UMLS unique concept code is "C0000005." The term is "(131)I-Macroaggregated Albumin."

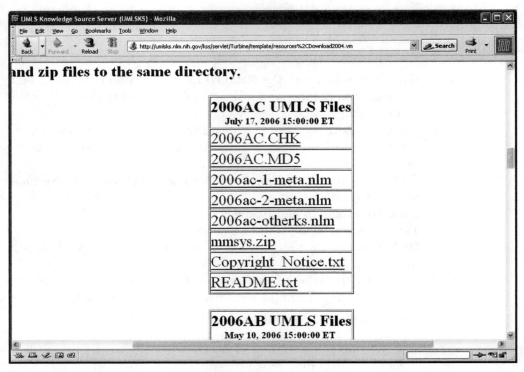

Figure 5-2 The UMLS download Web page.

LIST 5.7.1. FIRST RECORD OF THE UMLS METATHESAURUS MRCONSO FILE

C0000005 | ENG | X | L0000005 | X | S0007492 | X | A7755565 | | M0019694 |

D012711 | MSH | PEN | D012711 | (131)I-Macroaggregated Albumin | 0 | N | |

There are millions of unique medical terms in the 2006 UMLS.

MRSTY is another important UMLS file. Uncompressed, it exceeds 86 Megabytes. Each record in the MRSTY files lists a relationship term for a UMLS concept (List 5.7.2).

The first three records of MRSTY indicate that C0000005 is an amino acid, peptide or protein. C0000005 is also a pharmacologic substance and an indicator, reagent or diagnostic aid. However, what term is C0000005? The MRCON file indicates that one of the synonyms for C0000005 is "(131)I-Macroaggregated Albumin." You can see that the MRSTY file, in tandem with the MRCON file, can be used to extract terms that fit any desired MRSTY relation (see List 6.5.1).

LIST 5.7.2. THE FIRST FEW RECORDS FROM THE UMLS METATHESAURUS MRSTY FILE

C0000005 | T116 | A1.4.1.2.1.7 | Amino Acid, Peptide, or Protein | AT17648347 | |

C0000005 | T121 | A1.4.1.1.1 | Pharmacologic Substance | AT17575038 | |

C0000005 | T130 | A1.4.1.1.4 | Indicator, Reagent, or Diagnostic Aid | AT17634323 | |

C0000039 | T119 | A1.4.1.2.1.9 | Lipid | AT17617573 | |

C0000039 | T121 | A1.4.1.1.1 | Pharmacologic Substance | AT17567371 | |

C0000052 | T116 | A1.4.1.2.1.7 | Amino Acid, Peptide, or Protein | AT08381079 | |

C0000052 | T126 | A1.4.1.1.3.3 | Enzyme | AT08775334 | |

C0000074 | T119 | A1.4.1.2.1.9 | Lipid | AT17617801 | |

C0000084 | T116 | A1.4.1.2.1.7 | Amino Acid, Peptide, or Protein | AT17641823 | |

C0000084 | T123 | A1.4.1.1.3 | Biologically Active Substance | AT17597318 | |

C0000096 | T109 | A1.4.1.2.1 | Organic Chemical | AT17685682 | |

C0000096 | T121 | A1.4.1.1.1 | Pharmacologic Substance | AT17567369 | |

C0000097 | T109 | A1.4.1.2.1 | Organic Chemical | AT17685735 | |

C0000097 | T131 | A1.4.1.1.5 | Hazardous or Poisonous Substance | AT17619208 | |

C0000098 | T109 | A1.4.1.2.1 | Organic Chemical | AT17696093 | |

C0000098 | T131 | A1.4.1.1.5 | Hazardous or Poisonous Substance | AT17620025 | |

5.8. SQL FILE, THE FOUNDATIONAL MODEL OF ANATOMY

The Foundational Model of Anatomy (FMA) serves as both a dictionary of anatomic terms and their relationships and an encoded database that can support machine-based parsing and inferencing. The FMA is freely available to the public after an online registration process.

Registrants are asked to accept a 12-page license written in dense legalistic prose.

http://sig.biostr.washington.edu/projects/fma/FMA_License_Nov06.pdf

Registration is completed at *http://sig.biostr.washington.edu/cgi-bin/ fma_register.cgi*

The FMA is distributed to the public as an SQL file (List 5.8.1). The file used in this book is

fma_v1.4.0_06-13-06.sql, length 99,064,732

LIST 5.8.1. SOME DATA LINES OF THE FMA SQL FILE

(199227,5,2006,0,0,0,6,'10001',NULL),

(199227,5,181349,0,0,0,3,'English',NULL),

(199227,5,145199,0,0,0,3,'Mon Mar 10 11:45:20 PST 2003',NULL),

(199227,5,63840,0,0,0,3,'Nerve to right plantaris',NULL),

(199227,5,2002,0,0,0,3,'FM_live_10678',NULL),

(199227,5,63838,0,0,0,3,'Rosse MD',NULL),

(31233,6,2006,0,0,0,6,'31227',NULL),

(31233,6,63834,0,0,0,5,'141140',NULL),

(31233,6,2004,0,0,0,6,'31227',NULL),

(31233,6,2002,0,0,0,3,'Costal part of costal surface of right lung',NULL),

(31233,6,2003,0,0,0,3,'Concrete',NULL),

(34782,6,198693,0,0,1,6,'31233',NULL),

(31233,6,180803,0,0,0,6,'31235',NULL),

(31233,6,180803,0,0,1,6,'31237',NULL),

(31233,6,63836,0,0,0,3,'27402',NULL),

(102755,5,2006,0,0,0,6,'10001',NULL),

(102755,5,63839,0,0,0,3,'Thu Aug 12 11:30:30 PDT 1999',NULL),

Casual inspection of the file indicates that related lines are assigned a common number and that every set of lines corresponding to a unique number seems to hold the name of an anatomic part.

(199227,5,63840,0,0,0,3,'Nerve to right plantaris',NULL),

(31233,6,2002,0,0,0,3,'Costal part of costal surface of

right lung',NULL),

This goes to show that even database files can be interpreted after inspection and parsed much like any other type of file (see List 10.4.1).

5.9. NEOPLASM CLASSIFICATION (AN XML FILE)

The Developmental Lineage Classification and Taxonomy of Neoplasms contains over 145,000 names of neoplasms and has been described in several open access publications (3, 6–8). It is the world's largest source of names of human neoplasms. The most recent public version is available from the Association for Pathology Informatics Website (9), or from the author's Website: *http://www.julesberman.info/*.

It stands as an example of a comprehensive listing of all items in a circumscribed field of knowledge. Aside from its value to cancer researchers, it has value for software developers who are developing or testing autocoders, lexical parsers, term extractors, and a variety of data mining projects.

The Neoplasm Classification is distributed as an XML file. Readers should become familiar with the syntax and purpose of the XML format (List 5.9.1).

LIST 5.9.1. SIX EXTRAORDINARY PROPERTIES OF XML

Enforced and defined structure (XML rules and schema)

Formal metadata (through ISO11179 specification)

Namespaces (permits sharing of uniquely identifiable common data elements (CDEs))

Linking data via the Internet (through Unique Resource Identifiers)

Logic and meaning (the Semantic Web and Ontologies)

Self-awareness (software agents [see the glossary], artificialintelligence [see the glossary], embedded protocols and commands)

In XML, data descriptors (known as XML tags) enclose the data they describe with angle brackets.

```
<birthdate>September 28, 1950</birthdate>
```

<birthdate> is the XML tag. The tag and its end-tag enclose a data element, which in this case is the unabbreviated month, beginning with an uppercase letter and followed by lowercase letters, followed by a space, followed by a two-digit numeric for the date of the month, followed by a comma and space, followed by the four-digit year. The XML tag could have been defined in a separate document detailing the data format of the data element described by the XML tag. ISO-11179 (see the glossary) is a standard that tells people how they should specify the properties of metadata (10). In this case, the metadata is the XML tag, <birthdate>. If

we had chosen, we could have broken the <birthdate> tag into its constituent parts.

```
<birthdate>
<month_of_birth>September</month_of_birth>
<month_day_of_birth>28<month_day_of_birth>
<year_of_birth>1950<year_of_birth>
</birthdate>
```

These properties of XML are powerful because they permit us to fully describe the data that we use and because they permit us to reach data anywhere on the Internet (Figure 5-3).

An XML file is well formed if it conforms to the basic rules for XML file construction recommended by the W3C (Worldwide Web Consortium). This means that it must be a plain-text file, with a header indicating that it is an XML file, and must enclose data elements with metadata tags that declare the start and end of the data element. The tags must conform to a standard format (for example, alphanumeric strings without intervening spaces) and must also obey a specified nesting syntax.

Figure 5-3 XML is the father of all metadata.

Most browsers will parse XML files, rejecting files that are not well formed. The ability to ensure that every XML file conforms to basic rules of metadata tagging and nesting makes it possible to extract XML files as sensible data structures and to transform XML files into any other preferred format.

The neoplasm nomenclature is distributed in two gzipped files. Neoclxml.gz should be renamed neocl.xml when decompressed (List 5.9.2).

Neoself.gz, when decompressed is a flat file that lists each term's class ancestry.

LIST 5.9.2. THE FIRST FEW LINES OF THE `neocl.xml`

```
<tumor_classification>
<neoplasms>
<embryonic>
<primitive>
<primitive_differentiating>
<totipotent_or_multipotent_differentiating>
<name nci-code = "C3403000">teratoma</name>
<name nci-code = "C3752000">embryonal ca</name>
<name nci-code = "C3752000">embryonal cancer</name>
<name nci-code = "C3752000">embryonal carcinoma</name>
<name nci-code = "C3756000">mixed embryonal carcinoma and
    teratoma</name>
<name nci-code = "C3756000">teratocarcinoma</name>
<name nci-code = "C3856000">ovary with dermoid cyst</name>
<name nci-code = "C3856000">dermoid cyst arising in ovary</name>
<name nci-code = "C3856000">dermoid cyst involving ovary</name>
<name nci-code = "C3856000">dermoid cyst arising from
    ovary</name>
<name nci-code = "C3856000">dermoid cyst of ovary</name>
<name nci-code = "C3856000">dermoid cyst of the ovary</name>
<name nci-code = "C3856000">dermoid cyst arising in the
    ovary</name>
<name nci-code = "C3856000">dermoid cyst involving the
    ovary</name>
<name nci-code = "C3856000">dermoid cyst arising from the
    ovary</name>
<name nci-code = "C3856000">ovarian dermoid cyst</name>
<name nci-code = "C3856000">ovary dermoid cyst</name>
```

Neocl.htm corresponds to the unclassified names of neoplasms contained in the nomenclature.

http://www.julesberman.info/neocl.htm

5.10. STRUCTURED TEXT: MESH (MEDICAL SUBJECT HEADINGS)

One of the most important nomenclatures within UMLS is the U.S. National Library of Medicine's Medical Subject Headings (MeSH).

MeSH is used by the National Library of Medicine to index all biomedical abstracts included in MedLine and has been used to index medical terms found throughout the Internet. MeSH is a mature, well-curated, large, comprehensive, and publicly available nomenclature.

It contains descriptors in a hierarchical structure (usually referred to as a MeSH tree) that allows searching at higher levels of granularity.

Information on MeSH is found at *http://www.nlm.nih.gov/mesh/meshome.html*.

The MeSH download page is *http://www.nlm.nih.gov/mesh/filelist.html*.

The ftp site is *nlmpubs.nlm.nih.gov/online/mesh/.asciimesh/d2007.bin*.

The MeSH file we use in this book is "d2007.bin," the MeSH ASCII flatfile. In October 2006, this file was approximately 27 Mb (List 5.10.1).

LIST 5.10.1. THE FIRST RECORD IN MESH

```
*NEWRECORD
RECTYPE = D
MH = Calcimycin
AQ = AA AD AE AG AI AN BI BL CF CH CL CS CT DU EC HI IM IP
    ME PD PK PO RE SD ST TO TU UR
ENTRY = A-23187 | T109 | T195 | LAB | NRW | NLM (1991) | 900308 | abbcdef
ENTRY = A23187 | T109 | T195 | LAB | NRW | UNK (19XX) | 741111 | abbcdef
ENTRY = Antibiotic A23187 | T109 | T195 | NON | NRW | NLM
    (1991) | 900308 | abbcdef
ENTRY = A 23187
ENTRY = A23187, Antibiotic
MN = D03.438.221.173
```

PA = Anti-Bacterial Agents

PA = Ionophores

MH_TH = NLM (1975)

ST = T109

ST = T195

N1 = 4-Benzoxazolecarboxylic acid,

5-(methylamin

o)-2-((3,9,11-trimethyl-8-(1-methyl-2-oxo-2-(1H-pyrrol-2-yl)

ethyl)-1,7-dioxaspiro(5.5)undec-2-yl)methyl)-,

(6S-(6alpha(2S*,3S*),

8beta(R*),9beta,11alpha))-

RN = 52665-69-7

PI = Antibiotics (1973–1974)

PI = Carboxylic Acids (1973–1974)

MS = An ionophorous, polyether antibiotic from Streptomyces char-
treusensis. It binds and transports cations across membranes and uncou-
ples oxidative phosphorylation while inhibiting ATPase of rat liver
mitochondria. The substance is used mostly as a biochemical tool to
study the role of divalent cations in various biological systems.

OL = use CALCIMYCIN to search A 23187 1975–90

PM = 91; was A 23187 1975–90 (see under ANTIBIOTICS 1975–83)

HN = 91(75); was A 23187 1975–90 (see under ANTIBIOTICS 1975–83)

MED = *62

MED = 847

M90 = *299

M90 = 2405

M85 = *454

M85 = 2878

M80 = *316

M80 = 1601

M75 = *300

M75 = 823

M66 = *1

(continues)

M66 = 3

M94 = *153

M94 = 1606

MR = 20060705

DA = 19741119

DC = 1

DX = 19840101

UI = D000001

5.11. STRUCTURED TEXT: TAXONOMY

The taxonomy database of the International Sequence Database Collaboration contains the names of organisms represented in the sequence databases. Taxonomy.dat is available from *ftp://ftp.ebi.ac.uk/pub/databases/taxonomy/*.

On October 28, 2006, the taxonomy.data file was 83,247,987 bytes in length and contained 365,296 records.

So thorough is taxonomy.dat that it not only lists all known variations of an organism's name, it also lists commonly used misspellings of an organism (List 5.11.1).

LIST 5.11.1. A RECORD IN TAXONOMY

ID: 50

PARENT ID: 49

RANK: genus

GC ID: 11

SCIENTIFIC NAME: Chondromyces

SYNONYM: Polycephalum

SYNONYM: Myxobotrys

SYNONYM: Chondromyces Berkeley and Curtis 1874

SYNONYM: "Polycephalum" Kalchbrenner and Cooke 1880

SYNONYM: "Myxobotrys" Zukal 1896

MISSPELLING: Chrondromyces

Information about the taxonomy.dat file is found at

http://www.ebi.ac.uk/msd-srv/docs/dbdoc/ref_taxonomy.html

5.12. RDF SYNTAX FILE, GENE ONTOLOGY (GO)

GO is an ontology for the domain of cell biology. It can be thought of as three distinct domains, molecular function, biological process, and cellular components, combined under one ontology.

The GO Consortium Website is *http://www.geneontology.org/*

The GO Consortium distributes its products without a license, as long as users comply with its redistribution and citation policy.

http://www.geneontology.org/doc/GO.cite.html

The latest versions of GO can be downloaded from *http://archive. godatabase.org/latest-termdb/*

The GO XML document containing the ontology in RDF syntax is

```
go_daily-termdb.rdf-xml.gz
```

about 2 Mb in gzipped compressed document and 28 Mb uncompressed.

In Chapter 18, we explain RDF syntax files in detail. A few lines of the GO term file in RDF format are shown here (List 5.12.1).

LIST 5.12.1. FIRST LINES OF GO, LISTING THE FIRST TWO GO TERMS

```
<?xml version="1.0" encoding="UTF-8"?>
<!DOCTYPE go:go PUBLIC "-//Gene Ontology//Custom XML/RDF
    Version 2.0//EN" "http ://www.geneontology.org/dtd/go.dtd">



<go:go xmlns:go="http://www.geneontology.org/dtds/go.dtd#"
    xmlns:rdf="http://www.w3.org/1999/02/22-rdf-syntax-ns#">
    <rdf:RDF>
        <go:term rdf:about="http://www.geneontology.org/go#all">
            <go:accession>all</go:accession>
            <go:name>all</go:name>
<go:definition>This term is the most general term
    possible</go:definition>
        </go:term>
```

(continues)

```
<go:term
    rdf:about="http://www.geneontology.org/go#GO:0000001">
            <go:accession>GO:0000001</go:accession>
            <go:name>mitochondrion inheritance</go:name>
            <go:synonym>mitochondrial inheritance</go:synonym>
<go:definition>The distribution of mitochondria, including
    the mitochondrial genome, into daughter cells after mitosis
    or meiosis, mediated by interactions between mitochondria
    and the cytoskeleton.</go:definition>
<go:is_a
    rdf:resource="http://www.geneontology.org/go#GO:0048308" / >
<go:is_a
    rdf:resource="http://www.geneontology.org/go#GO:0048311" / >
        </go:term>
<go:term
    rdf:about="http://www.geneontology.org/go#GO:0000002">
            <go:accession>GO:0000002</go:accession>
            <go:name>mitochondrial genome maintenance</go:name>
<go:definition>The maintenance of the structure and
    integrity of the mitochondrial genome.</go:definition>
<go:is_a
    rdf:resource="http://www.geneontology.org/go#GO:0007005" / >
            <go:dbxref rdf:parseType="Resource">
<go:database_symbol>InterPro</go:database_symbol>
                <go:reference>IPR009446</go:reference>
            </go:dbxref>
            <go:dbxref rdf:parseType="Resource">
                <go:database_symbol>Pfam</go:database_symbol>
                <go:reference>PF06420 Mgm101p</go:reference>
            </go:dbxref>
        </go:term>
```

5.13. RDF SCHEMA FILE: DUBLIN CORE RDFS

The most popular CDEs (Common Data Elements) in existence are the Dublin Core CDEs. These are a set of file descriptors that were prepared by a committee of librarians who convened in Dublin, Ohio. The Dublin Core descriptors are XML tags that file creators should include in their XML files, along with the appropriate data, that provide basic information about the file, such as the title of the document, the name of the person who created the file, the date that the file was created, the date that the file was modified and a short description of the file. These are the items that a librarian or a software agent would need to retrieve if it were building an index of Internet documents. The world of informatics would be a better place if everyone who created an HTML, XML, or RDF file would remember to include the Dublin Core CDEs.

The Dublin Core RDF schema can be linked to (and downloaded from) *http://dublincore.org/schemas/rdfs/*

The downloaded RDF Schema document is a 14 Kb file: dces.rdf.

In Chapter 18, we learn about RDF syntax and RDF schemas.

The first few lines of the Dublin Core RDF schema file are shown in List 5.13.1.

LIST 5.13.1. FIRST LINES OF THE DUBLIN CORE RDF SCHEMA FILE

```
<rdf:RDF
    xmlns:rdf="http://www.w3.org/1999/02/22-rdf-syntax-ns#"
    xmlns:dcterms= "http://purl.org/dc/terms/"
    xmlns:dc="http://purl.org/dc/elements/1.1/" xmlns:rd
    fs="http://www.w3.org/2000/01/rdf-schema#">
<rdf:Description rdf:about="http://purl.org/dc/elements/1.1/">
<dc:title xml:lang="en-US">The Dublin Core Element Set v1.1
    namespace providing access to its content by means of an
    RDF Schema</dc:title>
<dc:publisher xml:lang="en-US">The Dublin Core Metadata
    Initiative</dc:publisher>
<dc:description xml:lang="en-US">The Dublin Core Element Set
    v1.1 namespace provides URIs for the Dublin Core Elements
    v1.1. Entries are declared using RDF schema language to
    support RDF applications.</dc:description>
```

5.14. IMAGE FILES: JPEG AND DICOM FILES

There are probably hundreds of image file formats in existence. As a Ruby programmer, you will be able to manipulate over 90 image file types with RMagick, Ruby's interface to the freely available ImageMagick image software. RMagick is not bundled into Ruby's standard distribution, but RMagick and ImageMagick can be obtained from RubyForge (see the Appendix).

In my experience, the most popular image format is JPEG (Joint Photographic Experts Group). JPEG is the format used for most of the images that you will find on the Web. JPEG images can be displayed by all popular web browsers.

In the field of biomedicine, DICOM (Digital Imaging and Communications in Medicine) has special significance because it is the format currently used for radiologic images. DICOM was developed over several decades as a standard of enormous complexity that uses a model for data storage that is unlike any other image file format. The DICOM standard includes a set of protocols for transferring information through networks and for communicating between different radiologic devices or different parts of a single device (for example, between CT machine and CT workstation). It creates a unique syntax and semantics for information and produces a file that contains a large number of descriptive information (including patient information and diagnostic information) and a binary representation of one or more images.

One of the best descriptions of the DICOM file format is available at

> http://www.dclunie.com/medical-image-faq/html/part1.html
> http://www.dclunie.com/medical-image-faq/html/part2.html

For the purposes of this book, all we need to know is that the header information in a DICOM file can be extracted (with a short Ruby script) and that the binary portion of a DICOM file can be converted to a JPEG file. The header data from the DICOM file can be reinserted into the header of a JPEG file, or it can be included in a special XML file that "points" back to the original DICOM file or to the JPEG file that contains the image representation (List 5.14.1).

LIST 5.14.1. TEXTUAL REPRESENTATION OF THE HEADER CONTENTS OF DICOM IMAGE, FIGURE 5-4

```
0002,0000,File Meta Elements Group Len=122

0002,0001,File Meta Info Version=1

0002,0002,Media Storage SOP Class UID=1.2.840.10008.5.1.4.1.1.7.

0002,0003,Media Storage SOP Inst UID=9999.20070123103417.100.10

0002,0010,Transfer Syntax UID=1.2.840.10008.1.2.1.

0002,0012,Implementation Class UID=960051513

0008,0008,Image Type=

0008,0012,Instance Creation Date=20070123

0008,0013,Instance Creation Time=103417

0008,0016,SOP Class UID=1.2.840.10008.5.1.4.1.1.7.

0008,0018,SOP Instance UID=9999.20070123103417.100.10
```

```
0008,0020,Study Date=20070123
0008,0030,Study Time=103417
0008,0050,Accession Number=
0008,0060,Modality=OT
0008,0064,Conversion Type=WSD.
0008,0090,Referring Physician's Name=
0010,0010,Patient's Name=gwmbw.jpg.
0010,0020,Patient ID=0.
0010,0030,Patient Date of Birth=
0010,0040,Patient Sex=M
0010,1010,Patient Age=0.
0020,000D,Study Instance UID=9999.20070123103417.100.20
0020,000E,Series Instance UID=9999.20070123103417.100.30
0020,0010,Study ID= 0
0020,0011,Series Number=0
0020,0013,Image Number=0
0020,0020,Patient Orientation=
0028,0002,Samples Per Pixel=1
0028,0004,Photometric Interpretation=MONOCHROME2
0028,0010,Rows=1536
0028,0011,Columns=2048
0028,0100,Bits Allocated=8
0028,0101,Bits Stored=8
0028,0102,High Bit=7
0028,0103,Pixel Representation=0
7FE0,0010,Pixel Data=3145728
```

Any JPEG image can be converted to a DICOM image. Figure 5-4 is a DICOM image representing a photomicrograph of human endocervix.

Image headers have great importance in the fields of biology and medicine. A biomedical image has no value unless it is accompanied by detailed information that describes the specimen that is imaged, the

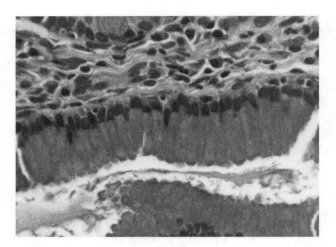

Figure 5-4 DICOM image of human endocervix.

conditions of acquisition of the specimen, clinical or biological properties of the specimen, and so on. Well-annotated images can be used for diagnosis, research, and consultation. Image libraries can be archived and later retrieved through queries tied to the annotations. The data elements in image annotations can be collected and merged with data from other databases. Using annotations, images can be linked back to specimens that can be used for additional studies. Unannotated images really cannot be used for any serious purpose.

What are the kinds of annotations that are important for medical images (List 5.14.2)?

If you keep an image's annotations in a text file or in some database separate from the actual image (the so-called image binary), you risk losing the annotation file or risk losing the data that links the annotation file from the image binary. A better idea is to embed the annotations within the image file.

DICOM images permit the inclusion of annotations. The content of List 5.14.1 was extracted from the DICOM image file, gwmbw.dcm, using a short Ruby script (see List 8.5.3).

We use DICOM headers in Chapter 8 when we learn how to interconvert DICOM images and JPEG images and how to insert, extract, or modify the clinical annotations conveyed in DICOM and JPEG headers. You can find thousands of radiologic images in DICOM format at

ftp://ftp.erl.wustl.edu/pub/dicom/images/version3/RSNA95/

LIST 5.14.2. IMAGE ANNOTATIONS FOR A MEDICAL IMAGE

1. General file properties, such as who created the file, when the file was created, the purpose of the file and any intellectual property rights and restrictions. This section may contain data elements that authenticate the file or its creator or that indicate that the image was acquired and distributed with the approval of an institutional review board.

2. Binary object properties, such as the organization, structure or mathematical properties of the binary image(s), so-called image header data, technical image or image display descriptors, and either the binary object itself (rendered in ASCII base64) or with a pointer to a URL holding the binary image file.

3. Image capture device information, specifying the microscope/camera and any other hardware devices contributing to the capture of the image.

4. Image acquisition information, such as device settings and physical/optical parameters related to the capture of the image and calibration data or protocols.

5. Image features, such as staining information, or pointers to experimental protocols for the preparation of the image.

6. Specimen information, which may include the methods used to procure or prepare the specimen and pointers to specific specimen-related records in tissue databases or specimen repositories.

7. Pathologic information pertaining to the image, including diagnosis or specific pathologic descriptions of defined regions of interest.

8. Clinical or demographic information related to the patient providing the specimen. This section can be provided with de-identified or encrypted data elements or with data intended to authenticate or otherwise ensure the confidentiality and privacy of the record or ensure legal compliances with federal regulations related to the use or transfer of patient record information.

CHAPTER

6

Using Ruby Strings, Hashes, Arrays, Files, and Directories (Level 1)

6.1. BACKGROUND

We promised that we would teach you how to program with Ruby without needing to write any of your own classes or modules. In this chapter, we show you how to use the built-in Ruby classes to write simple programs that solve your most common computational tasks (List 6.1.1).

LIST 6.1.1. SOME LEVEL 1 RUBY SCRIPTS

Reading Through Large Text and Data Files

Counting Occurrences in a Data File

Finding the Frequency of Occurrence of Each Word in a Text File

Preparing an ordered Zipf distribution

6.2. READING A LITTLE BIT OF A FILE (REGARDLESS OF ITS SIZE)

Sometimes, when you encounter a large file for the first time, you may want to peek at the first few lines, just to get an idea of what the file contains and how the data in the file is organized. The `readsome.rb` script extracts the first 20 lines from a large file and sends them to your monitor for viewing (List 6.2.1).

LIST 6.2.1. RUBY SCRIPT readsome.rb **READS THE FIRST 20 LINES OF THE MRCONSO FILE**

```
#!/usr/local/bin/ruby
f = File.open "MRCONSO"
(1..20).each do
     STDOUT.puts(f.gets)
end
exit
```

The script sends the open method to class File, automatically creating a new File object instance, f, assigning f the file "MRCONSO" located in the current directory, and preparing the object instance for reading (the default action for the open method). "MRCONSO" is the large, publicly available file that contains all the medical concepts in the UMLS metathaurus (see Chapter 5, Section 7).

For 20 iterations, the gets method is sent to f, yielding sequential line-reads from the "MRCONSO" file. In a chained command, the standard output receives the puts method, with the yielded line from the "MRCONSO" file as its argument. Consequently, the each block sends the first twenty lines of the "MRCONSO" file to the monitor.

The readsome.rb script can be easily modified to accept any text file and to send any number of lines to any desired output device (including a file).

6.3. A ZIPF DISTRIBUTION IN FOUR LINES OF RUBY CODE

George Kingsley Zipf (1902–1950) gave us Zipf's law, asserting that in a text corpus the frequency of any word is roughly inversely proportional to its rank in the frequency table (11). A practical way of interpreting Zipf's law is that a small amount of words accounts for most of the occurrences of words in any text. A Zipf distribution is a listing of the different words in a text in the descending order of their occurrences. The Zipf distribution of this paragraph is shown (List 6.3.1).

In this example, Zipf's law was not strictly obeyed. The second most frequently occurring word, "a," occurred at nearly the same frequency as the most frequently occurring word (not half the frequency). Zipf would surely have insisted that his law is tuned to large texts. A few sentences cannot serve to test Zipf's law.

LIST 6.3.1. THE WORD FREQUENCIES FOR THE PRIOR PARAGRAPH

```
00007 of
00005 a
00004 the
00003 words
00003 is
00003 in
00002 zipf
00002 text
00002 occurrences
00002 distribution
00001 zipf's
00001 way
00001 this
00001 their
00001 that
00001 small
00001 shown
00001 see
00001 practical
00001 paragraph
00001 order
00001 most
00001 listing
00001 list
00001 law
00001 interpreting
00001 for
00001 different
00001 descending
00001 any
00001 amount
00001 account
```

Computational linguists rely on Zipf distributions to identify high-frequency, low-information words that delimit phrases of high information content (sometimes called "stopwords"). Zipf distributions are also used to build nomenclatures and indexes. They can be useful for tracking the occurrence of misspelled words. Zipf distributions can be used as a "signature" for a text and as part of methods to detect plagiarized text or to rank textual concepts (List 6.3.2).

LIST 6.3.2. RUBY SCRIPT `zipf.rb` PRINTS THE NUMBER OF OCCURRENCES OF WORDS IN A STRING

```
#!/usr/local/bin/ruby
freq = Hash.new(0)
my_string = "A man, a plan, a canal, Panama"
my_string.downcase.scan(/\w+/){|word| freq[word] = freq[word]+1}
freq.keys.sort.each {|k| print k, " - ", freq[k], "\n"}
exit
```

LIST 6.3.3. PARTIAL OUTPUT OF `zipf.rb`

```
C:\ftp\rb>ruby zipf.rb
a - 3
canal - 1
man - 1
panama - 1
plan - 1
```

The `zipf.rb` script produces an alphabetized list of the words in a string, with the number of occurrences following each word (List 6.3.3).

Let us review the script line by line.

First, we declare a new Hash object and a string to be parsed.

```
freq = Hash.new(0)
my_string = "A man, a plan, a canal, Panama"
```

The Zipf distribution of the words in the sentence is created in a single line of Ruby code.

```
my_string.downcase.scan(/\w+/){|word| freq[word] = freq[word]+1}
```

The string is converted to lowercase and is then parsed by the scan iteration method.

The scan method matches a pattern against a string and pushes each matching substring into an array or passes each matching substring to a block. In this case, we provide the scan method with a block so that the latter behavior is followed. The matching pattern is /\w+/. The \w character represents alphanumerics (0–9 plus any alphabetic character) and the underscore. Words are essentially concatenations of alphanumerics bordered by nonalphanumerics, such as a space or a period or a newline character. Each matching word is passed to the block, where it is added as a key to the freq Hash object. Each time the same key occurs in the block, the value associated with key is incremented by one.

```
freq[word] = freq[word]+1
```

The initial value associated with each key is zero.

The next line of Ruby code takes the freq Hash object, produces an array from the keys (with the keys method), sorts the keys alphabetically and then, for each element in the array, prints to the monitor the element and the element's value (List 6.3.3).

```
freq.keys.sort.each {|k| print k, " - ", freq[k], "\n"}
```

There are a few problems with the zifp.rb script. In Ruby, most files can be ported into a string object with class IO's read method (see the Glossary); however, it is possible for a file to exceed your computer's ability to hold its string representation in memory and to perform a scan over the entire String object. In addition, the zipf.rb script produces an output that is arranged in the alphabetic order of the words in the string. Strictly speaking, a Zipf distribution should consist of a file that is ordered by the frequency of occurrence of the words.

With a few extra lines of Ruby, we can create zipf2.rb an improved Zipf distribution script that will parse files of any size (List 6.3.4).

The zipf2.rb script uses basically the same algorithm as the zipf.rb script. The differences are subtle.

First, we inspect the OMIM file and determine that it is composed of multiline records, with each record delineated by the line "*RECORD*." We reset Ruby's line-separator global variable (see List 5.3.1).

```
$/ = "*RECORD*"
```

We can scan each record in the OMIM file, incrementing the freq Hash object repeatedly.

When we scan each line in the file, we look for words that are composed exclusively of alphabetic letters (not alphanumerics) because we are not

LIST 6.3.4. RUBY SCRIPT `zipf2.rb` **CREATES A ZIPF DISTRIBUTION OF THE WORDS IN OMIM**

```
#!/usr/local/bin/ruby
start_time = Time.new.to_f
$/ = "*RECORD*"
freq = Hash.new(0)
zipf = Array.new
output = File.open("zipfomim.txt","w")
file1 = File.open("c\:\\entrez\\omim")
file1.each do
  |line|
  line.downcase.scan(/[a-z]+/) do
    |word|
    freq[word] = freq[word]+1 if word.length > 2
    end
end
freq.each do
  |key, value|
  occur = value.to_s.rjust(7,"0") + " #{key}"
  zipf.push(occur)
end
output.print(zipf.sort.reverse.join("\n"))
end_time = Time.new.to_f
puts "Execution time is #{end_time - start_time} seconds"
exit
```

interested in knowing the frequency of occurrence of numbers. Also, we restrict words to lengths of three or more letters, as we are not interested in shorter words.

```
line.downcase.scan(/[a-z]+/) do
  |word|
  freq[word] = freq[word]+1 if word.length > 2
  end
```

After the `freq` Hash object has been created and filled with key/value pairs, we create a string consisting of the justified and padded value for the number of occurrences of the word followed by the word itself.

```
freq.each do
  |key, value|
  occur = value.to_s.rjust(7,"0") + " #{key}"
  zipf.push(occur)
end
```

Because `value` is a number, we convert it to a string (with the `to_s` method). Then we pad the string with zeroes so that it is seven characters in length using the `rjust` method. The padded value is concatenated with its key and the resulting string is pushed into an array (see the `push` method, in the glossary).

The `rjust` method returns a string that is the length of the first parameter and padded with the second parameter (List 6.3.5).

LIST 6.3.5. EXAMPLES OF CLASS STRING'S `rjust` METHOD

```
irb(main):001:0> "7".rjust(3,"0")  => "007"
irb(main):002:0> "7".rjust(3)  => "  7"
irb(main):003:0> "45".rjust(15,"_")  => "_____45"
```

The utility of the `rjust` method, aside from neatly aligning a list, is to provide strings that can be alphabetically ordered by the `sort` method.

```
output.print(zipf.sort.reverse.join("\n"))
```

The sorted Zipf array is reversed (to put the most frequently occurring words on the top) and joined with a newline character to produce an output file with each key/value pair on a separate line (List 6.3.6).

The OMIM file is about 117 Mb in length. It took 192 seconds for the `zipf2.rb` file to parse the OMIM file and create the Zipf distribution file (on a modest desktop computer with a 2.5-gigahertz CPU).

The output file consisted of about 162,500 different words and their frequencies. Most texts (for example, novels) have about 20,000 different words. The average human has a vocabulary that does not far exceed 20,000 words and uses only a small portion of that vocabulary in ordinary speech. Technical texts, such as OMIM, have very large vocabularies because they cover multiple biological domains (names of genes, names of proteins, names of diseases, and so on). Most of the alphabetic strings that occur only once in the text are scarcely recognizable as words.

As a general cautionary tale, you should understand that the criteria for what constitutes a word in a file will change depending on the contents of the file and the intended uses of the word list. Also, some files make use of end-of-line hyphens to connect parts of a single word over two lines of text. For such texts, the programmer would need to include code to connect these words and remove the hyphen if necessary. Sometimes a hyphenated word break at the end of a line should preserve the hyphen (x-linked), and at other times, preserving the hyphen would be

LIST 6.3.6. FIRST 10 AND LAST 10 ITEMS FROM OUTPUT FILE OF `zipf2.rb`

```
0642293 the
0407626 and
0175090 with
0154735 that
0129853 field
0121657 gene
0085557 was
0084823 for
0061329 human
0058462 protein
.
.
.
0000001 aach
0000001 aaccct
0000001 aabt
0000001 aab
0000001 aaatc
0000001 aaap
0000001 aaaca
0000001 aaac
0000001 aaaac
0000001 aaaa
```

wrong (precancer). Sometimes, it is wise to include numerics in words (p53, cd117) and other times not (54 or even fifty four). The point is that many textual parsing tasks are not fully generalizable. If you are working in the fields of healthcare or biology, you cannot depend on off-the-shelf applications to parse files in a manner suitable to your specific needs. You will need to write your own scripts, with Ruby statements that suit your own purposes.

6.4. EXTRACTING SNOMED TERMS FROM THE UMLS

The UMLS metathesaurus is composed of over 100 different vocabularies (see Chapter 5). Once of the largest of these vocabularies is SNOMED-CT. It is easy to extract the terms from any of the vocabularies in the UMLS metathesaurus if you know the name of the UMLS files that contains all the vocabulary terms and if you know that each record in the file includes the name of its originating vocabulary source.

The file containing all of the UMLS terms is MRCONSO.RRF.gz. Decompressed (and renamed MRCONSO, this file exceeds 775 Mb.

Here is an example of a record in MRCONSO derived from SNOMED-CT:

C0000039 I ENG I S I L0012507 I PF I S0033298 I N I A8380106 I 166113012 I 102735002 I I SNOMEDCT I OP I 102735002 I Dipalmitoylphosphatidylcholine I 4 I O I 256 I

Each record is divided into elements by a vertical bar (" I "). The zeroth element is the UMLS concept unique identifier, C0000039. The 11th element is the name of the source vocabulary, SNOMED-CT. With Ruby, it is easy to parse through the file, line by line, extracting those lines that identify SNOMED-CT records (List 6.4.1).

LIST 6.4.1. RUBY SCRIPT snom_get.rb EXTRACTS SNOMED-CT TERMS FROM UMLS

```ruby
#!/usr/local/bin/ruby
f = File.open("c\:\\ftp\\entrez\\MRCONSO")
outf = File.open("snomed.out", "w")
f.each do
  |line|
  line_array = line.split("\|")
  next if (line_array[1] != "ENG")
  next if (line_array[11] != "SNOMEDCT")
  outf.print(line_array[0], " ", line_array[14], "\n")
end
exit
```

The resulting file, "snomed.out", is approximately 47.5 Mb in length. A sample of the "snomed.out" file is shown in List 6.4.2.

Let us review the Ruby script line by line.

```ruby
f = File.open("c\:\\ftp\\entrez\\MRCONSO")
```

This line opens the large MRCONSO file. By default, the file is opened for reading.

```ruby
outf = File.open("snomed.out", "w")
```

This line supplies the open method with the "w" argument, so that the open method will prepare the file for writing (receiving input).

```ruby
f.each do
  |line|
```

LIST 6.4.2. THE FIRST 10 RECORDS OF SNOMED TERMS EXTRACTED FROM UMLS

C0000039 Dipalmitoylphosphatidylcholine

C0000039 Dipalmitoylphosphatidylcholine (substance)

C0000052 1,4-alpha-Glucan branching enzyme

C0000052 Branching enzyme

C0000052 Amylo-(1,4,6)-transglycosylase

C0000052 Amylo-(1,4->,6)-transglycosylase

C0000052 1,4-alpha-Glucan branching enzyme (substance)

C0000097 Methylphenyltetrahydropyridine

C0000097 Methylphenyltetrahydropyridine (substance)

C0000163 17-Hydroxycorticosteroids

Class `File`'s each method, sent to the `File` instance object, `f`, iterates line by line through the file, executing a block of code with each iteration.

There are two syntax options for sending a block to an iterator method.

The most commonly used syntax is as follows:

```
{|<iterator value>| your code}
```

The value between the vertical bars is the iterator value for each loop. In the case of a file, it is each consecutive line of the file. For an array, it would be each index element in the array. For a hash, it would be each key/value pair in the hash. The other syntax, used here, is to enclose the block in a `do...end` loop.

The iterator block is one of the most ubiquitous and useful constructs in Ruby. In Ruby, everything is an object, including methods and code. Ruby has a special class, `Proc`, for blocks of code bound to local variables (see the Glossary).

```
line_array = line.split("\|")
```

The `split` method, sent to a string object, produces an array of string fragments delimited by an argument that serves as the data element delimiter. In this case, the delimiter is the vertical bar.

```
next if (line_array[1] != "ENG")
next if (line_array[11] != "SNOMEDCT")
```

Referring back to our sample record, the zeroth element of the array happens to be the UMLS concept unique identifier, "C0000039" in this case. The first element is the language of the term, English (represented as "ENG") in this case. The 11th element is the name of the source vocabulary, and the 14th element is the name of the term. We are only interested in English terms that derive from the SNOMED-CT source vocabulary, and the code rejects all other term occurrences from the MRCONSO file.

```
outf.print(line_array[0], " ", line_array[14], "\n")
```

As each line is parsed, we save the lines corresponding to English SNOMED-CT terms and print to the output file the 0th element (Concept Unique Identifier followed by a space), followed by the 14th element (the term itself), followed by a newline character. The output, snomed.out, is a 47+-Mb file of every SNOMED term.

Readers should be cautioned that the SNOMED terminology is encumbered by a special license included in the UMLS documentation. You should read SNOMED's usage restrictions before implementing the SNOMED terminology.

6.5. SELECTING A SUBSET OF SNOMED TERMS USING MRSTY

The MRSTY file contains the relationships that apply to individual UMLS concepts (see Chapter 5, Section 7).

Four sample records from MRSTY are as follows:

> C0000005 | T121 | A1.4.1.1.1 | Pharmacologic Substance |
>   AT17575038 | |
>
> C0000005 | T130 | A1.4.1.1.4 | Indicator, Reagent, or Diagnostic
>   Aid | AT17634323 | |
>
> C0000039 | T119 | A1.4.1.2.1.9 | Lipid | AT17617573 | |
>
> C0000744 | T047 | B2.2.1.2.1 | Disease or Syndrome | AT17683825 | |

Using the MRSTY, we can extract a subset of SNOMED-CT terms that fall under any desired MRSTY relationship.

Let us write a Ruby script that selects just those SNOMED terms from MRCONSO that have a Disease or Syndrome relationship in MRSTY (List 6.5.1).

LIST 6.5.1. RUBY SCRIPT disease.rb **COLLECTS SNOMED-CT DISEASES FROM UMLS**

```
#!/usr/local/bin/ruby
m = File.open("c\:\\entrez\\MRSTY")
hash_disease = Hash.new
m.each do
  |line|
  disease_array = line.split("\|")
  if (disease_array[3] == "Disease or Syndrome")
    hash_disease[disease_array[0]] = ""
  end
end
m.close
f = File.open("c\:\\entrez\\MRCONSO")
outf = File.open("snomed2.out", "w")
f.each do
  |line|
  line_array = line.split("\|")
  next if !(hash_disease.has_key?(line_array[0]))
  next if (line_array[1] != "ENG")
  next if (line_array[11] != "SNOMEDCT")
  outf.print(line_array[0], " ", line_array[14], "\n")
end
exit
```

A few lines from the output file, "snomed2.out" is shown in List 6.5.2.

LIST 6.5.2. A FEW LINES FROM THE OUTPUT FILE CREATED BY disease.rb

C0000774 Gastrin secretion abnormality NOS

C0000774 Abnormality of secretion of gastrin

C0000774 Abnormality of gastrin secretion

C0000774 Gastrin secretion abnormality NOS (disorder)

C0000774 Abnormality of secretion of gastrin (disorder)

C0000786 Spontaneous abortion

The Ruby script disease.rb is very similar to snom_get.rb (and just a few lines longer). Let us review the differences between the two scripts.

We first open the MRSTY file and create a new Hash object, hash_disease, that will contain the concept codes in UMLS that correspond to the name of a disease or a syndrome.

```
m = File.open("c\:\\entrez\\MRSTY")
hash_disease = Hash.new
m.each do
  |line|
  disease_array = line.split("\|")
  if (disease_array[3] == "Disease or Syndrome")
    hash_disease[disease_array[0]] = ""
  end
end
```

As each record in the MRSTY file is parsed, we look for the third item, which tells us the kind of term in the record (for example, Procedure, Chemical, and Disease or Syndrome. If record item 3 is "Disease or Syndrome," then we save the code (record item 0) as a key in the Hash item. We do not care what value is assigned to the key, and thus, we arbitrarily assign it the empty string.

We use the hash_disease object a few lines later, as we parse all of the lines of the MRCONSO file.

```
next if !(hash_disease.has_key?(line_array[0]))
next if (line_array[1] != "ENG")
next if (line_array[11] != "SNOMEDCT")
```

Remember that we are looking for SNOMED terms, in English, that correspond to diseases or syndromes. If a term is a disease or syndrome, then its code must occur as a key somewhere in the hash_disease object. The concept code is the first item (item 0) in the MRCONSO record. We test to see whether the code is a key in the hash_disease object. If not, the MRCONSO record is skipped. Next we determine whether the MRCONSO record is in English. If not, it is skipped. Finally, we test if the MRCONSO record is a SNOMED-CT term. If not, the record is skipped.

The final product is a file containing thousands of lines, each line consisting of a UMLS concept identifier followed by the name of a disease term.

6.6. CREATING A PERSISTENT DATABASE OBJECT (USING RUBY SDBM)

So far, we have written Ruby scripts that create data structures (hashes and arrays) on the fly, often from external data files. When the script ends, the data structures disappear into the bit void. Every time we run our Ruby scripts we need to wait while the data structures are reconstructed.

It would be nice if we had a way of conferring persistence on the data structures that we create in our scripts. The next time we ran a script, the data would be available to us. The most common method of achieving persistence is through the creation of a database. In fact, the chief purpose of any database is to provide persistent storage for data structures that will be retrieved by external software applications.

Ruby lets you write scripts that minimize your dependence on non-Ruby software applications (such as databases). Ruby bundles the SDBM (Simple DataBase Module) in the standard Ruby distribution (see Chapter 4). SDBM supports hash persistence. For most purposes, hashes are sufficient to represent most Ruby data structures; therefore, SDBM may be the only persistence implementation that you will ever need.

How does the SDBM library work? Basically, when you use SDBM, you tie an SDBM object to a hash in your script. Whenever you add a key/value pair to your hash, you are also adding the key/value pair to the SDBM object. The SDBM object stores its hashes in an external file. When the script ends, the external file persists. When you reopen the script or create a new script, the external SDBM file is available to you. You can tie a hash to the SDBM object and use the stored key/value pairs just as you would use the key/value pairs in a newly created hash object.

Let us see how the SDBM object can be implemented. In Chapter 2, we created two hashes from the Neoplasm Classification nomenclature (see List 2.8.4). We can modify that same script to store the hashes as SDBM objects (List 6.6.1).

LIST 6.6.1. RUBY SCRIPT neosdbm.rb CREATES THREE PERSISTENT DATABASE OBJECTS

```
#!/usr/local/bin/ruby
require 'sdbm'
begin_time = (Time.new).to_f
text = File.open("c\:\\ftp\\neocl.xml")
```

```
literalhash = Hash.new; doubhash = Hash.new
onewordhash = Hash.new
text.each do
  |line|
  next if (line !~ /\"(C[0-9]{7})\"/)
  line =~ /\"(C[0-9]{7})\"/
  code = $1;
  line =~ /\"\> ?(.+) ?\<\//
  phrase = $1;
  if (phrase !~ / /)
     onewordhash[phrase] = code
     next
  end
  literalhash[phrase] = code
  hoparray = phrase.split
  (0..hoparray.length).each do
     |i|
     doublet = "#{hoparray[i]} #{hoparray[i+1]}"
next if !(doublet =~ /[a-z]+[a-z0-9\-]* [a-z]+[a-z0-9\-]*/)
     doubhash[doublet] = ""
  end
end
text.close
f = File.open("hashes.txt", "w")
puts "Number of multi-word vocabulary terms is
  #{literalhash.length}"
puts "Number of doublets is #{doubhash.length}"
puts "Number of one-word vocabulary terms is
  #{onewordhash.length}"
SDBM.open("doubhash.dbm") do
  |dbm|
  doubhash.each{|key,value| dbm[key] = value}
end
SDBM.open("literalhash.dbm") do
  |dbm|
  literalhash.each{|key,value| dbm[key] = value}
end
SDBM.open("onewordhash.dbm") do
  |dbm|
  onewordhash.each{|key,value| dbm[key] = value}
end
exit
```

We start off by requiring the SDBM library into our script.

```
require 'sdbm'
```

The script creates three object instances of class Hash: doubhash, literal hash and onewordhash.

We open an SDBM object and pass it a name. We use "doubhash.dbm" in this case to remind us of its tied hash, but we could have used any-thing.

```
SDBM.open("doubhash.dbm") do
    |dbm|
    doubhash.each{|key,value| dbm[key] = value}
end
```

We send the each method to the doubhash Hash object, iterating over every key/value pair, and sending each pair to the dbm Hash object. This is standard syntax for the SDBM library. We do the same for the literalhash and onewordhash Hash objects. We can follow the screen output of the neosdbm.rb script and the list of files created by the script (Lists 6.6.2 and 6.6.3).

LIST 6.6.2. SCREEN OUTPUT OF neosdbm.rb

```
C:\ftp\rb>ruby neosdbm.rb
Number of multi-word vocabulary terms is 141518
Number of doublets is 30177
Number of one-word vocabulary terms is 857
```

LIST 6.6.3. FILES CREATED BY neosdbm.rb

```
doubhash.dbm.pag        1,048,576
doubhash.dbm.dir            4,096
literalhash.dbm.pag    31,753,216
literalhash.dbm.dir         4,096
onewordhash.dbm.pag        32,768
onewordhash.dbm.dir         4,096
```

In the next section, we learn how to retrieve persistent data. One word of caution: Persistence means that the object is not thrown into the garbage (Ruby's method for eliminating objects). This means that persis-tent objects can get bigger and bigger and bigger with multiple runs of a script that adds key/value pairs to the named object. It would be wise to keep this in mind and to check the size of your persistent objects (files ending in .dir and .pag) after every run of an SDBM script.

6.7. RETRIEVING INFORMATION FROM A PERSISTENT DATABASE OBJECT

Now that we have created persistent objects, we need a way to retrieve the encapsulated key/value pairs (List 6.7.1).

LIST 6.7.1. RUBY SCRIPT sdbmget.rb RETRIEVES DATA FROM PERSISTENT OBJECT

```
#!/usr/local/bin/ruby
require 'sdbm'
literalhash = SDBM.open("literalhash.dbm", nil)
onewordhash = SDBM.open("onewordhash.dbm", nil)
puts "Refractory anemia " << literalhash["refractory anemia"]
puts "Rhabdoid tumor " << literalhash["rhabdoid tumor"]
puts "Hepatoma " << onewordhash["hepatoma"]
puts "Nephroblastoma " << onewordhash["nephroblastoma"]
exit
```

Once more, we `require` the SDBM library into the script. We create an SDBM object using the open method and pass it the name of the external file for the hash (omitting the "`pag`" suffix). That is all there is to it. After the SDBM instance object is opened, you can retrieve key/value pairs just as though it was an instance of class `Hash` (List 6.7.2).

LIST 6.7.2. OUTPUT OF sdbmget.rb

```
C:\ftp\rb>ruby sdbmget.rb
Refractory anemia C4036100
Rhabdoid tumor C3808000
Hepatoma C3099000
Nephroblastoma C3267000
```

Pattern Searching with Regular Expressions (Level 1)

7.1. BACKGROUND

A regular expression is a linguistic device for expressing an abstract pattern in character strings. Ruby contains simple methods for matching the occurrences of such patterns in string objects. Regular expressions are incredibly important in all aspects of modern biomedical programming. The same regular expressions used in Ruby are also used in Perl, Python, Java, and XML Schemas. After you understand regular expressions, you will be able to write short, powerful programs that transform large data files into any format you prefer. You can also create simple scripts that search and extract (from any data collection) information that conforms to your particular interests. A one-line regular expression in Ruby can accomplish the equivalent of a full-length program in other languages (List 7.1.1).

LIST 7.1.1. THINGS YOU CAN DO WITH A ONE-LINE REGULAR EXPRESSION

Collect the lines from a file that contain a specific word, phrase, number, or character pattern.

Rearrange the content of lines based on matching words, phrases, numbers, or character patterns.

Substitute any alphanumeric character string for any other for the entire file.

Consider the following English expressions:

"I'm looking for strings that begin with an integer number followed by a period, followed by a space, followed by a capitalized word, followed by a space followed by words or numbers that may or may not contain uppercase letters but that must include the word 'notified' and ending with a period."

In many programming languages, it would literally take hundreds of lines of code to specify a parsing algorithm that satisfied this kind of description. In Perl, Python, and Ruby, these descriptions are described as regular expressions and can be represented and parsed with a single line of code.

```
/^\d+\. [A-Z]\w+ \w*notified\w*\./
```

By the end of this chapter, this regular expression will make some sense to you, and you will be able to compose some simple regular expressions of your own.

The purpose of this chapter is to explain regular expressions and to provide examples of some of the most useful patterns for matching, substituting, rearranging, and extracting data.

7.2. PSEUDOCODE FOR COMMON USES OF REGEX (REGULAR EXPRESSION PATTERN MATCHING)

Although simple minded, List 7.2.1 and List 7.2.2 describe a scripting process for the most common tasks performed by Ruby scripts. If you learn the basic scripting model for parsing files and extracting or substituting text elements based on regular expression matches, then you will have the basic set of Ruby skills used in biomedicine.

LIST 7.2.1. PSEUDOCODE FOR REGULAR EXPRESSIONS IN RUBY SCRIPTS

```
for all the lines of a given file
  put the next line from the file into some variable
  check the line to see if it matches your regular expression
  if the line matches the regular expression
    do something with it, like put it into another file
    or do an operation on the matching value
  end
end
```

LIST 7.2.2. PSEUDOCODE FOR SUBSTITUTIONS (WITH gsub)

```
for all the lines of a given file
   put the next line from the file into some variable
do a substitution on all of the parts of the line that
     match your regular expression
   do something with the revised line, like rearranging it
   then put the rearranged line into another file
end
```

7.3. A REGEX EXAMPLE

Let us use the script sentence.rb to parse a corpus of PubMed abstracts into sentences.

The script (List 7.3.1) parses through a PubMed output file consisting of titles and abstracts (see Chapter 5). The output file lists the sequentially occurring sentences from the text file, on separate lines.

LIST 7.3.1. RUBY SCRIPT sentence.rb, A SIMPLE SENTENCE PARSER

```ruby
#!/usr/local/bin/ruby
f = File.open("c:\\entrez\\tum_abs.txt")
fout = File.open("tum_abs.out", "w")
$/ = "\n\n"
f.each do
   |line|
   line.gsub!(/\n/, " ")
line.gsub!(/([^A-Z])(?=\.[\s]+[A-Z])/){|match| match + "\.\n"}
   line.gsub!(/^[ \.]+/,"")
   print(line + "\n")
end
exit
```

This sentence parser is not perfect, but it does a pretty good job in a short time. In this example, the input file "tum_abs.txt" is about 57 Mb in length. The sentence.rb script parses the entire file and produces a neat output file, "tum_abs.out", that is about 56 Mb in length and consists of sentences displayed one sentence per line (List 7.3.2). The script takes 47 seconds to execute on a modest 2.5-gigahertz CPU. A parsing speed faster than 1 Mb per second is adequate for many purposes.

LIST 7.3.2. SAMPLE OUTPUT OF sentence.rb, **WITH EACH LINE TRUNCATED AT CHARACTER 68**

The survival rates were significantly higher in the rats treated by . . .

Moreover, no lung metastasis was detected in some rats with 24 weeks . . .

Lower microvessel density, lower PCNA Index and higher Apoptotic Ind . . .

A beneficial effect of by early administration of MMI270 against pos . . .

PMID: 16003755 [PubMed—as supplied by publisher]

The sample output is truncated for display here, but in the actual output file, the full sentences extend to beyond the point that would correspond to the margin of a page (List 7.3.2).

By now, you should be familiar with most of the Ruby statements that compose the script. One line, however, contains a new trick and requires explanation.

```
line.gsub!(/([^A-Z])(?=\.[\s]+[A-Z])/){|match| match + "\.\n"}
```

This line uses class String's gsub! method, which looks for occurrences of a Regex pattern and substitutes the pattern with a specified string at every location in the string where the pattern matched. The gsub! method is a "destructive" method in the sense that the method returns a changed object. In this case, the method returns a modified line object. In Ruby, all methods that end with an exclamation point are destructive methods that return a modified receiver object. The gsub method (no exclamation point) is equivalent to gsub! but does not yield a modified receiver object.

Let us think about what constitutes a good marker for the end of a sentence:

There is a basal cell carcinoma. The margins are free of tumor.

The split between the two sentences consists of a lowercase letter ("a" in this case) followed by a period, followed by one or more space characters, followed by an uppercase letter.

We can create an abstract regular expression to match sentence breaks.

```
/([^A-Z])(\.[\s]+[A-Z])/)
```

Regular expressions are enclosed by a pair of slashes, (/ and /), and the parts of a regular expression can be enclosed by parentheses without modifying the meanings of the enclosed expressions. The first part of the regular expression is:

```
([^A-Z])
```

The complementary straight brackets ([and]) indicate a subpattern will match against any of the enclosed characters. If the enclosed expression is A-Z, this would mean that the pattern matches against any uppercase letter from A to Z. If the enclosed pattern were A-C, this would mean that the pattern would match against A, B, or C. In this case, A-Z is preceded by ^. The ^ character, within enclosing straight brackets, is a complement operator and indicates that everything EXCEPT the following characters will be matched. The expression [^A-Z] matches against any character that is not an uppercase letter.

The second part of the expression is(\.[\s]+[A-Z]), and the first part of this expression is "\.". The \ is an escape operator. It indicates to Ruby that the character following the \ (in this case, a period) should be interpreted as a literal character and not as an operator. In the case of a period, this is an important distinction, because in Ruby, the period serves as the operator that sends a method to an object. To confuse matters, there are some notable exceptions. For instance, the newline character is \n. The \ before the n does not indicate that the n should be interpreted as a character. Ruby knows that \n always means the newline character. Ruby also knows that \s always means a space character and \d always means a numeric character. This logical inconsistency is a holdover from languages that predate Ruby. Because so many different languages adopt traditional regular expressions, Ruby retains the somewhat confusing escape syntax.

Continuing through the parenthetic subpattern, the \s indicates a space character. The + following the enclosed \s indicates that the subpattern will match against one or more spaces. The enclosed A-Z indicates that the expression will match against an uppercase letter.

We will want to replace the interface between each sentence with a newline character, but we will want to preserve the sentence characters from either side of the interface. We can use the look-ahead assertion, ?=, which is a Regex device that lets us examine whether an expression matches in the text but that excludes the expression from the match. In other words, it looks ahead, beyond the matching part of the expression, to ensure that the expression exists.

```
/([^A-Z])(?=\.[\s]+[A-Z])/
```

The only matching part of the expression will be the final character of the first sentence, and we create a block for the gsub! method that substitutes the matching last character of the expression plus a period plus a new-line character for the end of each sentence and preserves the first characters of the following sentence.

```
line.gsub!(/([^A-Z])(?=\.[\s]+[A-Z])/){|match| match + "\.\n"}
```

This script is not foolproof, but it does a fair job of converting block-text into a list of sentences. The sentence is the basic unit for all natural language processing, and line-reads are the basic unit of file parsing. Having a corpus of text consisting of exactly one sentence per line will greatly facilitate any natural language processing project.

7.4. REGULAR EXPRESSION MODIFIERS AND EXAMPLES

Regular expressions are referred to in the shortened form, Regex, by most programmers. Virtually all languages that accommodate Regex will offer the identical modifiers to enhance the versatility of Regex (List 7.4.1).

LIST 7.4.1. PATTERN MATCH OPTIONS

g	Match globally, (find all occurrences).
i	Do case-insensitive pattern matching.
m	Treat string as multiple lines.
o	Compile pattern only once.
^	Match the beginning of the line.
.	Match any character (except newline).
$	Match the end of the line (or before newline at the end).
()	Grouping, designates a segment of the matching term that can be assigned to a variable. Strings matching group patterns are assigned variables $1, $2, $3 sequentially as they appear in the regex expressions.
$1	A variable containing the string that matched the first group in a regex pattern.
$2	A variable containing the string that matched the second group in a regex pattern.
[	Character class, tells Ruby to look for a match to any of the characters included within the square bracket.
*	Match 0 or more times.
+	Match 1 or more times.
?	Match 1 or 0 times.
{n}	Match exactly n times.
{n,}	Match at least n times.

```
{n,m}  Match at least n but not more than m times.
\n     newline(LF, NL).
\W     Match a non-word character.
\s     Match a whitespace character.
\S     Match a non-whitespace character.
\d     Match a digit character.
\D     Match a non-digit character.
```

7.5. USING RUBY REGULAR EXPRESSIONS

Here are some additional commonly used regular expressions. Readers are encouraged to study these or to include them in short Ruby test scripts to see how these regular expressions perform on sample text (List 7.5.1). It is easy to write simple Regex, but mastering the many subtleties of Regex can be daunting.

LIST 7.5.1. SAMPLE REGEX OPERATIONS

```
string.gsub(/^ +/, "")
```
Removes leading spaces from a character string.

```
string.gsub(/ +$/, "")
```
Removes trailing spaces from a character string.

```
string.gsub(/ +/, "")
```
Changes all sequences of one or more spaces to just a single space.

```
string.gsub(/\n/, "")
```
Gets rid of newline (sometimes called line break) characters in your string.

```
string.tr('A-Z', 'a-z')
```
Every uppercase letter is converted to a lowercase letter using the translate operator.

```
string.downcase
```
Every uppercase letter is converted to a lowercase letter using the `downcase` method. `string.upcase` does the opposite.

```
string.gsub(/\<[^\<]+\>/, "")
```
Removes angle-bracketed expressions, such as HTML or XML markup.

7.6. A SIMPLE SCRIPT FOR FILE SEARCHING USING REGEX

After you have learned to represent text patterns as Regex expressions, you can create amazing queries operating over text files.

The `search.rb` script provides a simple interface to a Regex query. The script asks you for a file and then asks you for a Regex expression. If you have weak Regex skills, you can always enter a plain word or a phrase, as these are legitimate Regex patterns.

The script opens the file, parses it line by line and prints out the lines that match your expression (List 7.6.1).

LIST 7.6.1. RUBY SCRIPT `search.rb` **SEARCHES THROUGH ANY FILE FOR LINES MATCHING A REGEX EXPRESSION**

```ruby
#!/usr/bin/ruby
puts "Enter your search file, including its path, if it is not"
puts "in the current directory, and press the return key"
filename = STDIN.gets.chomp!
puts "Enter your search Regex and press the return key"
regex = STDIN.gets.chomp!
searchfile = File.open("#{filename}")
searchfile.each{|line| puts line if (line =~ /#{regex}/i)}
exit
```

We have already seen how the `gets` method receives a line entered from your keyboard. After receiving a file name and a Regex pattern, the heart of the script beats on a single line (List 7.6.2):

```ruby
searchfile.each{|line| puts line if (line =~ /#{regex}/i)}
```

In the first run of `search.rb`, we looked for matches to the Regex expression `undif.+sarcoma` in the `neocl.xml` file (the Neoplasm Classification XML file). This expression finds lines that contain the string `undif` followed by one or more of any intervening characters followed by the string `sarcoma`.

One line was included in the list from among many different output lines.

```
<name nci-code = "C8972000">undifferentiated uterine sarcoma
</name>
```

The second run of the `search.rb` script searched the OMIM file for lines that matched the expression "`rhabd.+mor.`" The expression matches

LIST 7.6.2. PARTIAL OUTPUT OF TWO RUNS OF SCRIPT `search.rb`

```
C:\ftp\rb>ruby search.rb
Enter your search file, including its path, if it is not
in the current directory, and press the return key
c:\ftp\neocl.xml
Enter your search Regex and press the return key
undif.+sarcoma
<name nci-code = "C8972000">undifferentiated uterine
    sarcoma</name>


C:\ftp\rb>ruby search.rb
Enter your search file, including its path, if it is not
in the current directory, and press the return key
c:\entrez\omim
Enter your search Regex and press the return key
rhabd.+mor

chromosomal translocation breakpoint from a rhabdoid tumor,
within a progression of rhabdomyosarcoma tumorigenesis. Among
different types of teratoid/rhabdoid tumors (609322), and
malignant gliomas. They are also key mediators in the genesis
of rhabdoid tumors.

V.: Genetic ablation of cyclin D1 abrogates genesis of rhab-
doid tumors Caenorhabditis elegans homologs of the Rb tumor
suppressor complex rhabdomyomata are congenital; renal tumors
develop only later in life
```

strings beginning with `rhabd` followed by one or more of any intervening characters followed by the string `mor`.

Parsing through the 117 Megabyte OMIM file produced many matching lines, a few of which are shown (List 7.6.2). Look at some of the matching phrases within the lines (List 7.6.3).

When writing the Regex expression, I guessed that the only match would be the term "rhabdoid tumor"; however, some of the matching phrases were surprising (List 7.6.3). Whenever you create a Regex pattern, you can expect the unexpected.

The simple `search.rb` script can be easily expanded to search through a list of files or a list of Regex expressions or to parse through paragraphs or records or to return chunks of text larger than a line, or to

LIST 7.6.3. SOME STRINGS IN OMIM MATCHING REGEX PATTERN
`"rhabd.+mor"`

rhabdoid tumor

rhabdomyosarcoma tumorigenesis

teratoid/rhabdoid tumors

rhabdoid tumors.

rhabdoid tumors

Caenorhabditis elegans homologs of the Rb tumor

rhabdomyomata are congenital, renal tumors

look for co-occurrences of Regex expressions within a specified proximity of each other. The variations on `search.rb` are endless, if you can program in Ruby.

7.7. SAMPLE PROJECT: EXTRACTING E-MAIL ADDRESSES FROM A PUBMED SEARCH

In Chapter 5, there is a description of PubMed and of the kinds of data files that can be obtained through a PubMed search. In this example, we will be using the easily obtained file, named pubmed.txt, that we generated from a PubMed search on the word "neoplasm" over citations published in the past 5 years that link to free, full-text articles published. The pubmed.txt file is 14,258,404 bytes in length and contains 56,873 entries.

Every entry starts with a PubMed unique identifier number. List 5.4.1 contains a typical PubMed record. The record begins with the following:

PMID-15113444

About a third of the way through the entry, the author's e-mail address is listed.

AD-Cancer Diagnosis Program, National Cancer Institute, Bethesda, USA. bermanj@mail.nih.gov

We will write a short ruby script that parses through every entry in the long PubMed file, extracting every occurrence of an e-mail address in a PubMed download file (List 7.7.1).

LIST 7.7.1. RUBY SCRIPT pubemail.rb **EXTRACTS E-MAIL ADDRESSES FROM A PUBMED SEARCH**

```
#!/usr/bin/ruby
old_hash = Hash.new
corpus_file = File.open("pubmed.txt")
email_file = File.open("email.txt", "w")
$/ = "PMID-"
corpus_file.each do
    |line|
    line = line.downcase
    if (line =~ /\b[\w\d\_\-\.\~]+\@[\w\d\_\-\.\~]+\b/)
line = $&

next if (old_hash.has_key?(line))

old_hash[line] = 1

email_file.puts(line)

    end
end
exit
```

We begin by creating old_hash, an object of the built-in Hash class.

```
old_hash = Hash.new
```

We do not want to repeat any of the e-mail addresses that may be in the file. As we extract e-mail addresses from the text (a few lines further in the script), we will add them to old_hash and test each newly encountered e-mail address to see if it has an entry in the old_hash Hash object.

```
corpus_file = File.open("pubmed.txt")
```

We will prepare the pubmed.txt file for reading, using the File#open method. The open method creates a new object and opens it for file operations. This is one of the few Ruby examples in which a new Class object is created without involving the new method. The read status is the default parameter for the open method, and thus, we do not need to specify that the file is being opened for reading.

```
email_file = File.open("email.txt", "w")
```

We create a new, empty file for writing, using the File#open method and the "w" parameter. If the file "email.txt" does not exist, the open method will create a new file with that name. Otherwise, the open method prepares the existing file for writing, overwriting any pre-existing data in the file.

```
$/ = "PMID-"
```

The $/ line separator is a built-in Ruby variable that tells Ruby how to distinguish one line from the next when it parses through a file. Ruby's default line separator is the newline character, \n. If you don't want to use \n as the line separator, Ruby permits you to assign any character string your prefer. Because each PubMed entry begins with "PMID-", we will assign "PMID-" to the line separator variable. Each time Ruby grabs a line of the file, it will actually be grabbing all the text (including newline characters) between each occurrence of "PMID-".

```
corpus_file.each do
    |line|
    line = line.downcase
    if (line =~ /\b[\w\d\_\-\.\~]+\@[\w\d\_\-\.\~]+\b/)
line = $&\

next if (old_hash.has_key?(line))

old_hash[line] = 1

email_file.puts(line)

    end
end
```

Here we create a block that iterates over every line of the corpus_file, using the each iteration method. There are two equivalent formats for each iteration block.

```
object.each do
    |something|
    .

    .
    end
```

or

```
object.each {|something| . . }
```

Both these forms are ubiquitous in Ruby programs. The each iteration method tells Ruby to perform a block of code on each member of the object, assigning each member the variable something for the duration of the block.

File iterations using the `each` method are particularly useful because they allow Ruby to parse through a file of any length, performing operations line by line, with temporary variables that vanish at the end of each iteration.

In the `each` loop, successive lines are matched against the Regex for an e-mail pattern.

```
if (line =~ /\b[\w\d\_\-\.\~]+\@[\w\d\_\-\.\~]+\b/)
line = $&
```

Ruby looks for a break between words (designated by the zero-length `\b` character) followed by one or more characters that could be letters, digits, underscores, hyphens, periods, or tildas, followed by the @ symbol, followed by one or more of the same kinds of characters, followed by a break between words. This should match most e-mail addresses. The part of the line that matches the entire regular expression is held in Ruby's built-in global variable, `$&`. We assign the matching phrase (the e-mail address, in this case) to the `line` `String` object.

```
next if (old_hash.has_key?(line))

old_hash[line] = 1

email_file.puts(line)
```

As each e-mail address is assigned to the `line` `String` object, we check to see if the value of the line object already exists in the `old_hash` `Hash` object. If it already exists in our hash of e-mail addresses, we skip to the next iteration of the loop. Otherwise, we add it to our hash, with the e-mail address as a key, and with `"1"` as our value. We can then add the e-mail address in `line` to our file of e-mail addresses, using the `puts` method. After the entire `pubmed.txt` input file is parsed, we are left with our `email.txt` output file containing all the e-mail addresses from `pubmed.txt`.

CHAPTER 8

File/Dataset Transformations (Level I)

8.1. BACKGROUND

The purpose of this chapter is to begin to familiarize you with bits, bytes, files and directories, the building blocks of computational data.

Let us begin with ASCII, the American Standard Code for Information Interchange. ASCII is the binary code that your operating system uses to represent characters (including all the keyboard characters).

There are 256 (2^8) different characters in the ASCII character set. ASCII values under 128 are often referred to as 7-bit ASCII. All of the printable characters (that is, the characters that a keyboard can print) are assigned an ASCII number under 128 and can all be specified in 7 bits (List 8.1.1).

LIST 8.1.1. SEVEN AND EIGHT BIT ASCII CHARACTERS

128 in binary is 2^7	10000000
127 in binary is	1111111
256 in binary is 2^8 or	100000000
255 in binary is	11111111

8.2. ASCII CHARACTERS

All of the printed characters found in this book are ASCII characters from 33 to 126. The unprinted characters in this book are space and the doublet carriage return/line feed. These three unprinted characters are ASCII 32 (space), ASCII 13 (carriage return), and ASCII 10 (line-feed) (List 8.2.1).

LIST 8.2.1. THE ALPHANUMERIC 7-BIT ASCII CHARACTERS

32	space		62	>
33	!		63	?
34	"		64	@
35	#		65	A
36	$		66	B
37	%		67	C
38	&		68	D
39	'		69	E
40	(		70	F
41	)		71	G
42	*		72	H
43	+		73	I
44	,		74	J
45	-		75	K
46	.		76	L
47	/		77	M
48	0		78	N
49	1		79	O
50	2		80	P
51	3		81	Q
52	4		82	R
53	5		83	S
54	6		84	T
55	7		85	U
56	8		86	V
57	9		87	W
58	:		88	X
59	;		89	Y
60	<		90	Z
61	=		91	[

92	\		110	n
93	]		111	o
94	^		112	p
95	_		113	q
96	`		114	r
97	a		115	s
98	b		116	t
99	c		117	u
100	d		118	v
101	e		119	w
102	f		120	x
103	g		121	y
104	h		122	z
105	i		123	{
106	j		124	|
107	k		125	}
108	l		126	~
109	m			

8.3. CONVERTING BINARY TO BASE64

Although we distinguish text files from binary files, all files are actually binary files. Sequential bytes of 8 bits are converted to ASCII equivalents, and if the ASCII equivalents are alphanumerics, we call the file a text file. If the ASCII values of 8-bit sequential file chunks are nonalphanumeric, we call the files binary files.

Actually, any file can be converted into something akin to a text file by dividing the file into 6-bit chunks and assigning each 6-bit chunk an alphanumeric ASCII character with two leading zeros (that is, a 0-padded 6-bit ASCII value, which is equivalent to a Base64 character). Binary can be interconverted with Base64. Base64 conversion is sometimes used to represent a binary file as a Base64 alphanumeric file. Alphanumeric files are useful because they can be ported inside formats that require plain ASCII text (such as HTML and XML). It is easy to convert a text string into Base64 and to covert the Base64 representation back into ordinary text (Lists 8.3.1 and 8.3.2).

LIST 8.3.1. RUBY SCRIPT base64.rb ENCODES STRINGS IN BASE64 NOTATION

```
#!/usr/local/bin/ruby
require 'base64'
text = "The secret of life"
encoded = Base64.encode64(text)
puts("This is the encoded text ... #{encoded}")
decoded = Base64.decode64(encoded)
puts("This is the decoded text ... #{decoded}")
exit
```

LIST 8.3.2. OUTPUT OF RUBY SCRIPT base64.rb

```
C:\ftp\rb>ruby base64.rb
This is the encoded text ... VGhlIHNlY3JldCBvZiBsaWZl
This is the decoded text ... The secret of life
```

An entire file can be converted to Base64. The b64jpg.rb script prints the first 301 characters of the Base64 representation of the binary image file, walnut.jpg (List 8.3.3). The script also reconstructs the binary file from the Base64 representation, verifying that the reconstructed file is byte-for-byte identical to the original file.

LIST 8.3.3. RUBY SCRIPT, b64jpg.rb ENCODES A BINARY FILE IN BASE64

```
#!/usr/local/bin/ruby
require 'base64'
image_file = File.open("walnut.jpg").binmode
image_file_string = image_file.read
b64 = Base64.encode64(image_file_string)
puts b64.slice(0,300)
regular = Base64.decode64(b64)
out_file = File.open("walnew.jpg", "w").binmode
out_file.write(regular)
exit
```

The output of the `b64jpg.rb` script is shown in List 8.3.4.

LIST 8.3.4. OUTPUT OF RUBY SCRIPT, `b64jpg.rb`

```
C:\ftp\rb>ruby b64jpg.rb
/9j/4AAQSkZJRgABAgAAZABkAAD/7AARRHVja3kAAQAEAAAAHgAA/+4ADkFk
b2J1AGTAAAAAAf/bAIQAEAsLCwwLEAwMEBcPDQ8XGxQQEBQbHxcXFxcXHx4X
GhoaGhceHiMlJyUjHi8vMzMvL0BAQEBAQEBAQEBAQEBAAERDw8RExEVEhIV
FBEUERQaFBYWFBomGhocGhomMCMeHh4eIzArLicnJy4rNTUwMDU1QEA/QEBA
QEBAQEBAQEBA/8AAEQgEfgYQAwEiAAIRAQMRAf/EAJMAAQADAQEBAQAA
```

```
/9j/4AAQSkZJRgABAgAAZABkAAD/7AARRHVja3kAAQAEAAAAHgAA/+4ADkFk
b2J1AGTAAAAAAf/bAIQAEAsLCwwLEAwMEBcPDQ8XGxQQEBQbHxcXFxcXHx4X
GhoaGhceHiMlJyUjHi8vMzMvL0BAQEBAQEBAQEBAQEBAAERDw8RExEVEhIV
FBEUERQaFBYWFBomGhocGhomMCMeHh4eIzArLicnJy4rNTUwMDU1QEA/QEBA
QEBAQEBAQEBA/8AAEQgEfgYQAwEiAAIRAQMRAf/EAJMAAQADAQEBAQAA
```

The `b64jpg.rb` script first requires the Base64 library into the script.

```
require 'base64'
```

It then creates the `image_file` File object, sending the `open` method to class File, and sending the `binmode` method to the new File object. The `binmode` method tells Ruby to treat the file as a binary file, not as an ASCII file (see the Glossary).

```
image_file = File.open("walnut.jpg").binmode
```

The `read` method, sent to the `image_file` File object without arguments, deposits the entire binary file into the `image_file_string` string object.

```
image_file_string = image_file.read
b64 = Base64.encode64(image_file_string)
```

The string containing the binary file is converted to Base64, and the first 301 characters of the Base64 representation of the file are extracted with the `slice` method (see the Glossary).

```
puts b64.slice(0,300)
```

We use base64 encoding again in Chapter 18 when we embed a binary image in an XML file.

8.4. COPYING FILES FROM ONE DIRECTORY TO ANOTHER

Dircopy.rb is a simple Ruby script for copying files from one subdirectory to another (List 8.4.1).

LIST 8.4.1. RUBY SCRIPT dircopy.rb **COPIES FILES FROM ONE DIRECTORY TO ANOTHER**

```ruby
#!/usr/local/bin/ruby
require "ftools"
puts "What directory will receive files?"
receiver = gets.chomp
puts "From what directory would you like to send files?"
sender = gets.chomp
filearray = Dir.entries(sender)
filearray.each do
|filename|
sendernow = sender + filename
receivernow = receiver + filename
next if File.stat(sendernow).directory?
puts sendernow
puts receivernow
   if File.exist?(receivernow)
      if File.exist?(sendernow)
         stat = File.stat(receivernow)
         receiver_time = stat.ctime.to_f
         stat= File.stat(sendernow)
         sender_time = stat.ctime.to_f
         next if receiver_time >= sender_time
      end
   end
File.copy(sendernow,receivernow)
end
exit
```

This script is straightforward and does not require a line-by-line review, but we can examine a few highlights. The most important line in the script is:

```ruby
filearray = Dir.entries(sender)
```

Class Dir receives the class method, entries, with the name of the directory attached as the argument for the entries method. This yields the Array object, filearray, containing the list of files in the directory.

When copying files from one directory to another, it is important not to overwrite newer files with older files of the same name. The `stat` method, sent to file, collects a list of file information (see the Glossary). The `ctime` method extracts, from the `stat` list, the time that the file was created. The `to_f` method converts the time to epoch seconds. By comparing the creation times of files that exist in both the "copied from" directory and the "copied to" directory, we can avoid replacing an existing file with an older file of the same name.

```
stat = File.stat(receivernow)
receiver_time = stat.ctime.to_f
stat= File.stat(sendernow)
sender_time = stat.ctime.to_f
next if receiver_time >= sender_time
```

The copy method, sent to class File, copies a source file (the first argument), to the destination (the second argument).

```
File.copy(sendernow,receivernow)
```

The `copy` method is not a method of class `File`, or of any of the ancestor classes of class `File`. The `copy` method belongs to the `ftools` library required into the script on the very first line.

```
require "ftools"
```

`Ftools` is a very handy library that adds methods to class `File` for moving and copying files.

8.5. CONVERTING DICOM TO JPEG IMAGE FILES

DICOM and JPEG files were described in Chapter 5. If you work in a hospital, you are likely to encounter radiology files encoded in the DICOM format. Outside of hospitals, DICOM is rarely used. You may find it useful to transfer DICOM images to some other file format, such as JPEG, that can be used in off-the-shelf image software. It is easy to convert a DICOM image to a JPEG image, using DCM2JPG, a free command-line software application. Instructions for obtaining DCM2JPG are found in the Appendix. For this section, you will need to have a collection of DICOM images. You can download DICOM images from

ftp://ftp.erl.wustl.edu/pub/dicom/images/version3/RSNA95/

We will use

dcm2jpg.exe —converts DICOM to JPEG

dcm2txt.exe —converts the DICOM header to text

Ruby can simply call a command-line application from within a script using the exec method (Lists 8.5.1 and 8.5.2).

LIST 8.5.1. RUBY SCRIPT dcm2jpg.rb **CONVERTS A DICOM FILE INTO A JPEG FILE**

```
#!/usr/local/bin/ruby
exec("dcm2jpg.exe c\:\\ftp\\picker\\dicom\\CT4174\~1")
exit
```

The second argument to the exec method is a path and file name of a DICOM image.

LIST 8.5.2. SCREEN OUTPUT OF dcm2jpg.rb **SCRIPT**

```
c:\ftp>ruby dcm2jpg.rb
1 Creating: c:\ftp\picker\dicom\CT4174~1.jpg
1
```

The Ruby script uses just one line of code.

```
exec("dcm2jpg.exe c\:\\ftp\\picker\\dicom\\CT4174\~1")
```

The exec method runs an external command, just as though you had typed in the command line at the system prompt.

The exec method belongs to module Kernel, which is included in all Ruby objects. Kernel methods can be invoked without an explicit object receiver.

What is the advantage of having a Ruby script when you can access the application yourself from the command line? When you run a command-line application from within Ruby, you can add Ruby code that iteratively calls the external application, or that calls the application with arguments determined elsewhere in the script. Let us look at one more simple Ruby script that calls the conversion application twice (List 8.5.3).

LIST 8.5.3. RUBY SCRIPT dcmsplit.rb **CONVERTS A DICOM FILE INTO A JPEG AND A TEXT FILE**

```
#!/usr/local/bin/ruby
system("dcm2jpg.exe c\:\\ftp\\picker\\dicom\\CT4174\~1")
system("dcm2txt.exe c\:\\ftp\\picker\\dicom\\CT4174\~1")
exit
```

Here we make two consecutive calls to an external application. Notice that in the dcm2jpg.exe script we call the external application with Kernel's `system` method, whereas we call the application with Kernel's `exec` method in the prior script. The `exec` method replaces the current process with the external command. When the external command ends, the process ends, and any portions of the Ruby script after the `exec` method will be ignored. The `system` method returns to the script after the external operation is complete. Because we needed to call external applications twice, we switched to the `system` method. We could have written a Ruby script that converted thousands of DICOM images all at once by sending the `foreach` method to the class DIR object and iterating over a list of files (see List 2.10.3).

Let us look at the screen output of the `dcm2jpg.rb` script (List 8.5.4).

LIST 8.5.4. SCREEN OUTPUT OF dcm2jpg.rb SCRIPT

```
c:\ftp>ruby dcm2jpg.rb
1 Creating: c:\ftp\picker\dicom\CT4174~1.jpg
1
1 Creating: c:\ftp\picker\dicom\CT4174~1.txt
1
```

The DICOM script has been split into two output files, one a JPEG file (CT4174~1.jpg) and the other a text file (CT4174~1.txt) containing the header information for the DICOM file. The just-created JPEG file lacks the clinical JPEG information contained in the DICOM file, but this information is now available to us in our newly created text file. In the next section, we see how any textual information can be inserted back into a JPEG file using RMagick.

8.6. EXTRACTING AND INSERTING JPEG AND DICOM IMAGE HEADERS

As described in List 5.14.2, medical images must contain headers with information that describes the specimens represented by the images. Biomedical professionals need to have methods for adding textual annotations to an image file.

A simple Ruby script uses RMagick to insert any text into a JPEG image (Lists 8.6.1 and 8.6.2). RMagick, Ruby's interface to free and open source ImageMagick, is discussed in detail in the Appendix.

What just happened here? The Ruby script took the JPEG file `gwmbw.jpg` and inserted into its header a comment consisting of the

LIST 8.6.1. RUBY SCRIPT jpeg_add.rb INSERTS TEXTUAL INFORMATION INTO A JPEG IMAGE

```
#!/usr/local/bin/ruby
require 'RMagick'
include Magick
text = IO.read("gwmbw.txt")
orig_image = ImageList.new("gwmbw.jpg")
orig_image.cur_image[:Comment] = text
print "\nComment added, let's make a file to hold the
    modifications\n\n"
copy_image = ImageList.new
copy_image = orig_image.cur_image.copy
copy_image.write("c:\\ftp\\rb\\gwmout.JPG")
copy_image.properties{|name, value| print "#{name}\n#{value}\n"}
exit
```

LIST 8.6.2. OUTPUT OF jpeg_add.rb SCRIPT

```
C:\ftp\rb>ruby jpeg_add.rb
      Comment added, let's make a file to hold the modifications
Comment
0002,0000,File Meta Elements Group Len=122
0002,0001,File Meta Info Version=1
0002,0002,Media Storage SOP Class UID=1.2.840.10008.5.1.4.1.1.7.
0002,0003,Media Storage SOP Inst UID=9999.20070123103417.100.10
0002,0010,Transfer Syntax UID=1.2.840.10008.1.2.1.
0002,0012,Implementation Class UID=960051513
0008,0008,Image Type=
0008,0012,Instance Creation Date=20070123
0008,0013,Instance Creation Time=103417
0008,0016,SOP Class UID=1.2.840.10008.5.1.4.1.1.7.
0008,0018,SOP Instance UID=9999.20070123103417.100.10
0008,0020,Study Date=20070123
0008,0030,Study Time=103417
0008,0050,Accession Number=
0008,0060,Modality=OT
0008,0064,Conversion Type=WSD.
0008,0090,Referring Physician's Name=
0010,0010,Patient's Name=gwmbw.jpg.
0010,0020,Patient ID=0.
0010,0030,Patient Date of Birth=
0010,0040,Patient Sex=M
```

```
0010,1010,Patient Age=0.
0020,000D,Study Instance UID=9999.20070123103417.100.20
0020,000E,Series Instance UID=9999.20070123103417.100.30
0020,0010,Study ID=0
0020,0011,Series Number=0
0020,0013,Image Number=0
0020,0020,Patient Orientation=
0028,0002,Samples Per Pixel=1
0028,0004,Photometric Interpretation=MONOCHROME2
0028,0010,Rows=1536
0028,0011,Columns=2048
0028,0100,Bits Allocated=8
0028,0101,Bits Stored=8
0028,0102,High Bit=7
0028,0103,Pixel Representation=0
7FE0,0010,Pixel Data=3145728


JPEG-Colorspace
1
JPEG-Sampling-factors
1x1
```

entire contents of file `gwmbw.txt`. The `gwmbw.txt` file is the textual representation of the header information in the DICOM file gwmbw.dcm (see List 5.14.1). We extracted this file from gwmbw.dcm using a modification of `dcmsplit.rb` (see List 8.5.3).

The output JPEG image file (`gwmout.jpg`) contains the binary representation of the same image represented by `gwmbw.dcm` and `gwmbw.jpg`. In addition, it contains a comment field consisting of the contents of file gwmbw.txt, the textual representation of the original DICOM header. We can extract the comment field from the JPEG header whenever we wish using RMagick's `properties` method.

```
copy_image.properties{|name, value| print "#{name}\n#{value}\n"}
```

In this and the prior sections, we have shown how image annotations can be conveyed in an image header and extracted whenever they are needed. In biology and medicine, image annotations may convey important information relating to the content of the image and the methods by which the image was acquired. By including the annotations within the image file, we can be certain that the annotations will always be available to the entity (person or software agent) that gains access to the image file.

8.7. SAMPLE PROJECT: CREATING AN EXCEL-COMPATIBLE SPREADSHEET FROM PUBMED DATA

All spreadsheet applications recognize CSV-format files. CSV (Comma-Separated Values) is a format in which the rows of a spreadsheet are represented as lines in the file (character strings separated by the newline character) and the elements of the spreadsheet are separated by commas. If you have a file in which each line contains data elements separated by commas, with the same number of commas on every line, you can be confident that the file can be opened in a spreadsheet application.

If you like to work with spreadsheet applications, there will be occasions when you will want to parse a text file, extracting the data elements of interest and creating a new file in CSV format.

We have used PubMed output files in Chapters 7.3 and 7.6. We use the same PubMed file (pubmed.txt) in the following example (List 8.7.1).

LIST 8.7.1. RUBY SCRIPT comma.rb CREATES COMMA-SEPARATED VALUE FILE FROM TEXT DATA

```ruby
#!/usr/bin/ruby
old_hash = Hash.new
new_hash = Hash.new
corpus_file = File.open("pubmed.txt")
comma_separated_file = File.open("e_names.csv", "w")
email_file = File.open("email.txt", "w")
full_title_file = File.open("altmail.txt", "w")
$/ = "PMID-"
def csv(place,name,line)
    place.gsub!(/\n +/, "\,") if place =~ /\n +/
    name.gsub!(/\,/, "\_") if name =~ /\,/
    place.gsub!(/\,/, "\_") if place =~ /\,/
    line.gsub!(/\,/, "\_") if line =~ /\,/
    name.gsub!(/\n/, "") if name =~ /\n/
    place.gsub!(/\n/, "") if place =~ /\n/
    place.gsub!(/[\.\_ ]+$/, "") if place =~ /[\.\_ ]$/
    place.gsub!(/\_\_/, "\_") if place =~ /\_\_/
    place.gsub!(/\&/, "and") if place =~ /\&/
    line.gsub!(/\n/, "") if place =~ /\n/
    line = line, "\,", name, "\,", place
end
```

```
corpus_file.each do
    |line|
    next if (line !~ /\b[\w\d\_\-\.\~]+\@[\w\d\_\-\.\~]+\b/)
    name = $1 if (line =~ /FAU \- ([\w\'\.\, ]+)\n/m)
    if (line =~ /AD  \- ([\w\W\d\D\n]+)\n[F]?AU /m)
        place = $1
        place = $` if (place =~ /[F]?AU/)
  place = $` if (place =~ /\b[\w\d\_\-\.\~]+\@[\w\d\_\-\.\~]+\b/)
    end
    line = line.downcase
    if (line =~ /\b[\w\d\_\-\.\~]+\@[\w\d\_\-\.\~]+\b/)
        line = $&
      next if (old_hash.has_key?(line))
      old_hash[line] = 1
      email_file.puts(line)
      full_title_file.print("\"", name, "\"", " \<", line, "\>\n")
       line = csv(place,name,line)
       new_hash[line] = 1
    end
end
new_hash.each {|key,value| comma_separated_file.print(key,"\n")}
exit
```

The `comma.rb` script uses `pubmed.txt`, a 14,258,404 byte file, as its only input. In a little over 5 seconds, the script parses the `pubmed.txt` file and produces three output files:

   `email.txt`, 56,145 bytes, a simple list of 2366 e-mail addresses

   `altmail.txt`, 99,772 bytes, an e-mail list of addresses in angle brackets preceded by a name, in quotations, a popular format for associating a name with an e-mail address

   `e_names.csv`, 307,533 bytes, a line-record file with each line consisting of an e-mail address, a name, and a street address, all separated by commas

The `e-names.csv` file can be visualized and manipulated in any spreadsheet program (see Figure 8-1).

Let us review the `comma.rb` script. Every PubMed multiline record begins with the record separator `"PMID-"`. We set Ruby's line separator global variable to parse the `pumbed.txt` file one record at a time.

```
$/ = "PMID-"
```

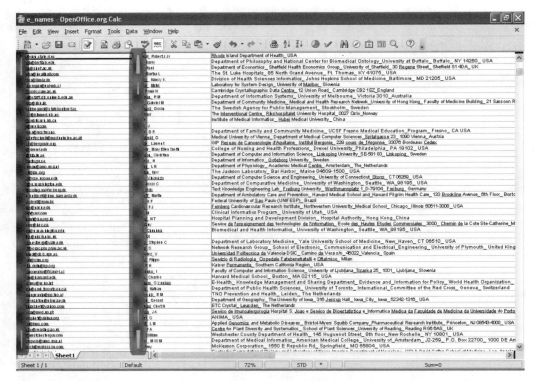

Figure 8-1 Output file, `e_names.csv`, **in spreadsheet viewer. Names are shaded for privacy.**

The address of the first author, including the e-mail address, appears after `"AD-"`.

```
AD=Cancer Diagnosis Program, National Cancer Institute, Bethesda, USA.
Bermanj@mail.nih.gov
```

The name of the first author of the paper is delineated in PubMed with `"FAU-"`.

```
FAU-Berman, Jules J
```

By now, it should be apparent that we must use Regex to parse out the name, the street address, and the e-mail address from each record and place them in data structures that can be ported into the appropriate files.

The bulk of the work is done in the last lines of the script.

```
if (line =~ /\b[\w\d\_\-\.\~]+\@[\w\d\_\-\.\~]+\b/)
  line = $&
    next if (old_hash.has_key?(line))
```

```
        old_hash[line] = 1
        email_file.puts(line)
        full_title_file.print("\"", name, "\"", " \<", line, "\>\n")
        line = csv(place,name,line)
        new_hash[line] = 1
    end
end
new_hash.each {|key,value|comma_separated_file.print(key,"\n")}
```

The PubMed records are matched against a general pattern for an e-mail address. If there is a match, the if-block is entered. Otherwise, the next PubMed record is examined.

```
    if (line =~ /\b[\w\d\_\-\.\~]+\@[\w\d\_\-\.\~]+\b/)
```

At this point, the line String object contains the matching e-mail address.

```
    line = $&
```

If we have already collected this e-mail address previously in the pubmed.txt file, we do not need to collect it again.

```
    next if (old_hash.has_key?(line))
```

Otherwise, we add the e-mail address to the old_hash Hash instance.

```
    old_hash[line] = 1
```

We can add the e-mail address to the e-mail_file file object, which is a simple collection of addresses.

```
    e-mail_file.puts(line)
```

We can add the e-mail address and the name of the author (previously assigned to the String object name in an earlier part of the script).

```
    full_title_file.print("\"", name, "\"", " \<", line, "\>\n")
```

We pass name, place (previously assigned in an earlier part of the script), and line to the csv method, defined earlier in the script. The csv method cleans the arguments so that they meet alphanumeric standards for names, place addresses and e-mail addresses and returns its value to the String object, line, replacing its prior value.

```
    line = csv(place,name,line)
```

The value of line serves as a key to a Hash instance object, new_hash.

```
    new_hash[line] = 1
```

Finally, the `new_hash` `Hash` instance object is iterated through a block, and each key is put into a file. This file is a comma-separated file suitable for use in any spreadsheet application.

This example was simple enough, but Ruby has its CSV standard library to make life even simpler for the spreadsheet enthusiast. The CSV library has methods for reading and writing cells and headers.

Indexing Text
(Level 1)

9.1. BACKGROUND

Books are like sequential files. You learn the contents of a book by starting at the first word in the file and reading until the file is exhausted. If you want to find a specific sentence or paragraph in the file and you have no index, the only certain way of locating the sentence or paragraph is to repeat the reading process, beginning with the first word, and stopping at the desired text. Some nonprogrammers believe that computers eliminate the need for indexes because a computer can rapidly parse books, beginning with the first word and sequentially reading words until any desired string is found. Experienced programmers know that sequential reading of text is impractical, even for fast computers, when the text is long, the searches are many, and the search fragment occurs at multiple locations through the file.

To find words or phrases in a large text quickly, you need an index, a key to the location of all the words or phrases in the text.

The purpose of this chapter is to describe some very simple indexing techniques that can be implemented in Ruby.

9.2. CONCORDANCE

A concordance is a complete listing of all of the words in a text, along with the locations in the text where they occur. Before the advent of computers, concordances were created for books of great significance, in which every word was deemed important. Not surprisingly, the bible has been the subject of numerous efforts of scribes and scholars to create a concordance for the many versions and translations of the New and Old Testaments. It is difficult to imagine the enormity of creating a concordance "by hand."

Luckily, with Ruby, a concordance can be constructed with just a few lines of code (List 9.2.1).

LIST 9.2.1. RUBY SCRIPT concord.rb **CREATES A CONCORDANCE**

```ruby
#!/usr/local/bin/ruby
f = File.open("fastcode.rb")
place = Hash.new(""); wordarray = Array.new
f.each do
  |line|
  line.downcase!
  line.gsub!(/[^a-z]/," ")
  wordarray = line.split.uniq
  next if wordarray == []
wordarray.each{|word| place[word] = "#{place[word]} #{f.lineno}"}
  wordarray = []
end
place.keys.sort.each{|key| puts "#{key} #{place[key]}"}
exit
```

The first 21 output lines of concord.rb are shown in List 9.2.2.

The concord.rb script creates a concordance for a text file. Each word in the concordance file is followed by the list of lines from the text on which the word appears. In this case, we chose fastcode.rb (see List 12.3.1) as our text file. If you wish, you can verify the output in List 9.2.2 by comparing the line occurrences in List 12.3.1 for each word in the concordance.

The concord.rb script parses each line of text and creates an array of the words from the line of text. The array is assigned to the wordarray instance object of class Array. For each word in wordarray, a key/value pair is created. The key is the word itself. The value is the line number in which the word appears (determined with class IO's lineno method) concatenated to the prior value associated with the key. This effectively builds a list of line numbers on which the key occurs. The key/value pair is assigned to the place Hash instance object.

```ruby
wordarray.each{|word| place[word] = "#{place[word]} #{f.lineno}"}
```

At the end of each line iteration through the file, the wordarray instance object is emptied in preparation for receiving the words on the next line.

LIST 9.2.2. PARTIAL OUTPUT OF RUBY SCRIPT concord.rb

```
C:\ftp\rb>ruby concord.rb
add   23 67 71
adenocarcinoma   56 58
anemia   56 57
are   57
array   36 37 38 40 42 44 46 54 60 62 64 65 66 67 70 73 74 75
    76 77 79
autocode   2 55
bin   1
blasts   58
class   2
codehash   8 25 27 32 49
coder   35 76
codes   23 67 71
cum   36 42 46
dbm   5 6 7
def   3 11 15 19 23 31 35
display   31 82
do   39 40 46 62
doub   7
doubhash   7 19 20 72
doublet   65 69 71 72
each   32 40 46 62
else   26 78
```

The keys in the `place Hash` instance object are extracted as an array using the `keys` method and are subsequently sorted before the next iteration with `each`. Every iteration through the sorted array of keys prints the key, followed by its value.

```
place.keys.sort.each{|key| puts "#{key} #{place[key]}"}
```

Remember, the "`#{object}`" notation is Ruby's way of retrieving the string assigned to the object.

This method may not work for very large files. At some point, the growing hash instance may surpass the limits of your computer's memory. For a large concordance, the hash can be tied to an external database or to a persistent DBM object (see Chapter 6, Section 6).

9.3. INDEXES

Indexes are somewhat different from concordances. An index is composed of a chosen subset of words and phrases from a text followed by their locations in the book. A concordance contains no multiword terms. To build an index, you start with a list of the words and phrases that you want to include, and then you write a script that identifies the locations of the index terms (List 9.3.1).

LIST 9.3.1. RUBY SCRIPT `indexer.rb` CREATES AN INDEX

```
#!/usr/local/bin/ruby
f = File.open("fastcode.rb")
wordplace = Hash.new("")
indexhash = Hash.new("")
indexarray = Array.new(["refractory anemia","rhabdoid tumor",
    "initialize"])
indexarray.each{|term|indexhash[term] = ""}
f.each do
    |line|
    line.downcase!
    indexhash.each do
      |key, value|
      if (line =~ /#{key}/)
        wordplace[key] = "#{wordplace[key]} #{f.lineno}"
      end
    end
end
wordplace.keys.sort.each{|key| puts "#{key} #{wordplace[key]}"}
exit
```

The heart of the script is the iterator that loops through every key in `indexhash`, the Hash object instance that holds index terms as keys.

```
indexhash.each do
    |key, value|
    if (line =~ /#{key}/)
      wordplace[key] = "#{wordplace[key]} #{f.lineno}"
    end
end
```

For each line of text, each key in index hash is matched to determine whether it is contained in the line. If so, the term and its location are added to the `wordplace` Hash instance object.

The last line of the script prints the sorted keys of `wordplace` followed by the value containing the key's line locations in the file. List 9.3.2 shows some of the output lines produced by the `indexer.rb` script.

LIST 9.3.2. AN EXCERPTED OUTPUT FOR THE INDEXING PROGRAM, LISTING ONLY THE TERMS "INITIALIZE, REFRACTORY ANEMIA, RHABDOID TUMOR" AND THE PAGES ON WHICH THEY ARE FOUND

```
C:\ftp\rb>ruby index.rb
initialize   3
refractory anemia   56 57
rhabdoid tumor   59
```

CHAPTER 10

Searching and Mining Data (Level 1)

10.1. BACKGROUND

Data mining is a special kind of data search and retrieval project in which a valued class of data is sought from within one or more datasets. The role of the biomedical data miner is to confer sense on an otherwise inchoate data collection (12).

People like to think that data mining has become an automatic process conducted with the help of sophisticated and expensive software applications. In my opinion, any value in biomedical datasets is conferred through a creative process that involves intense study leading to the discovery of generalizable trends and patterns in disease biology and patient care. Search software must be designed to complement the researcher's conceptualization of a problem or hypothesis. There is no substitute for writing your own search software. Datasets and projects vary to such an extent that off-the-shelf solutions often fail.

To be an effective data miner, you need to create and use large, comprehensive databases. There are some questions that cannot be answered by experience or by reviewing the literature or by experiment. Some questions can only be answered by reviewing all of the collected information in a knowledge domain and finding a trend or a class of cases or a shared property that reveals some new biomedical truth.

New searches on a dataset begin as tentative, unrefined queries. As query results are obtained, the searcher gets an idea of the range of subject information that is available and modifies the query until a final search item is chosen. The process of query refinement is crucial. The search engine must provide the searchers with a valid notion of the depth and breadth of contained information pertaining to a broad area of interest. The search engine must help the searcher determine what he or she can reasonably search.

Hospital information systems (HISs) store a lot of information, but they are almost useless for data mining projects. The primary search function of a HIS is to retrieve test results (for example, a biopsy, a blood analysis, an x-ray) for a particular patient when queried by a healthcare provider. Of course, accomplishing this service dependably and accurately is no simple feat. Still, data miners soon learn that the typical HIS cannot provide global analyses in which all of the patient records are collected and compared. For example, a relatively simple search for all the positive reports (reports that contained values exceeding normal limits) on all patients who are overweight would be highly problematic. HISs typically search on patient names (or patient identifiers), not fields within reports. HISs seldom support searches that collect collections of reports on multiple patients.

Some HISs may support global searches through all their hospital records, but with few exceptions, HISs will retrieve only those records that contain record fields exactly matched by the query. A medical report may be entered into a HIS as a record containing a patient name field and a date field and a procedure field, with the text of the report attached as a character string. In such a case, the database may accept queries on patient name and date and procedure but may not accept queries on expressions contained in a character string field. Consequently, biomedical professionals seldom have query access to data embedded within the text of medical reports.

Beyond this problem, most HISs do not provide access to all of the information on a given patient. A skin disease report may be sequestered in the dermatology department's database, and the patient may be registered under a different identifier in the dermatology clinic than in the medical clinic. These problems and many others have contributed to the current push for electronic medical records (EMRs) that attach all of a patient's clinic visits and test results to a single, comprehensive digital record.

In summary, if you are not sure of what you are looking for until you see it, and if you need to have access to all of the information, structured and unstructured, in the dataset, your HISs will likely disappoint you. You will need to develop your own methods to describe, search, and retrieve data. Because search and retrieval over large databases are slow unless the data are sorted or stored in a data structure designed for quick retrieval, programmers must learn to sort and structure large collections of data.

The purpose of this chapter is to provide practical approaches to finding data in large biomedical datasets.

10.2. FINDING NEEDLES FAST USING A BINARY-TREE SEARCH OF THE HAYSTACK

It is very easy for Ruby to find a specific item in an ordered list. If the list is ordered, it can be gigabytes in length, and Ruby can find any record almost instantly.

What is an ordered list? Examples are an index, an alphabetized list such as a dictionary or glossary, or a numbered array.

The haystack.rb script is shown in List 10.2.1. Sample searches are shown in List 10.2.2.

LIST 10.2.1. RUBY SCRIPT haystack.rb PERFORMS A BINARY SEARCH ON A FILE

```ruby
#!/usr/local/bin/ruby
text = File.open("terms.put", "r")
text.seek(0, IO::SEEK_SET)
puts "What would you like to find?"
findword = gets.chomp.downcase
puts "Let's begin....."
filesize = File.stat("terms.put").size
portionarray = Array.new; arraynumber = Numeric.new; place = Numeric.new
(1..128).each do
    |value|
    portion = ((filesize * value)/128).to_i
    portionarray << portion
end
arraynumber = 64
[4,8,16,32,64,128].each do
    |division|
    place = portionarray[arraynumber-1]
    text.seek(place, IO::SEEK_SET)
    line = text.readline
    line = text.readline
    line =~ /^([a-z]+) /
    estimate_word = $1
    puts estimate_word
    comp_result = (estimate_word <=> findword)
    arraynumber = (arraynumber + (128/division).to_i) if (comp_result == -1)
    arraynumber = (arraynumber - (128/division).to_i) if (comp_result != -1)
end
text.seek((place - 100000), IO::SEEK_SET)
holder = text.read(200000)
```

```
if (holder =~ /#{findword}.+\n/)
    puts $&
elsif
    puts "Sorry.  Couldn't find #{findword} in the index.\n"
end
exit
```

LIST 10.2.2. SAMPLE OUTPUTS OF haystack.rb

```
C:\ftp\rb>ruby haystack.rb
What would you like to find?
accessory
Let's begin.....
mesiobuccal
distal
branch
articular
anterior
anterior
accessory parotid gland

What would you like to find?
jugum
Let's begin.....
mesiobuccal
distal
lateral
glandes
insular
intervertebral
jugum of sphenoid

What would you like to find?
wall
Let's begin.....
mesiobuccal
set
trabecular
trunk
vasculature
wall
wall of urinary bladder
```

The algorithm for binary searches is very simple. A search term is provided along with the name of a file containing ordered items, with one item on each line of the file. Ruby opens the file and goes to the middle of the file. Ruby then determines whether the item at the middle of the file precedes (alphabetically) the search term. If the item at the middle of the file precedes the search term, then the search term must reside in the latter half of the file. Otherwise it resides in the top half of the file. In either case, Ruby has reduced the size of the search space by one-half and proceeds to the middle item of the appropriate half-file, where it repeats the process. In just a few iterations, Ruby always manages to get close to the search item. Once Ruby has narrowed the location of the search item, it can do a simple Regex search for the item on a small block of the file.

The `haystack.rb` script begins by opening the `"terms.put"` file, an alphabetized list of medical terms, for reading. It sets the `text` file object instance to the beginning of the file using the seek method (see the Glossary).

```
text.seek(0, IO::SEEK_SET)
```

The script asks the user to supply a search word.

```
puts "What would you like to find?"
findword = gets.chomp.downcase
```

The script determines the size of the file by sending the `size` method to the object yielded by the `stat` method sent to the file (see the Glossary).

```
filesize = File.stat("terms.put").size
```

An array consisting the the approximate byte number for each 1/128th portion of the file is calculated and stored in the `portionarray` Array object.

```
(1..128).each do
    |value|
    portion = ((filesize * value)/128).to_i
    portionarray << portion
end
```

The middle portion is number 64.

```
arraynumber = 64
```

For 6 iterations, and beginning with the middle of the file, the search term is compared with the term at the chosen file location, using the `<=>` comparison operator.

```
[4,8,16,32,64,128].each do
    |division|
    place = portionarray[arraynumber-1]
    text.seek(place, IO::SEEK_SET)
    line = text.readline
    line = text.readline
    line =~ /^([a-z]+) /
    estimate_word = $1
    puts estimate_word
    comp_result = (estimate_word <=> findword)
```

The `<=>` comparison operator is a polymorphic method included in several different classes with a distinctly non-Ruby syntax that traces back to its roots in Unix scripting languages. In the `String` class, the `<=>` operator returns a `0` if the string on the left of the operator has the same alpabetic rank as the string on the right of the operator. It returns `-1` if the string to the left of the operator precedes the string to the right, alphabetically. It returns `1` if the string to the left succeeds the string to the right.

For example:

```
irb>"hello" <=> "yesterday" => -1
irb>"zoo" <=> "apple" => 1
```

If the current word in the file (`estimate_word`) precedes the search word (`findword`), the next loop moves up the file, by half. Otherwise, the next loop moves back in the file by half.

```
arraynumber = (arraynumber + (128/division).to_i) if
(comp_result == -1)
arraynumber = (arraynumber - (128/division).to_i) if
(comp_result != -1)
```

By examining the sample searches in List 10.2.2, you can see how the successive jumps in the file come closer and closer to the desired matching term. It never takes more than six jumps to come close to the match.

Binary searches can be performed on any ordered list of any length at great speed. Because this trick works on files with ordered content, programmers may prefer binary searches on files, rather than database programs, for rapid record lookups.

10.3. SORTING LARGE FILES QUICKLY

It is incredibly easy to sort the lines of a file in Ruby.

As an example, let us sort the line of the file `icd.out`, which we create in Chapter 12, Section 4. The `icd.out` file is 1,384,365 bytes and contains about 26,000 lines, each consisting of an ICD (International Classification of Diseases) code followed by the name of a disease (List 10.3.1).

LIST 10.3.1. FIRST FIVE LINES OF ICD.OUT FILE

R10.0 Acute abdomen

Q89.9 Congenital malformation, unspecified

K00.2 Abnormalities of size and form of teeth

E16.4 Abnormal secretion of gastrin

O03 Spontaneous abortion

The file can be sorted with the `tinysort.rb` script. After the read and write file objects are created, the sort routine is composed of a single line of code (List 10.3.2).

LIST 10.3.2. RUBY SCRIPT `tinysort.rb` SORTS THE LINES OF A FILE

```
#!/usr/local/bin/ruby
text = File.open("icd.out", "r")
out = File.open("icdsort.out", "w")
out.print(text.readlines.sort.join)
exit
```

The output file is sorted alphabetically (not numerically). Digits are string characters and have their place in the ASCII chart just like any alphabetic character. Consequently, the sort order for strings that contain alphabetic and numeric characters assigns the numeric characters a precedent position in the alphabetic order (see List 8.2.1). The first few lines of output of the `tinysort.rb` script are shown in List 10.3.3.

LIST 10.3.3. FIRST SIX LINES OF OUTPUT OF THE `tinysort.rb` SCRIPT

```
1 Examination of skull, meninges or brain
10 Postoperative reopening of craniotomy or craniectomy site
1000 Other repair procedures on abdomen, peritoneum or omentum
1001 Revision procedures on abdomen, peritoneum or omentum
1002 Procedures for hydatid cyst of peritoneum or abdominal organs
1003 Procedures for gastroschisis
```

The parsing and sorting work of the `tinysort.rb` script is contained in a single line of Ruby code.

```
out.print(text.readlines.sort.join)
```

The IO object `readlines` method is sent to a `File` instance object and converts the `File` object's lines into an array. The array is sorted and then joined into a long character string. The string is printed to the IO object named `out`.

The problem with this script is that it requires the input file to be placed into an array, with each array element corresponding to a sequential line of text. Large files (hundreds of megabytes) may exceed your computer's maximum array size. Even if your computer's memory can accommodate a large array file, you may find that Ruby's built-in sort routine has an unacceptably long execution time.

It is easy to write a Ruby script that sorts large files quickly, if you are willing to accept a few shortcuts (List 10.3.4).

LIST 10.3.4. RUBY SCRIPT `bigsort.rb` **SORTS LARGE FILES QUICKLY**

```ruby
#!/usr/local/bin/ruby
text = File.open("terms.txt", "r")
out = File.open("terms.put", "w")
linearray = Array.new
text.each_line do
    |line|
    linelength = line.size
    begin_position = text.pos - linelength - 1
    linearray << line.chomp!.slice(0..9) + begin_position.to_s
end
linearray.sort!
linearray.each do
  |value|
  seekplace = value.slice(10..20).to_i
  text.seek(seekplace, IO::SEEK_SET)
  out.puts(text.readline)
end
exit
```

Let us review the script line by line.

```
text = File.open("terms.txt", "r")
```

First, we open a file, `terms.txt`, for reading. We sort this file.

```
out = File.open("terms.put", "w")
```

We open a second file, terms.put, for writing, to receive the sorted lines from file `terms.txt`.

```
linearray = Array.new
```

We start with an empty array.

```
text.each_line do
   |line|
```

We will be parsing each line of text (the recently created file object that refers to the terms.txt file). For each iteration, a successive file line will be referred by the temporary variable `line`.

```
linelength = line.size
begin_position = text.pos - linelength - 1
linearray << line.chomp!.slice(0..9) + begin_position.to_s
end
```

For each iteration, we will be adding an element to the array instance, `linearray`. The element that we add will consist of the first nine characters of the line followed by the byte location at which the iteration line appears in the input file.

Because each element in `linearray` is relatively short (just 10 characters plus a byte location), you can load a great many elements into `linearray` without exceeding your computer's memory.

```
linearray.sort!
```

After you have the sorted array of the first 10 characters from each line, you can reconstruct the full sorted file using the file location for each line.

```
linearray.each do
   |value|
   seekplace = value.slice(10..20).to_i
   text.seek(seekplace, IO::SEEK_SET)
   out.puts(text.readline)
end
exit
```

For each element in `linearray`, we slice off characters beginning at character 10 and extending to the end of the string. This part of the `linearray` element is the file position for the full line in the original file. We set the range as 10...20 knowing that none of the strings will exceed 10 characters.

We send the string the `to_i` method because we will be using the file position as a numeric in the next line.

We send the `seek` method to the original IO object, `text`. The `seek` method sets the current byte position in the receiving IO object. The parameters for the `seek` method are the number of bytes (first parameter), beginning from a designated byte position (the second parameter). When the second parameter of the `seek` method is IO::SEEK_SET, this tells Ruby to start from the beginning of the file. After the `seek` method brings you to the beginning of the line, the line is read into the output file by sending the `readline` method to the text IO object and sending the `puts` method to the output file.

This strategy is fast and can sort large files. Its drawbacks are that it alphabetically sorts on the first 10 characters of a line. If multiple lines share the same first 10 characters, those lines will be unsorted with respect to each other. The purpose of the script is to do a good (not perfect) job of sorting so that every line will be in its approximate sort position. This is sufficient to support binary searches over a file when the final line selection is done through a Regex match on a chunk of text (see List 10.2.1).

10.4. EXTRACTING TERMS FROM THE FUNCTIONAL MODEL OF ANATOMY'S SQL DATABASE

The Functional Model of Anatomy (FMA, see Chapter 5, Section 8) is downloaded as an SQL file. In this section, the file downloaded was fma_v1.4.0_06-13-06.sql.

We can easily write a Ruby script to extract a list of all the anatomic terms from the FMA (List 10.4.1).

LIST 10.4.1. RUBY SCRIPT `anatomy.rb` EXTRACTS SQL DATA FROM THE FUNCTIONAL MODEL OF ANATOMY

```
#!/usr/local/bin/ruby
termhash = Hash.new
althash = Hash.new
arrayline = Array.new;
$/ = "),("
text = File.open("fma_v1\.4\.0_06-13-06\.sql", "r")
out = File.open("anatomy.put", "w")
text.each do
    |line|
```

```
        line.sub!("\)\,\($/", "")
        arrayline = line.split(/\,/)
        number = arrayline.fetch(0)
        valuekind = arrayline.fetch(2)
        line = $' if (line =~ /\,\'/)
        line = $` if (line =~ /\'\,/)
        line = line.downcase
        if ((valuekind.eql?("63840")) or (valuekind.eql?("199449")))
          if (termhash.has_key?(number))
            termhash[number] = termhash[number], "\| ", line
          else
            termhash[number] = line
          end
        end
        if (valuekind.eql?("2002"))
          althash[number] = line
        end
end


termhash.each_value do
    |value|
    out.print(value, "\n")
end


althash.each do
    |key, value|
    next if (termhash.has_key?(key))
    next if (value =~ /\_/)
    value.sub!(/^\|/) if (value =~ /^\|/)
    out.print(value, "\n")
end
exit
```

The anatomy.rb script is a straightforward passing exercise designed for a particular file format.

10.5. UNITED STATES CENSUS DATA

We discussed the comma-delimited United States census files in Chapter 5, Section 5. After the key is studied, it is easy to parse the data file to collect the information you need (List 10.5.1).

LIST 10.5.1. FIRST FEW LINES OF ALLDATA6 U.S. CENSUS FILE

```
040,01,3,06,1,1,01,0,19163,19164,19291,19157,18607,18511,18707
040,01,3,06,1,2,01,0,866,866,892,1019,1145,1266,1277
040,01,3,06,2,1,01,0,18034,18035,18169,18318,17736,17678,17721
040,01,3,06,2,2,01,0,869,869,895,951,1126,1202,1222
040,01,3,06,1,1,02,0,9148,9148,9391,10199,9676,9601,9699
040,01,3,06,1,2,02,0,98,98,89,6,14,11,11
040,01,3,06,2,1,02,0,8957,8957,9187,9858,9366,9233,9423
040,01,3,06,2,2,02,0,88,88,80,10,11,14,12
040,01,3,06,1,1,03,0,128,128,128,63,69,64,58
```

The script `alldata.rb` opens the census file and sums the data to determine the total number of people counted in the census (List 10.5.2).

LIST 10.5.2. RUBY SCRIPT `alldata.rb` SUMS THE CENSUS DISTRICTS TO YIELD THE TOTAL U.S. POPULATION

```ruby
#!/usr/local/bin/ruby
f = File.open("alldata6")
total = 0
f.each do
    |line|
    lineitems = line.split(',')
    lineval = lineitems[8].to_i
    total = total + lineval
end
f.close
puts "The total US population is #{total}"
exit
```

It takes just a few seconds for Ruby to parse the file and compute the U.S. population counted in the census (List 10.5.3).

LIST 10.5.3. OUTPUT OF `alldata.rb` **SCRIPT**

```
C:\ftp\rb>ruby alldata.rb
The total US population is 281421906
```

The U.S. census files have many uses. A common and important task for epidemiologists is to prepare a listing of the number and percentage of the U.S. population for each decade of age. These numbers are used to adjust incidence statistics based on the proportion of people of the age groups at risk. This would be a simple task for Ruby programmers.

CHAPTER
11

Scrubbing Confidential Medical Data (Level 1)

11.1. BACKGROUND

One of the biggest challenges in biomedicine today relates to data privacy and security. Because medical data are often extracted from private and legally protected medical records, people who work with medical data must be versed in the legal and ethical issues related to medical data protections. In the United States, private medical data are protected by two Federal Regulations: HIPAA and the Common Rule (13, 14).

Both HIPAA and the Common Rule permit the use of confidential medical data in your research when the patient is informed of the research risks and provides consent. When a research project uses a small number of medical records, it may be feasible to obtain patient consent for each record; however, if large numbers of records are needed, the consent option is impractical. In the absence of patient consent, HIPAA and the Common Rule permit research on pre-existing records that have been stripped of all information that could identify the patient.

Latanya Sweeney was an early proponent of technical approaches to medical record deidentification and has published extensively on the subject (15–17). Her work formed the foundation for current multistep approaches to deidentification encompassing the following tasks (see List 11.1.1).

HIPAA lists 18 identifiers that must be absent from any deidentified medical records (see List 11.1.2).

Data scrubbing involves removing HIPAA identifiers and private information that are present in medical records (18). What is "private" text? Private text is text that is nobody's business and that does not enhance the intended use of the deidentified patient record. In many cases, private text

LIST 11.1.1. STEPS TOWARD RENDERING MEDICAL DATA HARMLESS

1. Deidentification of data fields that specifically characterize the patient (name, social security number, hospital number, address, age, and so forth)
2. Free-text data scrubbing, removing identifiers from the textual portion of medical reports (18)
3. Rendering the dataset ambiguous, ensuring that patients cannot be identified by data records containing a unique set of characterizing information
4. Free-text data privatizing, removing any information of a private nature that may be contained within the report

LIST 11.1.2. HIPAA-SPECIFIED IDENTIFIERS

Names

Geographic subdivisions smaller than a state

Dates (except year) directly related to patient

Telephone numbers

Fax numbers

E-mail addresses

Social security numbers

Medical record numbers

Health plan beneficiary numbers

Account numbers

Certificate/license numbers

Vehicle identifiers and serial numbers

Device identifiers and serial numbers

Web URLs

Internet protocol (IP) address numbers

Biometric identifiers, including finger and voice prints

Full-face photographic images and any comparable images

Any other unique identifying number, characteristic, or code, except as permitted under HIPAA to reidentify data is written by hospital personnel with the expectation that it will be shared only among the persons directly responsible for the care of the patient. This may include notes documenting errors, misjudgments, warnings, and complaints. Most hospital personnel are expected to exclude information of an incriminating nature from the patient's medical record. Incident reports and quality-assurance reports exist for this purpose. In reality, medical records often contain information that is best removed from shared datasets.

There is a general understanding that when medical data are shared for the purposes of conducting research, there is an ethical obligation to share only that portion of the patient's record that is actually needed to conduct the research. This is sometimes referred to as the "minimum necessary" principle.

One strategy for data scrubbing is the subtractive algorithm. In this algorithm, the text is parsed, sentence by sentence, and the computer program extracts words and numbers that match any item from an exclusion list (List 11.1.3).

LIST 11.1.3. SOME ITEMS THAT MAY BE KEPT IN EXCLUSION LISTS

List of patient names

List of staff names

List of patient hospital identifiers or social security numbers

List of hospitals, departments, wards, and rooms

Geographic locations, including street names and zip codes

List of expletives

Additionally, subtractive scrubbers typically filter text through dozens or even hundreds of Regex expressions, extracting text that matches patterns consistent with dates, times, and words, followed by honorifics (for example, Mr., Ms., Dr.) and certain data formatted within the report in a manner specific to the institution (for example, report identifiers).

Subtractive strategies mimic the way that a human might censor a text. The human reads the text with a marker in hand, prepared to strike out any words or phrases that he or she knows are offensive. In my opinion, subtractive algorithms for data scrubbing are ineffective and counterproductive (List 11.1.4).

Two other approaches to data scrubbing are the concept-match algorithm and the doublet-preserving algorithm, both of which are fast and do not rely on exclusion lists.

LIST 11.1.4. DEFICIENCIES OF SUBTRACTIVE DATA SCRUBBING ALGORITHMS

Requires the creation and continuous maintenance of an identifier list consisting of names of patients, staff and medical centers as well as addresses and other geographic minutiae.

Requires the creation and continuous maintenance of rules for excluding text based on co-locations or patterns of expression that might signify a HIPAA identifier (for example, a sequence of digits and slashes that might represent a date).

Does not exclude private information that is nonidentifying but which may be incriminating or distasteful.

Does not satisfy the "minimum necessary" (see Glossary) principle, holding that medical data used in research should convey only that information which is needed for research purposes.

Slow. Each parsed sentence is typically evaluated through the entire list of pattern rules. This means that parsing a long corpus of medical text will take considerable time.

Complex. Maintaining the rule list and the identifier list will add to the overall complexity of the software. Each institution that implements the software will need to maintain its own lists created for their patients and for their textual styles and formats.

Inadequate. Subtractive scrubbers, under the best of circumstances, will occasionally miss an identifier. If a scrubber is 99% accurate, it may miss thousands of identifiers in a large text.

The purpose of this chapter is to provide simple and effective Ruby scripts that can scrub and deidentify confidential biomedical data.

11.2. SCRUBBING TEXT USING THE DOUBLET ALGORITHM

I have written a much-improved version of my concept-match software that uses doublets (2 grams). The algorithm is now simpler than ever. There is an external list of "approved" word doublets (about 80,000 of them). The doublet list is chosen to contain no identifying terms. My current list of doublets was derived from two open source medical vocabularies (MeSH and the Neoplasm Classification, see Appendix). The algorithm is simple. The text is parsed, and all of the doublets in the text that match a term in the approved list are retained. Everything else is replaced by an asterisk. It works fast (1 Mb per second on my 1.6-gigahertz

CPU) and does not allow any unlisted doublets to slip through. It retains more words from the text than the original concept match algorithm.

The value of the use of doublets (instead of approved words) is that a single seemingly innocuous word (such as "No") can be a person's name ("Dr. No is in the hospital"). Because the doublets, "Dr. No" and "No is" are not included in the approved doublet list, the identifying text will be excluded. On the other hand, accepted doublets, such as "no way" or "no food" would be saved if they were included in the list of approved doublets.

The algorithm can be scripted in less than 20 Ruby command lines (List 11.2.1).

LIST 11.2.1. RUBY SCRIPT scrubit.rb SCRUBS AND DEIDENTIFIES ANY INPUT LINE

```ruby
#!/usr/local/bin/ruby
f = File.open "doubdb.txt"
outf = File.open("scrub.out", "w")
doubhash = Hash.new
while line = f.gets
    line = chomp
    doubhash[line] = " "
end
f.close
#doubhash.each_key{|k| puts "#{k}"}
puts "What would you like to scrub?"
line = gets.chomp
linearray = line.split
arraysize = linearray.length - 2
lastword = "*"
for arrayword in (0 .. arraysize)
    phrase = linearray[arrayword] + " " + linearray[arrayword+1]
    if doubhash.key?(phrase)
      print " " + linearray[arrayword]
      lastword = " " + linearray[arrayword+1]
    else
      print lastword
      lastword = "*"
    end
    if arrayword == arraysize
      print lastword
    end
end
end
exit
```

LIST 11.2.2. EXAMPLES OF SCRUBBED TEXT

Basal cell carcinoma, margins involved

Scrubbed text . . . basal cell carcinoma margins involved

Rhabdoid tumor of kidney

Scrubbed text . . . rhabdoid tumor of kidney

Mr Brown has a basal cell carcinoma

Scrubbed text . . . * * has a basal cell carcinoma

Mr. Brown was born on Tuesday, March 14, 1985

Scrubbed text . . . * * * * * * * * *

The doctor killed the patient

Scrubbed text . . . * * * * *

The heart of the script is shown in just a few lines of Ruby code:

for arrayword in (0 .. arraysize)

```
phrase = linearray[arrayword] + " "+linearray[arrayword+1]
if doubhash.key?(phrase)
     print " " + linearray[arrayword]
     lastword = " " + linearray[arrayword+1]
else
     print lastword
lastword = " *"
```

The text words to be parsed are held in the linearray Array object. The first two words in the array are checked against the hash of acceptable doublets, doubhash, using the key? method. If the doublet exists, it is added to the front of the deidentified output. Otherwise, an asterisk is added to the front of the deidentified output. Then the second and third words in the text array are examined. The procedure is repeated until every word is either added to the deidentified output or replaced with an asterisk. The output text will contain only doublets found in a nomenclature and would not be expected to contain any patient identifiers, or names of staff, or expletives, or language specific for other knowledge domains (for example, legalistic terms). The script requires an external file consisting of medical word doublets. As demonstrated in Chapter 2, Section 8, a doublet list can be compiled in about a second from any nomenclature (see List 2.8.4).

Autocoding Biomedical Data Using Nomenclatures (Level 3)

12.1. BACKGROUND

Modern nomenclatures are used to organize, index, and retrieve biomedical data. Most modern nomenclatures are prepared as taxonomies, collections of the relevant items in a data domain wherein synonymous terms are grouped together and assigned a unique concept code.

For instance, in the Developmental Lineage Classification and Taxonomy of Neoplasms (hereinafter called the Neoplasm Classification), prostate cancer is assigned the unique concept code C4863000, and all of the term variants for this concept are attached to the same concept code (3, 6, 7, 9) (List 12.1.1).

When a nomenclature collects synonymous terms under unique concept identifiers, medical text expressed as any of the terms corresponding to a single concept can be assigned the unique concept code. When all of the terms in a medical text have been assigned codes, they can be retrieved through a concept search that collects all synonymous terms by their unifying concept identifier.

Medical autocoding can be considered a specialized form of machine translation (19). Machine translation is a large field that covers direct translations between different languages (that is, Russian to and from English), the interconversion of language modes (for example, spoken words to and from narrative text), the interpretation of signals (for example, military SIGINT, deriving INTelligence from the analysis of intercepted SIGnals), the annotation of text through the extraction of terms and concepts (that is, medical autocoding) and the transformation of text into desired data structures (for example, converting narrative text to tagged XML).

LIST 12.1.1. EQUIVALENT TERMS FOR THE CONCEPT IDENTIFIER C4863000

C4863000	prostate with adenoca
C4863000	adenoca arising in prostate
C4863000	adenoca involving prostate
C4863000	adenoca arising from prostate
C4863000	adenoca of prostate
C4863000	adenoca of the prostate
C4863000	prostate with adenocarcinoma
C4863000	adenocarcinoma arising in prostate
C4863000	adenocarcinoma involving prostate
C4863000	adenocarcinoma arising from prostate
C4863000	adenocarcinoma of prostate
C4863000	adenocarcinoma of the prostate
C4863000	adenocarcinoma arising in the prostate
C4863000	adenocarcinoma involving the prostate
C4863000	adenocarcinoma arising from the prostate
C4863000	prostate with ca
C4863000	ca arising in prostate
C4863000	ca involving prostate
C4863000	ca arising from prostate
C4863000	ca of prostate
C4863000	ca of the prostate
C4863000	prostate with cancer
C4863000	cancer arising in prostate
C4863000	cancer involving prostate
C4863000	cancer arising from prostate
C4863000	cancer of prostate
C4863000	cancer of the prostate
C4863000	cancer arising in the prostate
C4863000	cancer involving the prostate

C4863000	cancer arising from the prostate
C4863000	prostate with carcinoma
C4863000	carcinoma arising in prostate
C4863000	carcinoma involving prostate
C4863000	carcinoma arising from prostate
C4863000	carcinoma of prostate
C4863000	carcinoma of the prostate
C4863000	carcinoma arising in the prostate
C4863000	carcinoma involving the prostate
C4863000	carcinoma arising from the prostate
C4863000	prostate adenoca
C4863000	prostate adenocarcinoma
C4863000	prostate ca
C4863000	prostate cancer
C4863000	prostate carcinoma
C4863000	prostatic cancer
C4863000	prostatic carcinoma
C4863000	prostatic adenocarcinoma
C4863000	prostate gland adenocarcinoma
C4863000	adenocarcinoma of the prostate gland
C4863000	adenocarcinoma of prostate gland
C4863000	prostate gland carcinoma
C4863000	carcinoma of the prostate gland
C4863000	carcinoma of prostate gland

Several computational approaches to machine translation exist. You can parse sentences into grammatic units permitting a program to reorder component parts of the sentence into a sequence of phrases that make grammatic sense in the target language. The sequential phrases of the transformed sentence can then be matched against a controlled vocabulary (in the target language), yielding translated text. The problem with this approach is that it is computationally intensive (resulting in slow execution speed) and prone to errors when sentences are long or complex. For this reason, much of machine translation work depends on the creation of elaborate grammar rule systems and exception lists that account for idiomatic language.

A second approach is "lexical" parsing, in which text is parsed and any phrases in the text that exactly match terms held in a nomenclature are extracted. The lexical parser does not tokenize a sentence into grammatic parts and does not reorder component parts of a sentence into alternate forms of statements. Lexical parsers are a simple but somewhat brutish approach to machine translation. The lexical parser depends on terms existing in medical text just as they appear in standard nomenclatures. Wherever medical text contains splitting modifiers, most lexical parsers will fail. For instance, the term "flat feet," appearing in a medical text and included in a medical nomenclature, would be easily extracted by a lexical parser. If the phrase "flat erythemic feet" appeared in a medical text, the lexical parser would miss the term, unless flat erythemic feet were included in the nomenclature (as a specially denoted form of flat feet).

As used in this chapter, the term "autocoder" refers to a software program capable of parsing large collections of medical records (for example, radiology reports, surgical pathology reports, autopsy reports, admission notes, discharge notes, operating room notes, medical administrative e-mails, memoranda and manuscripts), capturing the medical concepts contained in the text and assigning them an identifying concept code from a nomenclature.

The term "autocoding" should be distinguished from "computer-assisted manual coding." Healthcare workers may use a software enhancement of their hospital information systems to code a section of text as they enter reports into the computer system. Typically, candidate terms and term codes are displayed on the same screen as the entered report. The person entering text is often given the option of editing the proffered codes. This process should not be confused with "autocoding" and is not equivalent to the fully automatic and large-scale coding required in biomedicine.

Finding all of the concepts in a corpus of text is a necessary and early step in all data mining efforts. The autocoded terms can be used individually as index terms for the document, or on a record-by-record basis to produce a concept "signature" that is highly specific for each report, or collectively to relate the frequency of terms within records with the frequency of terms in the aggregate document (20).

The purpose of this chapter is to demonstrate some of the freely accessible nomenclatures in biomedicine and to provide some techniques for autocoding biomedical text.

12.2. DOUBLET ALGORITHM FOR A FAST LEXICAL AUTOCODER

The doublet algorithm is a novel approach to autocoding. It can autocode 0.8 Mb of text per second on a computer having a modest 1.6-gigahertz processor. This section describes the doublet autocoding algorithm.

One of the many problems in the field of machine translation is that expressions (multiword terms) convey ideas that transcend the meanings of the individual words in the expression. Consider the following sentence:

"The ciliary body produces aqueous humor."

The example sentence has unambiguous meaning to anatomists, but each word in the sentence can have many different meanings. "Ciliary" is a common medical word and usually refers to the action of cilia. Cilia are found throughout the respiratory and gastrointestinal tract and have an important role locomoting particulate matter. The word "body" almost always refers to the human body. The term "ciliary body" should (but does not) refer to the action of cilia that move human bodies from place to place. The word "aqueous" always refers to water. Humor relates to something being funny. The term "aqueous humor" should (but does not) relate to something that is funny by virtue of its use of water (as in squirting someone in the face with a trick flower). Actually, "ciliary body" and "aqueous humor" are each examples of medical doublets whose meanings are specific and contextually constant (that is, always mean one thing). Furthermore, the meanings of the doublets cannot be reliably determined from the individual words that constitute the doublet because the individual words have several different meanings. Basically, you either do or do not know the correct meaning of the doublet.

Any sentence can be examined by parsing it into an array of intercalated doublets:

"The ciliary, ciliary body, body produces, produces aqueous, aqueous humor."

The important concepts in the sentence are contained in two doublets (ciliary body and aqueous humor). A nomenclature containing these doublets would allow us to extract and index these two medical concepts. A nomenclature consisting of single words might miss the contextual meaning of the doublets.

What if the term were larger than a doublet? Consider the tumor "orbital alveolar rhabdomyosarcoma." The individual words can be misleading. This orbital tumor is not from outer space, and the alveolar tumor is not from the lung. The three-word term describes a sarcoma arising from the orbit of the eye that has a morphology characterized by tiny spaces of a size and shape as may occur in glands (alveoli). The term "orbital alveolar rhabdomyosarcoma" can be parsed as "orbital alveolar, alveolar rhabdomyosarcoma." Why is this any better than parsing the term into individual words, as in "orbital, alveolar, rhabdomyosarcoma"? The doublets, unlike the single words, are highly specific terms that are unlikely to occur in association with more than a few specific concepts.

Very few medical terms are single words. In the developmental lineage classification of neoplasms, there are 102,271 unique terms for neoplasms (6). All but 252 of these terms are multiword terms.

Medical autocoding can be considered a specialized form of machine translation. Medical autocoders transform text into an index of coded nomenclature terms (sometimes called a "concept index" or "concept signature"). Several innovative approaches to autocoding have used the higher information content of multiword terms (also called word n-grams) to match terms in text with terms in vocabularies or to enhance the content of vocabularies by identifying n-grams occurring in text that qualify as new nomenclature terms (21).

The doublet method uses the higher term specificity of doublets (bigrams) to construct a simple and fast lexical parser. Lexical parsers are types of string-matching algorithms. In general, the overall speed of lexical parsers is determined by the speed with which the parser can prepare an array of all possible words and phrases contained in a block of text, coupled with the speed with which each of these phrases can be compared against all the terms in the nomenclature.

The algorithm for the doublet autocoder is shown in List 12.2.1.

The Ruby script, autocode.rb, is shown in List 12.2.2.

LIST 12.2.1. ALGORITHM FOR THE DOUBLET AUTOCODER autocode.rb

1. Each phrase (term) in the nomenclature (neocl.xml) is converted into intercalated doublets, and each doublet is assigned a consecutive number.

2. Each nomenclature phrase is assigned the concatenated list of numbers that represent the ordered doublets composing the phrase.

3. Text is split into an array consisting of the consecutive words in the text.

4. The text array is parsed as intercalated doublets. Intercalated doublets from the text that match doublets found anywhere in the nomenclature are assigned their numeric values (from the doublet index created for the nomenclature). Runs of consecutive doublets from the text that match doublets from the nomenclature are built into concatenated

strings of doublet values. The occurrence of a text doublet that does not match any doublet in the nomenclature cannot possibly be part of a nomenclature term. Such text doublets serve as "stop" doublets between candidate runs of text doublets that match nomenclature doublets.

5. The runs of matching doublets are tested to see whether they match any of the runs of doublets that compose nomenclature terms or if they contain any subsumed terms that match nomenclature terms.

6. The array of doublet runs extracted from the text that match nomenclature terms are printed.

The `autocode.rb` script computes all possible phrases in an input line and matches each phrase against a list of vocabulary terms.

LIST 12.2.2. RUBY SCRIPT `autocode.rb` PROVIDES NOMENCLATURE TERMS AND CODES FOR AN INPUT SENTENCE

```
#!/usr/local/bin/ruby
require 'sdbm'
literalhash = SDBM.open("literalhash.dbm", nil)
onewordhash = SDBM.open("onewordhash.dbm", nil)
sentence = "refractory anemia with excess blasts in
    adenocarcinoma of prostate"
puts sentence
cum_array = Array.new
sentence_array = sentence.split
length = sentence_array.size
length.times do
    (1..sentence_array.size).each do
        |place_length|
cum_array = cum_array <<
    sentence_array.slice(0,place_length).join(" ")
    end
    sentence_array.shift
end
cum_array.each do
  |term|
puts "#{term} #{literalhash[term]}" if
    (literalhash.has_key?(term))
puts "#{term} #{onewordhash[term]}" if
    (onewordhash.has_key?(term))
end
exit
```

The persistent objects literalhash.dbm and onewordhash.dbm were created for us in List 6.6.1.

The heart of the autocode.rb script is contained in the following lines of code.

length.times do

```
        (1..sentence_array.size).each do
            |place_length|
    cum_array = cum_array <<
        sentence_array.slice(0,place_length).join(" ")
        end
        sentence_array.shift
    end
```

The words of the input sentence are held in the sentence_array Array object and the number of elements in the sentence_array Array object are held in the length Integer object. This snippet of code creates cum_array, a new Array object that contains all of the possible phrases in the input sentence. The cum_array instance object is built with a nested iteration. The nested blocks take the first word in the sentence and determine all the possible slices of the sentence beginning with the first word (that is, the first word plus the second word, the first word plus the second word plus the third word, etc.). The successive slices of the array are provided by sending the slice method to the sentence_array object. The array slices are concatenated into a string, with the join method. The " " argument puts a space between each word. After all of the slices are put into the cum_array instance object, the first word in the array is removed with the shift method. The outer loop repeats, adding slices to cum_array that begin with the second word of the sentence (for example, the second word, the second word plus the third word, the second word plus the third word plus the fourth word, etc.). After the nested loops have executed, cum_array array contains every occurring phrase of all possible size in the input sentence.

It is a simple matter to test each phrase in cum_array to determine if it is included in the nomenclature (stored as Hash instance objects with terms as keys and identifier codes as values). The inclusion of a candidate phrase in a Hash instance object can be tested by sending the has_key? method to the Hash object, with the candidate term included as the method's argument.

```
    cum_array.each do
        |term|
    puts "#{term} #{literalhash[term]}" if
        (literalhash.has_key?(term))
    puts "#{term} #{onewordhash[term]}" if
    (onewordhash.has_key?(term))
```

The output of autocode.rb is shown in List 12.2.3.

LIST 12.2.3. OUTPUT OF autocode.rb

```
C:\ftp\rb>RUBY AUTOCODE.RB
refractory anemia with excess blasts in adenocarcinoma of
    prostate
refractory anemia C4036100
refractory anemia with excess blasts C7506000
anemia C0000000
adenocarcinoma C0000000
adenocarcinoma of prostate C4863000
```

12.3. CLASSY AUTOCODER

We can rewrite autocode.rb as fastcode.rb, defining abstract methods for an Autocode class (List 12.3.1). This script saves time by only matching phrases composed of concatenated doublets contained in the nomenclatures.

Sample output is shown in List 12.3.2.

LIST 12.3.1. RUBY SCRIPT fastcode.rb IMPROVES PERFORMANCE COMPARED WITH autocode.rb

```ruby
#!/usr/local/bin/ruby
class Autocode
  def initialize
    require 'sdbm'
    @literalhash = SDBM.open("literalhash.dbm", nil)
    @onewordhash = SDBM.open("onewordhash.dbm", nil)
    @doubhash = SDBM.open("doub.dbm", nil)
    @codehash = Hash.new
  end



  def exists_onehash(key)
    return true if (@onewordhash.has_key?(key))
  end



  def exists_literalhash(key)
    return true if (@literalhash.has_key?(key))
  end
```

(continues)

```ruby
    def exists_doubhash(key)
      return true if (@doubhash.has_key?(key))
    end


    def add_to_codes(key)
      if (key !~ / /)
        @codehash[key] = @onewordhash[key]
      else
        @codehash[key] = @literalhash[key]
      end
    end


    def display
      @codehash.each{|key,value| puts "#{key} #{value}"}
    end


    def coder(sentence)
      cum_array = Array.new
      sentence_array = sentence
      length = sentence_array.size
      length.times do
          (1..sentence_array.size).each do
              |place_length|
    cum_array << sentence_array.slice(0,place_length).join(" ")
          end
          sentence_array.shift
      end
      cum_array.each do
          |term|
          next if (term.length < 3)
    @codehash[term] = @literalhash[term] if
    (@literalhash.has_key?(term))
      end
    end
end


increment_array = Array.new
store = Autocode.new
text = "adenocarcinoma refractory anemia hidalgo someplace "
```

```
text = text + "when Irish eyes are smiling refractory anemia "
text = text + "with excess blasts in transformation
    adenocarcinoma "
text = text + "of prostate of the peritoneum rhabdoid tumor"
text_array = text.split


text_array.each_index do
  |x|
  next if (x == text_array.size - 1)
  doublet = text_array[x] + " " + text_array[x+1]
  if store.exists_onehash(text_array[x])
    store.add_to_codes(text_array[x])
  end
  if store.exists_literalhash(doublet)
    increment_array << text_array[x]
    store.add_to_codes(doublet)
  elsif store.exists_doubhash(doublet)
    increment_array << text_array[x]
  elsif (increment_array.length > 1)
    increment_array << text_array[x]
    store.coder(increment_array)
    increment_array = []
  else
    increment_array = []
  end
end
store.display
exit
```

LIST 12.3.2. OUTPUT OF fastcode.rb

```
C:\ftp\rb>ruby fastcode.rb
anemia C0000000
rhabdoid tumor C3808000
adenocarcinoma C0000000
refractory anemia with excess blasts C7506000
adenocarcinoma of prostate C4863000
refractory anemia with excess blasts in transformation C7506100
refractory anemia C4036100
```

12.4. COLLECTING THE ICD CODES FROM THE UMLS METATHESAURUS

Any individual vocabularies can be easily extracted from the UMLS metathesaurus if you know the abbreviated name of the vocabulary, as used by UMLS. These abbreviations can be obtained from the UMLS Website. Alternatively, you can parse the MRCONSO file to extract the abbreviated names of the contained vocabulary sources.

```ruby
#!/usr/local/bin/ruby
f = File.open("c\:\\entrez\\MRCONSO")
vocab_hash = Hash.new("")
f.each do
  |line|
  line_array = line.split("\|")
next if line_array[1] != "ENG"
  #vocabularies with English terms
  vocab_hash[line_array[11].downcase] = ""
end
print vocab_hash.keys.sort.join(",")
exit
```

In the MRCONSO file, the abbreviated name of a term's vocabulary source is contained in the 11th data element (List 12.4.1).

LIST 12.4.1. A TYPICAL ICD RECORD WITHIN MRCONSO; ICD10AM IS THE 11TH ELEMENT

C0001422 | ENG | P | L0001422 | VO | S1275197 | N | A1233953

| | | | ICD10AM | PT | M9013/0 | Adenofibroma NOS | 3 | N | |

The list of abbreviated source vocabularies is shown in List 12.4.2.

We will extract all of the ICD10AM terms from the UMLS Metathesaurus.

ICD-10-AM was created from the *International Statistical Classification of Diseases and Related Health Problems,* 10th Revision (ICD-10) and broadened to include the Australian Classification of Health Interventions (List 12.4.3).

The output file consists of all codes and terms in the 25,891 ICD10AM records in the UMLS MRCONSO file (List 12.4.4).

LIST 12.4.2. OUTPUT OF vocabs.rb, A LIST OF UMLS VOCABULARIES

```
air,alt,aod,bi,ccpss,ccs,cdt,costar,cpm,cpt,csp,cst,
ctcae,ddb,dsm3r,dsm4,dxp,go,hcdt,hcpcs,hcpt,hhc,hl7v2.5,
hl7v3.0,hugo,icd10,icd10ae,icd10am,icd10amae,icd9cm,
icpc,icpc2eeng,icpc2icd10eng,icpc2p,icpcpae,jabl,lch,
lnc,mcm,mddb,mdr,medlineplus,mim,mmsl,mmx,msh,mth,mthch,
mthfda,mthhh,mthhl7v2.5,mthicd9,mthicpc2eae,mthicpc2icd107b,
mthicpc2icd10ae,mthmst,mthpdq,nan,ncbi,nci,nci-ctcae,nddf,
ndfrt,neu,nic,noc,oms,pcds,pdq,pnds,ppac,psy,qmr,ram,rcd,
rcdae,rcdsa,rcdsy,rxnorm,snm,snmi,snomedct,spn,src,ult,umd,
uspmg,uwda,vandf,who
```

LIST 12.4.3. RUBY SCRIPT icd.rb COLLECTS ICD10AM CODES FROM THE UMLS METATHESAURUS

```
#!/usr/local/bin/ruby
f = File.open("c\:\\entrez\\MRCONSO")
outf = File.open("icd.out", "w")
f.each do
  |line|
  line_array = line.split("\|")
  next if (line_array[1] != "ENG")
  next if (line_array[11] != "ICD10AM")
  outf.print(line_array[13], " ", line_array[14], "\n")
end
exit
```

LIST 12.4.4. FIRST FEW LINES OF OUTPUT FILE, ICD.OUT

R10.0 Acute abdomen

Q89.9 Congenital malformation, unspecified

K00.2 Abnormalities of size and form of teeth

E16.4 Abnormal secretion of gastrin

O03 Spontaneous abortion

N96 Habitual aborter

P96.4 Termination of pregnancy, fetus and newborn

O02.1 Missed abortion

(continues)

O20.0 Threatened abortion

O45 Premature separation of placenta [abruptio placentae]

O45.9 Premature separation of placenta, unspecified

L83 Acanthosis nigricans

Q77.0 Achondrogenesis

Q77.4 Achondroplasia

E87.2 Acidosis

L70.0 Acne vulgaris

L73.0 Acne keloid

H93.3 Disorders of acoustic nerve

D68.4 Acquired coagulation factor deficiency

M95.4 Acquired deformity of chest and rib

E24.3 Ectopic ACTH syndrome

A42 Actinomycosis

We will use the list of ICD codes in the next section.

12.5. ANALYSIS OF THE SEER PUBLIC USE DATASETS

Many people do not like byte-designated data files, finding them inscrutable and useless. Actually, they are a simple and convenient way of conveying well-organized, large datasets. With a little patience, it is possible to understand their organization and fathom their content. The SEER files, in particular, contain a wealth of information related to the cancers that occur in the U.S. population. The information in SEER files can be integrated with other datasets by clever data miners.

The SEER data files were described in Chapter 5. Here is a Ruby script that parses the bytes from SEER tumor records that contain the ICD codes for the neoplasm described by the records. By comparing codes with the names of tumors in the ICD nomenclature, we can tabulate the occurrence rates of all the tumors contained in the SEER database (List 12.5.1). To accomplish this, we use "icd.out", the file that lists the ICD codes and terms that we extracted from the UMLS Metathesaurus in the prior section (List 12.4.3).

Here are the first 20 lines of output from the seer.rb script (List 12.5.2). The most frequently occurring diagnosis in the SEER dataset is

LIST 12.5.1. RUBY SCRIPT seer.rb DETERMINES THE OCCURRENCES IN THE U.S. OF TUMOR TYPES FOUND IN THE SEER PUBLIC-USE DATA FILES

```ruby
#/usr/local/bin/ruby
f = File.open("ICD.OUT")
fout = File.open("SEER.OUT", "w")
codehash = Hash.new("")
subhash = Hash.new(0)
f.each do
  |line|
  next unless (line =~ /^M([0-9]{4})\/([0-9]{1}) /)
  icdcode = $1 << $2
  term = $'.chomp!
  codehash[icdcode] = term
end
filelist = Dir.glob("c:/ftp/rb/seer/*.TXT")
print filelist.inspect
begin_time = Time.new.to_f
filelist.each do
  |filepathname|
  seer_file = File.open(filepathname)
  seer_file.each do
    |line|
    code = line.slice(44,5)
    subhash[code] = subhash[code] + 1
  end
end
subhash.each do
  |key,value|
  if codehash.has_key?(key)
    fout.printf("%-8.06d  %-s \n", value, codehash[key])
  end
end
fout.close
fout = File.open("SEER.OUT")
end_time = Time.new.to_f
puts(fout.readlines.sort.reverse.join)
puts "Time to parse SEER files - #{end_time - begin_time}
  seconds"
exit
```

LIST 12.5.2. FIRST 20 LINES OF TUMOR OCCURRENCES FROM SCRIPT seer.rb*

401947	Adenocarcinoma NOS
133958	Infiltrating duct carcinoma
078938	Squamous cell carcinoma NOS
064993	Carcinoma NOS
038011	Papillary transitional cell carcinoma
031461	Intraepithelial neoplasia, grade III, of cervix, vulva, and vagina
023821	Neoplasm, malignant
018961	Small cell carcinoma NOS
018572	Malignant melanoma NOS
018433	Mucinous adenocarcinoma
017729	Intraductal carcinoma, noninfiltrating NOS
017556	Renal cell carcinoma
016681	Superficial spreading melanoma
015785	Transitional cell carcinoma NOS
015583	Lobular carcinoma NOS
013534	Multiple myeloma
013532	Malignant lymphoma, large cell, diffuse NOS
012910	Squamous cell carcinoma in situ NOS
012825	Endometrioid carcinoma
011423	Large cell carcinoma NOS

*NOS = not otherwise specified.

adenocarcinoma, NOS (not otherwise specified). There were 401,947 SEER records with this diagnosis. The second most frequently occurring diagnosis was infiltrating duct carcinoma, the most common type of breast cancer, with 133,958 occurrences.

How did the seer.rb script extract this data? First, the icd.out file (assigned to file object, f) is parsed. The M codes in ICD correspond to names of malignancies. In native ICD, the M codes are broken by a slash, but in SEER, the slash is omitted. We parse the ICD entries (see List 12.4.4) extracting and modifying codes and terms and putting them into a Hash instance object, codehash, with the ICD codes as keys and terms as values. How did we know that M codes are neoplasms and that SEER contains modified M codes? Basically, this knowledge came from past experiences. Sometimes the programmer runs up against obstacles that only the biologist can climb.

```
f.each do
  |line|
  next unless (line =~ /^M([0-9]{4})\/([0-9]{1}) /)
  icdcode = $1 << $2
  term = $'.chomp!
  codehash[icdcode] = term
end
```

We create a list of all the SEER files and parse through each file in the list. For each record in each file, we extract five bytes, beginning with byte 44. These five bytes correspond to the ICD code. The code is assigned a key to the subhash Hash instance, and each time the code occurs in the SEER files, we increment the value of the key by 1. In this manner, the value for any ICD code corresponds to the number of occurrences of the ICD code in the SEER files.

We then parse through the SEER files.

```
seer_file.each do
  |line|
  code = line.slice(44,5)
  subhash[code] = subhash[code] + 1
end
```

All that remains to do is to iterate through the key/value pairs in subhash, substituting the ICD term name for the ICD code and printing out the values in a pretty format, using printf (see the Glossary).

```
subhash.each do
  |key,value|
  if codehash.has_key?(key)
  fout.printf("%-8.06d  %-s \n", value, codehash[key])
  end
end
```

Some Mathematical and Statistical Methods (Level 2)

13.1. BACKGROUND

Ruby contains abundant math primitives, the basic functions on which advanced mathematical algorithms are built. These include arithmetic functions, trigonometric functions, the modulus operator, a built-in pseudorandom number generator, exponential operations, and logical (bit-based) operators.

The purpose of this chapter is to list some of the wide variety of mathematics resources available to Ruby programmers and to demonstrate how mathematics can be employed by biomedical professionals to solve common tasks.

13.2. CUMULATIVE ADDITION

Summing a range or a list of numbers is easily accomplished with inject, a handy iterator method from module Enumerable.

```
irb>[2,3,5,6].inject(0){|accum,x|accum + x} => 16
```

Inject iterates over a set of elements, applying the code block to a variable that maintains its value from the end of one iteration to the beginning of the next iteration.

There is an optional start value for the accumulating variable, called accum in this example, and the start value is supplied as the argument for the inject method (in this case, 0).

The inject method operates over ranges as well as arrays.

```
irb>(1..30).inject(0){|accum,x|accum + x} => 465
```

You may wonder why, in the above examples, instance objects of classes `Array` and `Range` can receive methods from module `Enumerable`. This is because the `Array` and `Range` classes mix the module `Enumerable` into their class definitions. This allows instance objects of classes `Array` (`[2,3,5,6]` in this case) and `Range` (`(1..30)` in this case) to receive `Enumerable` methods. This is another example of the transparent power of Ruby.

13.3. MODULE MATH

Ruby provides a variety of trigonometric and exponential methods in module Math.

```
irb>Math.methods - Module.methods => ["sinh", "exp", "acos",
"ldexp", "tanh", "atan2", "log", "asin", "hypot", "acosh",
"cos", "log10", "atan", "erf", "asinh", "sin", "sqrt",
"cosh", "erfc", "atanh", "tan", "frexp"]
```

Examples for some of these methods are shown.

```
irb>Math.sqrt(4) => 2.0
```

```
irb>Math.log10(1000) => 3.0
```
Returns the base 10 logarithm

```
irb>Math.log(3) => 1.09861228866811
```
Returns the natural logarithm

```
irb>Math.sin(3.14) => 0.00159265291648683
irb>Math.sin(1.57) => 0.999999682931835
```
Uses degrees expressed as radians

```
irb>Math.cos(3.14) => -0.99999873172754
irb>Math.cos(1.57) => 0.000796326710733263
```

In each case, the method is sent directly to the `Math` module because the code does not include instance objects of classes that mix `Math` into their class definitions. Modules, unlike classes, have no instance objects, and module methods that have no qualified instance object receiver must be sent directly to the module.

13.4. MATH STANDARD LIBRARIES

Four mathematical libraries come in Ruby's standard distribution and can be required into any Ruby script: Mathn, Matrix, Complex, and Rational.

As we have seen, several built-in Ruby operators (particularly the division operator "/") have polymorphic behavior for the subclasses of class Numeric. This is a potential source of error in Ruby scripts. Mathn provides methods that work in an expected manner for objects of the different subclasses of class Numeric.

```
irb>5/4 => 1
irb>3/4 => 0
irb>require 'mathn' => true
irb>5/4 => 5/4
irb>3/4 => 3/4
```

Matrix provides classes Matrix and Vector and methods for each class.

A simple example of matrix multiplication:

```
irb>Matrix[[1,2,3,4],[1,2,3,4],[1,2,3,4]] *
Matrix[[1,2,3],[1,2,3],[1,2,3],[1,2,3]]
=> Matrix[[10, 20, 30], [10, 20, 30], [10, 20, 30]]
```

13.5. FIBONACCI SERIES

Bacterial organisms grow exponentially (1, 2, 4, 8, 16 . . .), producing rapidly growing masses of round or spherical colonies that double their size in periodic cycles. Animals and plants have evolved a different strategy for growth that permits organisms to achieve remarkable geometric forms in a more leisurely fashion. In nature, Fibonacci growth (unlike exponential growth) slows and eventually stops.

In mathematical terms, the Fibonacci series is a progressive expansion wherein each element (after the second) is the sum of the two preceding elements (List 13.5.1). The first two elements are one. In most computer simulations of the Fibonacci series, there is a zeroth element (zero) included in the output (List 13.5.2).

LIST 13.5.1. RUBY SCRIPT `fibo.rb` **COMPUTES THE FIRST 20 ELEMENTS OF THE FIBONACCI SERIES**

```
#!/usr/local/bin/ruby
fib = Hash.new{|fib, n|n<2? fib[n]=n:
   fib[n]=fib[n - 1]+fib[n - 2]}
fib[30]
print(fib.values.sort.join(", "))
exit
```

LIST 13.5.2. OUTPUT OF `fibo.rb`

```
C:\ftp\rb>ruby fibo.rb
0, 1, 1, 2, 3, 5, 8, 13, 21, 34, 55, 89, 144, 233, 377, 610,
987, 1597, 2584, 4181, 6765, 10946, 17711, 28657, 46368,
75025, 121393, 196418, 317811, 514229, 832040
```

The series does not grow as rapidly as a doubling series (seen in bacterial growth). The Fibonacci series, as it occurs in nature, seems to be an invention of evolution, allowing the cells in an organism to grow slowly, with more morphologic complexity. Each Fibonacci generation retreats two generations to accumulate the members in the next Fibonacci cycle. The accumulating members in the Fibonacci cycle produce a lateralized, nonspherical form. The result, confined to plants and metazoan organisms, goes a long way toward explaining the distribution of petals in a flower, florets in a seed head, spirals in a pinecone and turns in a sea shell. The ratio of a Fibonacci element to its preceding element reaches a limit as the series progresses. The limiting ratio is the Golden Mean (1.618034), which also serves as the natural limit on growth for many plant and animal forms.

13.6. STATISTICS

The easiest and most fundamental statistical tests involve computing the mean and the variance of a population (List 13.6.1).

LIST 13.6.1. RUBY SCRIPT `mean.rb` **COMPUTES THE MEAN FROM AN ARRAY OF NUMBERS**

```
#!/usr/bin/ruby
my_array = Array.new([1000,1201,1500,3000])
arraysize = my_array.size
puts(my_array.inject(0){|accum,x|accum + ((x.to_f)/arraysize)})
exit
```

The mean is 1675.25.

Again, this approach uses the `inject` method from module `Enumerable`. With each iteration, the element of an array is divided by the number of elements in the array, and this is added to the accumulator variable (named `accum`). It is important, in this example, to convert each element of the array to class `Float` (with `to_f`). Otherwise, the division operator will only provide integer arithmetic, and you will not like the results.

13.7. COMPUTING THE STANDARD DEVIATION FROM AN ARRAY OF NUMBERS

The standard deviation is a commonly used quantifier of population scatter from the mean. The following Ruby script is modified from a Perl program appearing in the superb resource book *Mastering Algorithms with Perl* (22) (List 13.7.1).

LIST 13.7.1. RUBY SCRIPT `std_dev.rb` COMPUTES THE STANDARD DEVIATION FOR AN ARRAY OF NUMBERS

```ruby
#!/usr/bin/ruby
include Math
diffsquarearray = Array.new;
numbersarray = Array.new([1,2,3,4,5,6,7,8,9,10])
arraysize = numbersarray.size
sum = 0
numbersarray.each{|value| sum = sum + value}
samplemean = sum / arraysize
numbersarray.each do
  |value|
  diffsquare = (value - samplemean)**2
  diffsquarearray << diffsquare
end
sum = 0
diffsquarearray.each{|value| sum = sum + value}
samplediffsquaremean = (sum / arraysize)
diffsquaremean = (sum / (arraysize - 1))
samplestd = sqrt(samplediffsquaremean)
std = sqrt(diffsquaremean)
#puts "The sample standard deviation is #{samplestd}"
puts "The standard deviation is #{std}"
puts "The mean is #{samplemean}"
exit
```

The standard serves as an approximation of the deviations from the mean of the elements of a population, n, with n − 1 degrees of freedom (List 13.7.2).

LIST 13.7.2. OUTPUT OF std_dev.rb

```
C:\ftp\rb>ruby stdv.rb
The standard deviation is 3.02765035409749
The mean is 5.5
```

13.8. USING RANDOM NUMBERS

Many simulation programs rely on a random number generator. The random numbers are used to simulate probabilistic events.

Let us imagine that you are not exactly a whiz at probability. You have a pair of dice and would like to know how often you might expect each of the numbers (from one to six) to appear after you have thrown one dice.

Six throws of a dice can be simulated with a Ruby statement.

```
irb>one_of_six = (rand(6)+1).to_i => 2
irb>one_of_six = (rand(6)+1).to_i => 6
irb>one_of_six = (rand(6)+1).to_i => 6
irb>one_of_six = (rand(6)+1).to_i => 4
irb>one_of_six = (rand(6)+1).to_i => 4
irb>one_of_six = (rand(6)+1).to_i => 1
```

How does it work? The rand method returns a random fractional number greater than or equal to 0 and less than the value of its argument. If an argument is omitted, the value 1 is used.

We are not interested in decimal fraction, and thus, we send the to_i method to the object created from the output of the rand method. This yields integers 0, 1, 2, 3, 4, or 5. Because we want our output to be a nonzero integer (that is 1, 2, 3, 4, 5, or 6), we simply add 1 to the output number.

Randtest.rb simulates the results you may encounter when you throw a die 600,000 times, checking each time to see what number came up (List 13.8.1).

Output is shown in List 13.8.2.

Randtest.rb starts by setting a loop, simulating 600,000 casts of the dice. Each loop uses the rand method.

We make a hash of the frequency of occurrence of the different integer outcomes for all of the 600,000 simulations.

LIST 13.8.1. RUBY SCRIPT randtest.rb **SIMULATES 600,000 CASTS OF THE DIE**

```ruby
#!/usr/bin/ruby
hashrandom = Hash.new(0)
(1..600000).each do
   |value|
   one_of_six = (rand(6)+1).to_i
   hashrandom[one_of_six] = hashrandom[one_of_six] + 1
end
hashrandom.each{|key,value| puts "#{key} #{value}"}
exit
```

LIST 13.8.2. OUTPUT OF FIRST TEST OF randtest.rb

```
C:\ftp\rb>ruby randtest.rb
5 99760
6 100592
1 99873
2 100023
3 99375
4 100377
```

The results are as one might expect. Each number "came up" about 100,000 times. Just for fun, we repeated the script output, with much the same result.

There are many uses of random numbers, particularly in the fields of cryptography and probability.

13.9. RESAMPLING AND MONTE CARLO STATISTICS

Random numbers are used in many artificial life programs. These programs are based on simulating objects that obey prescribed rules of behavior (for example, move one square in any direction, duplicate yourself, disappear, etc.) and events that are triggered by probabilistic outcomes occurring within specified times.

In simulations, there are many outcomes that could result from a small set of initial conditions. It is much easier to write these programs and observe their outcomes than to calculate outcomes directly from a set of governing equations.

13.10. HOW OFTEN CAN I HAVE A BAD DAY?

Imagine this scenario. One of the pathologists on service has just made a diagnostic error on each of three consecutive reports. Luckily, they were detected at the pathology review conference and corrected before the report was released.

The chair of the department calls the pathologist to her office and berates her for a completely unacceptable error rate. No pathologist should be permitted to diagnose three consecutive cases incorrectly.

The pathologist defends herself, saying that a long-term review of her cases shows that she has a 2% error rate, which is the national average for pathology errors. She cannot explain why three errors occurred consecutively, but she supposes that if you sign out enough cases, you will eventually make three consecutive errors. The chair is not persuaded by this analysis.

Who is right? A few lines of Ruby can resolve the issue (List 13.10.1).

LIST 13.10.1. RUBY SCRIPT error.rb USES RESAMPLING TO SIMULATE RUNS OF ERRORS

```
#!/usr/local/bin/ruby
errorno = Numeric.new
(1..100000).each do
  |count|
  x = rand(100)
  errorno = (errorno + 1) if (x < 2)   #simulates a 2% error rate
  errorno = 0 if (x >= 2)
  if (errorno == 3)
    puts "Uh oh. 3 consecutive errors"
    errorno = 0
  end
end
exit
```

The output is shown in List 13.10.2.

The Ruby script simulates 100,000 diagnoses, which is a fair estimate of the total number of diagnoses a pathologist might render in their entire career (at 4000 diagnoses per year over 25 years of service). Each diag-

LIST 13.10.2. OUTPUT OF error.rb **AS SEVEN TRIAL RUNS AT 100,000 SIMULATIONS PER RUN**

```
C:\ftp\rb>ruby error.rb
    Uh oh. 3 consecutive errors
    Uh oh. 3 consecutive errors
    Uh oh. 3 consecutive errors


C:\ftp\rb>ruby error.rb


C:\ftp\rb>ruby error.rb
    Uh oh. 3 consecutive errors


C:\ftp\rb>ruby error.rb
    Uh oh. 3 consecutive errors


C:\ftp\rb>ruby error.rb


C:\ftp\rb>ruby error.rb


C:\ftp\rb>ruby error.rb
    Uh oh. 3 consecutive errors
    Uh oh. 3 consecutive errors
```

nosis is assigned a random number between 0 and 100. The "diagnosis" loop is repeated 100,000 times. In each loop, if the randomly assigned number is less than 2, the pathologist's error number is incremented by 1 (simulating an error). If the next diagnosis is randomly assigned a number greater than 2, the error number is dropped back down to 0 (that is, the next diagnosis is correct, and the run of errors is broken). If an error occurs on 3 consecutive occasions, the event is printed to the computer monitor (List 13.10.1).

In these trials of 100,000 diagnoses, using a 2% error rate, the modeled pathologist had several runs of three consecutive errors (List 13.10.2). Because 100,000 diagnoses represents about the number of diagnoses rendered by a pathologist in her entire career, one can say that she can be permitted a 3-error day about twice in her career.

CHAPTER 14

Cryptography and De-identification (Level 2)

14.1. BACKGROUND

The field of cryptography encompasses a variety of useful techniques (see List 14.1.1) (23, 24). Most of these methods involve using a one-way hash algorithm and/or a pseudorandom number generator. One-way hash algorithms can be easily implemented in Ruby scripts using either the MD (Message Digest) or the SHA (Secure Hash Algorithm) modules (List 14.1.1).

LIST 14.1.1. CRYPTOGRAPHIC METHODS VITAL TO BIOMEDICINE

Encrypting and decrypting messages

Electronic signatures

Message authentication

Time stamping

Creating unique identifiers

Reconciling patients across institutions

De-identification and re-identification

Privatizing data sharing protocols

Data referencing (with message digests)

Watermarking and steganography utilities

The purpose of this chapter is to explain how readily available cryptographic techniques can be used in Ruby scripts to provide powerful and elegant solutions to biomedical problems related to identification, de-identification, data authentication, and data privatization.

14.2. USING THE STANDARD LIBRARY DIGEST

A digest or a one-way hash is an algorithm that transforms a string into another string in such a way that the original string cannot be discovered by operations on the output (hence the term "one-way" hash). These popular algorithms are discussed in the Health Insurance Portability and Accountability Act (HIPAA) where they are referred to as Hashed Message Authentication Codes (HMACs). Examples of public domain one-way hash algorithms are MD5 (25) and SHA (26). These differ from encryption protocols that produce an output that can be decrypted by a second computation on the encrypted string.

The resultant one-way hash values for text strings consist of near-random strings of characters. The length of the hash strings can be increased so that the possible different values available to a one-way hash algorithm (the so-called namespace of the algorithm) is enormous. Namespaces for one-way hashes can be so large that the chance of hash collisions (two different names or identifiers hashing to the same value) is negligible.

In Ruby, it is easy to produce one-way hashes of strings using the MD5 algorithm or the SHA algorithm. Both algorithms are made available through `Digest`, a standard library distributed with Ruby. We can use the Ruby `irb` to demonstrate how `Digest` delivers one-way hash values on strings and files.

First, `require` Digest

```
irb>require 'digest/md5' => true
```

Ruby `irb` returns a true value when the `require` method successfully loads its passed filename.

The `hexdigest` method is sent to `Digest::MD5` with a string parameter.

```
irb>Digest::MD5.hexdigest("John Q. Public")
=> "03b266048c0c200b4e5da6832b226262"
```

A 32-character one-way hash string is returned.

When we repeat the same command on the same string, we get the same output.

```
irb>Digest::MD5.hexdigest("John Q. Public")
=> "03b266048c0c200b4e5da6832b226262"
```

We can just as easily require the `sha1` algorithm and perform an SHA digest on the string.

```
irb> require 'digest/sha1'=> true
irb> Digest::SHA1.hexdigest("John Q. Public")
=> "5397ff039aa279f29cae5b08ee63e79df3a0ca6d"
```

The SHA algorithm produces a different output than the MD5 algorithm.

If we change any character in the string, we get a completely different one-way hash.

```
irb> Digest::SHA1.hexdigest("John Q. Mublic")
=> "212b101beaa1d8f1ce60e6d58e854ff580e92d80"
```

We can also use the RIPEMD-160 digest algorithm.

```
irb> require 'digest/rmd160' => true
irb> Digest::RMD160.hexdigest("John Q. Public")
=> "09081079b359bf31875e209ba59458eb45aab8f6"
```

Ruby lets us use a 512-bit SHA digest. The syntax is shown:

```
irb> require 'Digest/sha2' => true
irb> Digest::SHA512.hexdigest("John Q. Public")
=>"03ff869947d3ecfdd5c2851b444fe95422a0e8ddf831b7ed8d38
eccd8f87decf07c7e48f1e2c05afccf518b10ea2faffd42511127d
98c550b60b9d8964218d1e"
```

When we use 512-bit hash values, it is virtually impossible that two different strings will yield the same digest values.

If we want to produce a one-way hash on a file, we provide the entire file using the IO class `read` method.

```
irb>Digest::MD5.hexdigest(File.open("walnut.jpg").binmode.read)
=> "aa6b413f5b34cfd7785fec0a1098580b"
```

When opening files, we send the `binmode` method to File object, which ensures that the file is read in binary mode (see the Glossary). We send the `read` method, without arguments, to the binary file object to capture the entire file. We used the `hexdigest` method because we like Hex notation. Hex notation is base-16 ASCII and uses an alphabet composed of (0, 1, 2, 3, 4, 5, 6, 7, 8, 9, a, b, c, d, e, f). Hex notation is useful because all possible hex strings appear as simple alphanumerics.

One-way hashes are useful for authenticating files. A file can be hashed, just as a character string can be hashed, producing a string of characters that is virtually unique for the file. If a single byte in the file is changed, the one-way hash for the file is completely changed. If a file always produces the same one-way hash value, it is a safe bet that the file has not been modified.

14.3. ANONYMIZATION USING ONE-WAY HASHING ALGORITHMS

One-way hashes can be used to anonymize patient records while still permitting researchers to accrue data over time to a specific patient record (List 14.3.1).

LIST 14.3.1. EXAMPLE PROTOCOL FOR A ONE-WAY HASH DE-IDENTIFIED RECORD LINKAGE

1. John Q. Public arrives for the first time in your medical clinic.
2. John Q. Public has a glucose test ordered and receives a glucose value of 85.
3. Using the MD5 one-way hash algorithm, on the character string "John Q. Public," a hash value of "3f875ec450dfbb07ed889e7b9c36da92" is generated.
4. In addition to John Q. Public's identified medical record, a de-identified record is prepared substituting the hash value for the patient name. 3f875ec450dfbb07ed889e7b9c36da92^^glucose^^85

   No computational efforts applied to the one-way hash value can yield the patient's name. The de-identified record is given to a trusted database administrator who adds it to the database of de-identified records. The database administrator cannot identify any of the patients whose records are included in the database.
5. Ten years later, John Q. Public returns to the medical clinic and has another glucose test. This time the glucose value is 95. A one-way hash is performed on the string "John Q. Public" yielding 3f875ec450dfbb07ed889e7b9c36da92, and a new de-identified record is prepared: 3f875ec450dfbb07ed889e7b9c36da92^^glucose^^95. The de-identified record is given to the trusted database administrator, who adds it to the aggregate database. The database program finds a match to the one-way hash and concatenates the new record to the old record: 3f875ec450dfbb07ed889e7b9c36da92^^glucose^^85^^glucose^^95.

What has this accomplished? It achieves the seemingly impossible feat of accruing clinical data over time for de-identified data records.

14.4. ONE-WAY HASH WEAKNESSES: DICTIONARY ATTACKS AND COLLISIONS

Insightful readers will notice that this approach has a flaw. Attacks on one-way hash data may take the form of hashing a list of names and looking for matching hash values in the dataset (the so-called dictionary attack). Efforts to overcome this limitation include encrypting the hash or hashing a secret combination of identifier elements or keeping the hash value private (hidden). As in any privacy protocol, success is almost always achieved with a realistic assessment of the risks pertaining to your particular situation. Regarding implementation, issues often arise when biomedical institutions have a flawed system for identifying patients. If a person is identified within a hospital system as Tom Peterson on Monday and Thomas Peterson on Tuesday, this system will fail because you cannot uniquely de-identify someone who has no unique name. If the hash is performed on unique, persistent patient identifiers, the system will have a better chance of success.

Technical problems may also arise. One-way hash collisions occur when two different strings yield the same hash value. Because hash values are pseudorandom character strings, the chance of a hash collision between two patients with different identifiers is very small. A variety of solutions have been suggested for large database implementations (where collisions may rarely occur). The most straightforward maneuver, as noted, is to use a longer hash value. SHA has different algorithmic forms (SHA-1, SHA-256, SHA-384, and SHA-512) with message digest (hash) lengths up to 512 bits. As the length of the message digest increases, the chance of having a digest collision diminishes.

14.5. THE THRESHOLD PROTOCOL

A threshold protocol is a cryptographic technique that splits information into pieces, none of which contains sufficient information to recreate the original text (23). These protocols permit the original information in a confidential message to be reconstructed from some number of the derived pieces. Threshold protocols have been used since antiquity, commonly appearing as plot devices in adventure novels. A map to buried treasure is divided among the central characters. A puzzle is reconstructed when five missing pieces are assembled. Measured turns of the combination lock are distributed to three untrustworthy coconspirators. Matching rings in a set are destroyed and so on. We describe a simple threshold protocol that can be used to search, annotate, or transform confidential data without breaching patient confidentiality (27).

The threshold protocol yields two threshold pieces with the following basic properties:

Neither piece 1 nor piece 2 contains confidential information.

The original text can be reconstructed from piece 1 and piece 2.

In typical use, piece 2 will be held by the data owner, and piece 1 will be freely distributed. Piece 1 can be annotated and returned to the owner of the original data to enhance the complete dataset. Collections of piece 1 files can be merged and distributed without breaching patient confidentiality. Variations of the threshold protocol are described.

Threshold files are safe in the sense that they contain no confidential information and can be used for research purposes. The threshold protocol is particularly useful when the receiver of the threshold file needs to obtain certain concepts or data types found in the original data but does not need to fully understand the original dataset.

The purpose of this section is to describe and implement a threshold protocol that can render confidential medical records harmless while permitting the exchange of information for research purposes.

A generalized confidentiality problem can be presented as a negotiation protocol between Alice and Bob. Bob has a file containing the medical records of millions of patients. Alice has secret software that can annotate Bob's file, enhancing its value manyfold. Alice will not give Bob her secret algorithm, but is willing to demonstrate the algorithm if Bob gives her his database. Bob will not give Alice the database, but he can give her little snippets of the database containing insufficient information to infer patient identities.

Bob prepares an algorithm that transforms his file into two threshold pieces (see List 14.5.1).

LIST 14.5.1. THE BASIC THRESHOLD PROTOCOL

1. Text is divided into short phrases.
2. Each phrase is converted by a one-way hash algorithm into a seemingly random set of characters.
3. Threshold piece 1 is composed of the list of all phrases, with each phrase followed by its one-way hash.
4. Threshold piece 2 is composed of the text with all phrases replaced by their one-way hash values and with high-frequency words preserved.

Piece 1 is a file that contains all of the phrases from the original file, with each phrase attached to its one-way hash value.

As discussed in the prior section, every one-way hash has two important properties:

1. A phrase will always yield the same hash value when it is operated on by the one-way hash algorithm.
2. There is no feasible way to determine the phrase by inspecting or manipulating the hash value. This second property holds true even if the hashing algorithm is known.

Bob will give Alice piece 1.

Piece 2 is a file wherein each phrase from the original file is replaced by its one-way hash value. High-frequency words (so-called stop words, such as the, and, an, but, and if) are left in place in piece 2. The use of stop words to extract useful phrases from text is a popular indexing technique. The list of stop words used in the threshold algorithm was taken directly from the National Library of Medicine's PubMed resource.

http://www.ncbi.nlm.nih.gov/books/bv.fcgi?rid=helppubmed.table.pubmedhelp.T42

Piece 2 will be used to reconstruct the original text or an annotated version of the original text, using Alice's modifications to piece 1.

The following is an example of a single line of Bob's text that has been converted into two threshold pieces according to the described algorithm.

Bob's original text said this: "They suggested that the manifestations were as severe in the mother as in the sons and that this suggested autosomal dominant inheritance."

Bob's piece 1, which can be freely distributed, is shown in List 14.5.2.

Bob's piece 2, which Bob keeps private, is shown in List 14.5.3.

LIST 14.5.2. BOB'S PIECE 1

```
684327ec3b2f020aa3099edb177d3794 => suggested autosomal
    dominant inheritance
3c188dace2e7977fd6333e4d8010e181 => mother
8c81b4aaf9c2009666d532da3b19d5f8 => manifestations
db277da2e82a4cb7e9b37c8b0c7f66f0 => suggested
e183376eb9cc9a301952c05b5e4e84e3 => sons
22cf107be97ab08b33a62db68b4a390d => severe
```

(continues)

LIST 14.5.3. BOB'S PIECE 2

```
they db277da2e82a4cb7e9b37c8b0c7f66f0 that the
8c81b4aaf9c2009666d532da3b19d5f8 were as
22cf107be97ab08b33a62db68b4a390d in the
3c188dace2e7977fd6333e4d8010e181 as in the
e183376eb9cc9a301952c05b5e4e84e3 and that this
684327ec3b2f020aa3099edb177d3794.
```

14.6. IMPLEMENTATION OF THE THRESHOLD PROTOCOL

If Alice had piece 1 and piece 2, she could simply use piece 1 to find the text phrases that match the hash values in piece 2. Substituting the phrases back into piece 2 will recreate Bob's original line of text. Bob must ensure that Alice never obtains piece 2. The negotiation between Alice and Bob is as follows:

Bob prepares threshold pieces 1 and 2 and sends piece 1 to Alice. Alice may require Bob to prove the authenticity of piece 1, but Bob has no reason to care if piece 1 is intercepted by an unauthorized party. Alice uses her software (which may be secret, or it may require computational facilities that Bob does not have, or it may require large databases that Bob does not have) to transform or annotate each phrase from piece 1. The transformation product for each phrase can be almost anything that Bob considers valuable (for example, a UMLS code, a genome database link, an image file URL, or a tissue sample location). Alice substitutes the transformed text (or simply appends the transformed text) for each phrase back into piece 1, collocating it with the original one-way hash number associated with the phrase.

The threshold protocol can be implemented with two files, a list of stop words (List 14.6.1) and a Ruby script that converts text into two threshold pieces (List 14.6.2).

LIST 14.6.1. PARTIAL LIST OF STOP WORDS IN FILE STOP.TXT

a

about

again

all

almost

also

although

always

among

an

and

another

any

are

as

at

be

LIST 14.6.2. RUBY SCRIPT `thresh.rb` DIVIDES A TEXT FILE INTO TWO THRESHOLD FILES

```
#!/usr/bin/ruby
require 'digest/md5'
index = Hash.new; stophash = Hash.new; phrasearray = Array.new
stop = File.open("stop.txt")
onefile = File.open("onefile.txt","w")
twofile = File.open("twofile.txt","w")
stop.each{|line|stophash[line.chomp]=""}
stop.close
text = IO.read("AA.TXT")
text = text.downcase
text.gsub!(/\.\n/, " ") if (text =~ /\.\n/)
text = text + " the"
textarray = text.split(/\s+/)
textarray.each do
    |word|
    if (stophash.has_key?(word))
      phrase = phrasearray.join(" ")
      phrasearray = []
      if !(phrase == "")
        hexstring = Digest::MD5.hexdigest(phrase)
```

(continues)

```
                index[hexstring] = phrase;
                twofile.print "#{hexstring} #{word} ";
                phrase = ""
            else
                twofile.print " #{word} "
            end
        else
            phrasearray << word
        end
end
index.each{|key,value|onefile.puts "#{key} => #{value}"}
exit
```

The two output files are piece 1 (List 14.6.3) and piece 2 (List 14.6.4).

LIST 14.6.3. PARTIAL OUTPUT FILE ONE, OF `thresh.rb`

```
b7bd39c79003dbbe065e3b601a0abe1b => shawl scrotum
33c9b363aa666f43190fa83fce543646 => pair
cf6b47ebefc36d1d8d8ea413d9f267fa => affected mother
c30635cc93c51c6f6731806dbd149a51 => suggested
8758e8af7c90217a6dc951e07b4bd97e => 2 different husbands.
b9a1cf2f3e81afe9c10271494c251359 => 2 sons
4b477f80238207af231e8f90193c69e4 => genetic heterogeneity
2ea618a65da7c9641888862cec6d86d2 => autosomal dominant
9040fdd3ea9e447e321e222efdd79a82 => affected males
```

LIST 14.6.4. PARTIAL OUTPUT FILE TWO, OF `thresh.rb`

```
1a829c58a155fdda58f3e73ab38ba9a0 and b9a1cf2f3e81afe9c1027149
4c251359 with e4c20e775401062d7f8016c201eb4347and b7bd39c790
03dbbe065e3b601a0abe1b they cb52faa26d48a2b1eb53a125f5fad3c3
the f85b785512fe9685dde7fda470fe2b9fin b9a5510e1972f78267041c
4e24f23a9d has been 717fbd16ccccd34c2ac2111d1481e213 the e9e3
5b4383108cddadc92eb9ec030fcf by df9743bca80d21a3f028c9ed331005a
6 had 9040fdd3ea9e447e321e222efdd79a82 in 0c235ed8228b9f540379
3526b285c021 there is either 4b477f80238207af231e8f90193c69e4 or
this is an
```

The two pieces can be recombined in another Ruby script to yield the original file (List 14.6.5).

LIST 14.6.5. RUBY SCRIPT threshrv.rb **COMPUTES ORIGINAL FILE FROM TWO THRESHOLD FILES**

```
#!/usr/bin/ruby
index = Hash.new
threshtext = IO.read("twofile.txt")
threshtext.chop!.chop!.chop!.chop!
onefile = File.open("onefile.txt")
result=File.open("result.txt", "w")
onefile.each do
  |line|
  array=line.chomp.split(/ \=\> /)
  index[array[0]] = array[1]
end
threshtext.gsub!(/[0-9a-f]{32}/){|m| m=index[$&]}
puts threshtext
exit
```

Other than obfuscating our original text, what is the practical value of the threshold protocol? Let us pretend that Alice has an autocoder that provides a standard nomenclature code to medical phrases that occur in text. Alice's software transforms the original phrases from piece 1, preserving the original hash values. Phrases from piece 1 that occur in the Unified Medical Language System now have been given code numbers by Alice's software.

```
684327ec3b2f020aa3099edb177d3794 => suggested (autosomal
    dominant inheritance=C0443147)
3c188dace2e7977fd6333e4d8010e181 => (mother=C0026591)
8c81b4aaf9c2009666d532da3b19d5f8 => manifestations
db277da2e82a4cb7e9b37c8b0c7f66f0 => suggested
e183376eb9cc9a301952c05b5e4e84e3 => (son=C0037683)
22cf107be97ab08b33a62db68b4a390d => (severe=C0205082)
```

Alice returns the coded phrase list from piece 1 to Bob. Bob now takes the transformed piece 1 and substitutes the transformed phrases for each occurrence of the hash values occurring in piece 2, which he has saved for this very purpose.

The reconstructed sentence is now

```
they suggested that the manifestations were as
(severe=C0205082) in the (mother=C0026591) as in the
(son=C0037683) and that this suggested (autosomal
dominant heritance=C0443147)
```

The original sentence is now annotated with UMLS codes. It was accomplished without sharing confidential information that might have been contained in the text. Bob never had access to Alice's software. Alice never had the opportunity to see Bob's original text. The useful properties of piece 1 and piece 2 are summarized in Lists 14.6.6 and 14.6.7.

LIST 14.6.6. PROPERTIES OF PIECE 1 (THE LISTING OF PHRASES AND THEIR ONE-WAY HASHES)

Contains no information on the frequency of occurrence of the phrases found in the original text (because recurring phrases map to the same hash code and appear as a single entry in piece 1).

Contains no information that Alice can use to connect any patient to any particular patient record.

Contains no information on the order or locations of the phrases found in the original text.

Contains all the concepts found in the original text. Stop words are a popular method of parsing text into concepts.

Bob can destroy piece 1 and recreate it later from the original file.

Alice can use the phrases in piece 1 to transform and annotate or search the concepts found in the original file.

Alice can transfer piece 1 to a third party without violating HIPAA privacy rules or Common Rule human subject regulations (in the United States). For that matter, Alice can keep piece 1 and add it to her database of piece 1 files collected from all of her clients.

Depending on the type of file that needs to be converted into threshold pieces, some data preparation may be useful. In particular, it may be useful to encrypt or delete specific identifiers found in the original file, such as surgical pathology numbers. The file that is actually used by the algorithm should itself be assigned a hash number by the algorithm, as should file 1 and file 2. These three hash numbers could be saved and

LIST 14.6.7. PROPERTIES OF PIECE 2

Contains no information that can be used to connect any patient to any particular patient record.

Contains nothing but hash values of phrases and stop words in their correct order of occurrence in the original text.

Anyone obtaining piece 1 and piece 2 can reconstruct the original text.

Bob can lose or destroy piece 2 and recreate it later from the original file.

used for authentication purposes in later stages of a data negotiation protocol. Issues of data space collisions arise when using very large files. A data space collision occurs when two different phrases are assigned the same hash value by the hashing algorithm. This problem can be handled by adding a block of code that tests for collisions and assigns an alternate hash value (by rehashing the original hash) in such cases.

The original text has been converted into two pieces, neither of which contains any identifying information. There is sufficient information in piece 1 for Alice to annotate the text and return it to Bob (annotated piece 1). Bob can reconstruct his original text, including Alice's annotations, thus adding value to his original data without breaching patient confidentiality. Bob can pay Alice for her services. Alice can keep piece 1 and use it for her own purposes. Alice can make a large database consisting of all of the piece 1 files she receives from all of her customers. Alice can sell piece 1 to a third party if she wishes. Alice can update or otherwise enhance her annotations on piece 1 and sell the updated files to Bob.

The same protocol could have been implemented in a three-party negotiation. Bob may have been a data supplier with no interest in using the data himself. Suppose Carol was interested in Alice's annotations of Bob's file. Bob may have given Alice threshold piece 1 and Carol threshold piece 2. Alice may have made her transformation of the phrases in piece 1 and sent the transformed version of piece 1 to Carol. Carol could use Alice's transformed version of piece 1 and her copy of piece 2 to create a transformed version of Bob's original text. This would only work, of course, if the transformed version of Bob's original file (produced by Carol) contains no confidential information. A variation may involve assigning Bob as the trusted broker, who uses piece 2 and the transformed version of piece 1 to create a file for Carol. In this variation, Carol receives nothing until the end of the negotiation, and Bob can take measures to ensure that the file that Carol receives is "safe."

The threshold negotiation need not be based on text exchange. The same negotiation would apply to any set of data elements that can be transformed or annotated. The threshold protocol has greatest practical value in instances when data elements inform on other data elements that reside in the same data record. The protocol teases apart the data records and substitutes one-way hash values back into the record. The ways in which individual pieces of data can be transformed or annotated are limited only by the imagination. As an example, sequences of DNA can be annotated with positional mappings or standard nomenclature codes or similarity information.

CHAPTER 5

Common Gateway Interface (Level 4)

15.1. BACKGROUND

Until this point, you have seen examples of Ruby scripts that operate only on your own computer. The Ruby interpreter, input files, class libraries and your own Ruby scripts reside on your computer and respond to your commands. In my opinion, this is what computation is all about: an individual with a deep understanding of the tools and data residing on her computer, synthesizing a new and beneficial hypothesis, process, conclusion, or idea. Today, however, most people would disagree with this paradigm, opting for an environment in which data are updated, condensed, and sent through the Internet via Web applications.

Web applications are typically services that reside on servers that search databases when requests come from Web browsers or from automated query agents. The query agent may be a semiautonomous software application that requests services from multiple servers, collecting data relevant to its program and drawing inferences from the collected data that trigger subsequent actions.

These ideas seem grandiose, but they spring from some very simple capabilities afforded through standard Internet protocols (Lists 15.1.1 and 15.1.2).

A full discussion of these protocols would be beyond the scope of this book (and beyond the scope of the author). Readers should know that most popular scripting languages, including Ruby, provide open source modules for the less complex protocols (FTP, TELNET, HTTP, RPC, and SOAP). There is an enormous literature available on these topics. Web Services, P2P, and GRID have complex architectures. Software packages

LIST 15.1.1. BASIC PROPERTIES OF THE INTERNET THAT SUPPORT COMPLEX DATA INTERCHANGES

1. All computers connected to the Internet have a unique address.

2. All computers connected to the Internet can act as either servers (responding to clients), clients (sending requests to servers) or peers (participants in protocols that distribute queries and responses via many different computers).

3. We now have language frameworks in which queries and responses can be packaged into standard messages equally recognizable to computers, regardless of their resident operating system. A succession of increasingly complex networking protocols characterizes the evolution of network-based computational tasking.

LIST 15.1.2. INCREASINGLY COMPLEX TASK-SHARING NETWORK PROTOCOLS AND METHODS

1. FTP (file transfer protocol)
2. TELNET
3. HTTP (hypertext transfer protocol)
4. CGI (Common Gateway Interface)
4. RPC (remote procedure calls)
5. XML-RPC (XML-based remote procedure calls)
6. SOAP (simple object access protocol)
7. P2P (peer-to-peer networking)
8. WEB applications (includes Ruby on Rails)
9. WEB Services (written in Web Services Description Language)
10. GRID computing

based on these technologies typically require participation by a group of computer scientists blessed with time and expertise.

Two data sharing tools that have wide popularity are Common Gateway Interface (CGI) scripts and Ruby on Rails (RoR). RoR is the subject of numerous books and articles (28–30), and you will be learning more about RoR in Chapter 16.

The purpose of this chapter is to provide sufficient description of CGI so that you will have an idea of the power of this technique. CGI is suffi-

ciently simple in concept and execution so that you can write simple
CGI scripts by applying the lessons learned here.

15.2. CGI SCRIPTS

From the user's point of view, CGI scripts can be perceived as server-side
Ruby scripts that are called from Web pages. A CGI script looks just like
any other Ruby script. The only difference is that it sits in a special Web
server directory called cgi-bin.

Typically, Web pages call CGI scripts discretely. The Web surfer is never
intended to know what transpires between browser and server. Here is
how it is done.

1. The Web page contains a link (usually in the form of an active link or
   a "submit" button on a Web form) that sends the name and location
   of the Ruby CGI script along with the Web server name, as a URL,
   using the standard HTTP protocol (Figure 15-1, List 15.2.1).
2. The server receives the data sent through the HTTP protocol and acti-
   vates the specified Ruby CGI script.

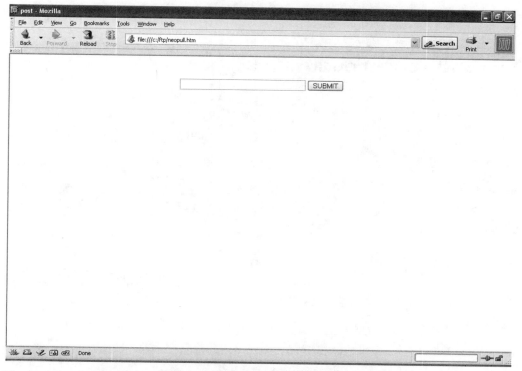

Figure 15-1 A simple Web page that calls a CGI script (neopull.tif).

LIST 15.2.1. HTML SOURCE FOR neopull.htm WEB PAGE TO CALL A CGI SCRIPT

```
<html>
<head>
<title>GET</title>
</head>
<body>
<br><form name="sender" method="GET"
    action="http://www.julesberman.info/cgi-bin/neopull.rb">
<br><center><input type="text" name="tx" size=38
    maxlength=48 value="">
<input type="submit" name="bx" value="SUBMIT"></center>
</form>
<br><br>
</body>
</html>
```

3. The Ruby script requires the CGI library and creates a CGI object (List 15.2.2).

LIST 15.2.2. RUBY SCRIPT neopull.rb SEARCHES A SERVER FILE FOR A WEB CLIENT QUERY

```
#!/usr/bin/ruby
print "Content-type: text/html\r\n\r\n"
print "<html><body></body></html>\r\n"
require 'cgi'
cgi = CGI.new
query_term = cgi.params["tx"]
print "\<br\>Your query term is #{query_term}\<br\>\<br\>\r\n"
text = File.open("neoself", "r")
text.each do
  |line|
  if (line =~ /#{query_term}/)
    line.gsub!(/[\|\>]/,"\<br\>\r\n")
    puts "\<br\>#{line}\r\n"
  end
end
print "</body></html>\r\n"
exit
```

4. The Ruby script executes and returns a chunk of HTML-formatted text to the client (the sending URL).

5. The newly composed HTML page is displayed in the client's Web browser (Figure 15-2).

The `neopull.htm` HTML file (List 15.2.1), appears in a Web browser as shown in Figure 15-1. The first 5 lines of `neopull.htm` are the minimal HTML header lines for a Web page. The title of the Web page is "GET".

```
<html>
<head>
<title>GET</title>
</head>
<body>
```

The next lines create the input box seen in Figure 15-1. The location of the server, with a complete path to the CGI script, `neopull.rb` (List 15.2.2) is specified. The CGI method for sending the input box contents to the server is "GET". The GET method appends input box text to the HTTP request received by the server named in the "action" parameter.

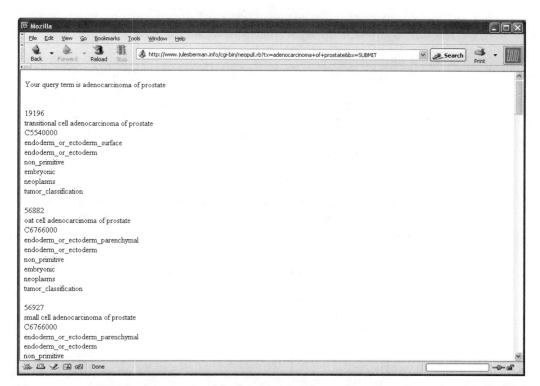

Figure 15-2 HTML page received by browser and sent by `neopull.rb` **(cgi_reply.tif).**

```
<br><form name="sender" method="GET"
    action="http://www.julesberman.info/cgi-bin/neopull.rb">
<br><center><input type="text" name="tx" size=38
        maxlength=48 value="">
<input type="submit" name="bx" value="SUBMIT"></center>
</form>
```

The last few lines are the minimal footer for an HTML file.

```
</body>
```

The server's Ruby script `neopull.rb`, receives the HTTP request from the client and returns a Web page to the same client, in HTML format (List 15.2.2).

Here is the composed Web page (Figure 15-2) that would be returned if the client had entered "adenocarcinoma of prostate" into the input box of Figure 15-1.

Let us review how the `neopull.rb` script works. The script must send back a chunk of text as a valid HTML Web page. It begins by printing a detailed header for an HTML page:

```
print "Content-type: text/html\r\n\r\n"
print "<html><body></body></html>\r\n"
```

It requires the CGI library and creates a CGI instance object.

```
require 'cgi'
cgi = CGI.new
```

It sends the `params` hash value to the `cgi` instance object, passing `"tx"` as its argument. List 15.2.1 indicates that the name of the text submitted by the form is `"tx."` The value associated with `"tx"` is the query phrase that the client submits.

```
query_term = cgi.params["tx"]
```

The next lines open a dataset file on the server side and parse through every line of the file, extracting those lines that match the example query term ("adenocarcinoma of prostate"). In this script, we use `"neoself"` as the dataset file. This is the previously described text file composed of all the terms in the Neoplasm Classification (see Chapter 5, Section 9).

```
text = File.open("neoself", "r")
text.each do
    |line|
    if (line =~ /#{query_term}/)
```

```
        line.gsub!(/[\|\>]/,"\<br\>\r\n")
        puts "\<br\>#{line}\r\n"
    end
  end
```

Every output line contains a `<br>` HTML formatting instruction. The `<br>` is HTML's equivalent to a newline character.

```
        puts "\<br\>#{line}\r\n"
```

The last line adds an HTML closer.

```
        print "</body></html>\r\n"
```

Most CGI scripts are constructed to do a few basic chores (List 15.2.3).

LIST 15.2.3. BASIC TASKS OF A CGI SCRIPT

1. Send print instructions that create a header for an HTML page.
2. Accept a GET or a POST message from a Web-client form.
3. Do something with the GET or POST message. This may involve adding the message contents to a database or using the message contents as a database query.
4. Print out a body of text in HTML format.
5. Print the footer of an HTML page.

In a CGI script, all print commands are sent back to the client. Thus, print commands that constitute a well-formed HTML page will create a response Web page that the client can view.

15.3. SECURITY CONSIDERATIONS

CGI programming is not particularly safe for either the client or the server. Clients can include intrusive code within GET or POST messages. This is usually accomplished through an `eval` statement, which tells Ruby to execute a character string. When the CGI script receives the client data, Ruby may innocently evaluate the client's input as though it were a command line. Obviously, a CGI program that does not guard against this, and other deceptions may be vulnerable to client attack.

Ruby includes some features that can improve the security of your CGI scripts. These features are referred to as "data tainting" and "safe" levels. Data tainting is a method of marking types of data. Ruby automatically marks all data received from external data sources (such as the Internet) as tainted. You can determine whether any object is tainted by sending it the `tainted?` method.

```
irb>1.tainted? => false
```

The number 1, entered on my keyboard, is not tainted. A CGI object's `param` data would be tainted and would return `"true"` if sent the `tainted?` method.

You can write Ruby scripts that handle tainted and untainted data differently.

Ruby also has safe levels. Safe levels are constraints imposed on Ruby scripts. The safe levels are determined by the global variable `$SAFE`. There are four safe levels built into Ruby. We use safe level 1 (in List 15.3.1). A safe level of 1 puts some restrictions of the use of tainted data.

List 15.3.1 demonstrates how safe levels and tainting can somewhat reduce your exposure to a malicious attack.

The script is essentially the same as the `neopull.rb` script from the prior section. The modified lines are as follows:

```
$SAFE = 1
cgi = CGI.new
query_term = cgi.params["tx"].to_s
if (query_term =~ /^[a-z\s]+$/i)
   query_term.untaint
```

We set the safe level to 1, thus restricting the use of tainted data. We obtain the query term by sending the hash accessor method (`params["tx"]`) to the CGI object. We then test the query term to ensure that it consists of a simple string of alphabetic letters and spaces. If it contained a "." or a quotation or a parenthesis or a block character, the match would not occur. These characters might appear in a stealth command. On the condition that data are simple text, the taint is lifted, and the script can resume. If you are concerned about security, you will need to prepare CGI scripts very carefully, providing a level of security proportionate to your level of concern.

We have seen that clients can hurt servers. Servers can also hurt clients. A CGI script can be programmed to send countless annoying HTML pages to clients or to use the server–client connection for other devious purposes. If you use CGI, you should be aware of your risks and responsibilities.

LIST 15.3.1. RUBY SCRIPT neosafe.rb **IMPROVES THE SECURITY OF** neopull.rb

```ruby
#!/usr/bin/ruby
print "Content-type: text/html\r\n\r\n"
print "<html><body></body></html>\r\n"
require 'cgi'
$SAFE = 1
cgi = CGI.new
query_term = cgi.params["tx"].to_s
if (query_term =~ /^[a-z\s]+$/i)
  query_term.untaint
else
  print "\<br\>Only alphabetic letters and spaces are"
  print "\<br\>permitted in the query box\n"
  exit
end
print "\<br\>Your query term is #{query_term}\<br\>\<br\>\r\n"
text = File.open("neoself", "r")
text.each do
  |line|
  if (line =~ /#{query_term}/)
    line.gsub!(/[\|\>]/,"\<br\>\r\n")
    puts "\<br\>#{line}\r\n"
  end
end
print "</body></html>\r\n"
exit
```

15.4. CGI PROGRAMMING AS A MODEST INTRODUCTION TO DISTRIBUTED COMPUTING

The only drawback in CGI programming is that you need to have access to a server's cgi-bin (List 15.4.1). This book emphasizes self-reliance and open source solutions, and we have tried to avoid solutions that require proprietary software, proprietary hardware, or complex protocols that require advanced training. In the next section, we use Ruby's WEBrick to demonstrate that every networked computer (including your own) can be a server.

LIST 15.4.1. THE ADVANTAGES OF CGI PROGRAMMING

1. The computations are performed on the server side, not the client side. A Web surfer can blithely send a request (via a CGI-calling Web form) that initiates a massive server-side computational effort. A fraction of a second later, a calculated reply appears on her screen.

2. CGI accepts input from the client. This is done through GET or POST messages.

3. The data resources are stored on the server side, not the client side. A Web request may require the participation of an enormous database or a federation of databases distributed throughout the world. A server-side CGI script can implement and coordinate complex database queries.

4. A server-side CGI script can be easily modified and improved. There is no need to change the client-side Web pages that call the CGI script.

5. CGI scripts are easy to write. They are basically the same as any other Ruby script except they accept input from client forms, and they format their output so that there is an HTML header and footer and the intervening output has HTML tags that format the output lines.

CHAPTER

16

Enter Ruby on Rails (Level 4)

16.1. BACKGROUND

Ruby on Rails (RoR), sometimes referred to as Rails, is a Ruby environment that supports the streamlined production of Web applications. Web applications are generally sophisticated programs with appealing graphic user interfaces that accept input from aesthetically pleasing Web forms and that query server-side database applications. For the most part, RoR applications are built by professional developers who invest the time to learn this fascinating Ruby tool. RoR programmers boast that they can develop Web applications 10 times faster with Rails than with Java (31). If you are a full-time biomedical professional and a sometime programmer, you may find RoR seductive.

In most cases, RoR programs are run from dedicated servers or from Internet server provider (ISP) accounts. Those ISPs that provide RoR support will typically have their own procedures for customers to access the RoR environment.

This chapter shows how you can use your Internet-connected computer as a server that provides full RoR functionality. The inspiration for this approach to learning Rails came from Curt Hibbs' article "Rolling with Ruby on Rails" (31).

16.2. INSTALLING RUBY ON RAILS

We will be installing RoR on a desktop computer connected to the Internet (the localhost), using Ruby's built-in WEBrick server. RoR is designed with the expectation that RoR applications will connect to a database. MySQL is an open source, free and publicly available database and is the default database for RoR.

RoR can be easily installed from GEMS.

C:\ftp>gem install rails—remote

WEBrick comes bundled in Ruby (versions 1.8 and later). It lets you turn your own computer into a server that can handle HTTP requests and responses. To test RoR, you will use WEBrick to turn your computer into a server that sends an HTTP request to your RoR applications and that receives a Web page in response to the request. We will not be creating a database for our short RoR application, but if you wish to explore a higher level of functionality for your RoR application, the Curt Hibbs article is recommended as a starting point (31).

16.3. STEP-BY-STEP RUBY ON RAILS EXAMPLE

After RoR is installed, you can create the framework for a Web application with a two-word command at the system prompt.

```
c:\ftp>rails trial
```

Our application will be named "`trial`." Invoking this simple command results in the automatic creation of dozens of Rails template files, all added to a new subdirectory, labeled "`trial`" (List 16.3.1).

The "`trial`" application will be prepared by modifying some of the provided files.

LIST 16.3.1. OUTPUT OF "`rails trial`" COMMAND

```
Directory of C:\ftp\trial
12/30/2006   08:55 AM    <DIR>          .
12/30/2006   08:55 AM    <DIR>          ..
12/30/2006   08:55 AM    <DIR>          app
12/30/2006   08:55 AM    <DIR>          components
12/30/2006   08:55 AM    <DIR>          config
12/30/2006   08:55 AM    <DIR>          db
12/30/2006   08:55 AM    <DIR>          doc
12/30/2006   08:55 AM    <DIR>          lib
12/30/2006   08:55 AM    <DIR>          log
12/30/2006   08:55 AM    <DIR>          public
12/30/2006   08:55 AM              307  Rakefile
12/30/2006   08:55 AM            7,353  README
12/30/2006   08:55 AM    <DIR>          script
12/30/2006   08:55 AM    <DIR>          test
12/30/2006   08:55 AM    <DIR>          tmp
12/30/2006   08:55 AM    <DIR>          vendor
```

For the application to work, we need to have an active WEBrick server. This is accomplished with another two-word command launched from the `trial` subdirectory (List 16.3.2).

```
C:\ftp\trial>ruby script/server
```

LIST 16.3.2. OUTPUT OF "ruby script/server" COMMAND LINE

```
=> Booting WEBrick...
=> Rails application started on http://0.0.0.0:3000
=> Ctrl-C to shutdown server; call with —help for options
[2006-12-30 09:05:37] INFO   WEBrick 1.3.1
[2006-12-30 09:05:37] INFO   ruby 1.8.4 (2006-04-14)
   [i386-mswin32]
[2006-12-30 09:05:37] INFO   WEBrick::HTTPServer#start:
   pid=2564 port=3000
```

Believe it or not, your computer has just been turned into a server, with a `localhost` address of http://127.0.0.1 and a listening port of 3000. The server will be active while your computer is turned on, your Internet connection is active and your DOS command window (that is, the WEBrick server window) is not closed. Text will automatically appear in the WEBrick server window as the RoR application receives and responds to HTTP requests. You can minimize the command window (without closing it) and forget about it until you have finished the exercise.

Now, open your preferred Web browser and enter your own address (localhost, http://127.0.0.0:3000/) in the URL box (see Figure 16.1, ror_home.tif).

You are now connected to the RoR developer's environment.

We will want a short script that controls our application. We create the script with Rails by entering a simple command line.

```
C:\ftp\trial>ruby script/generate controller MyTrial
```

Rails creates the controller files (List 16.3.3).

We are ready to "fill in" our RoR application. We will be using the controller file that was just automatically created; however, we wanted to have a controller named MyTrial. When we look at the created list of files, we find this:

```
create  app/controllers/my_trial_controller.rb
```

MyTrial has been automatically converted to `my_trial_controller.rb`, with underscores added between words.

Figure 16-1 Ruby on Rails environment page viewed from the localhost.

Here are the contents of the `my_trial_controller.rb` file:

```
class MyTrialController < ApplicationController
end
```

There is not much to the file, but it provides the framework for our short application.

LIST 16.3.3. OUTPUT OF `"ruby script/generate controller mytrial"` **COMMAND**

```
C:\ftp\trial>ruby script\generate controller MyTrial
      exists   app/controllers/
      exists   app/helpers/
      create   app/views/my_trial
      exists   test/functional/
      create   app/controllers/my_trial_controller.rb
      create   test/functional/my_trial_controller_test.rb
      create   app/helpers/my_trial_helper.rb
```

Let us revise the file with an RoR command. RoR expects us to start the controller file with a method named `index`, and we will use the `render_text` command.

```
class MyTrialController < ApplicationController
    def index
        render_text "Here I am!!"
    end
end
```

We have finished our modest RoR application.

Now we can call the RoR application from the Web browser by entering its full address: *http://127.0.0.1:3000/My_Trial/*

RoR executes the application and returns a Web page to the server (Figure 16-2, ror_my_trial.tif-1).

Remember that we began by generating a MyTrial application request, but we finished with a My_Trial application. This is a small RoR quirk that users must anticipate.

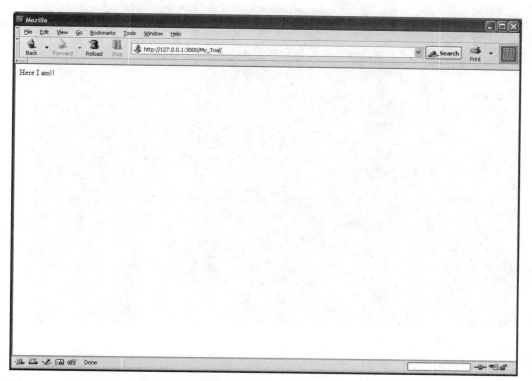

Figure 16-2 The My_Trial application.

The RoR application is finished. You can maximize your WEBrick application command window and review the server activity (Figure 16-3).

Remember to close the command window to end the WEBrick session. Although obscenely simple, this short application serves as an introduction to RoR programming. You will need to read dedicated RoR books to master the RoR syntax and command structure.

16.4. RUBY ON RAILS SUMMARY

RoR uses a popular model-view-controller paradigm for Web application development. The model layer contains data objects tied to a database. The view layer controls the HTML format of the application, and the controller layer controls the actions of the application. Web application developers understand this model and feel comfortable working in the framework provided by RoR. This framework, plus the ease of programming in Ruby, has contributed to the enormous success of RoR.

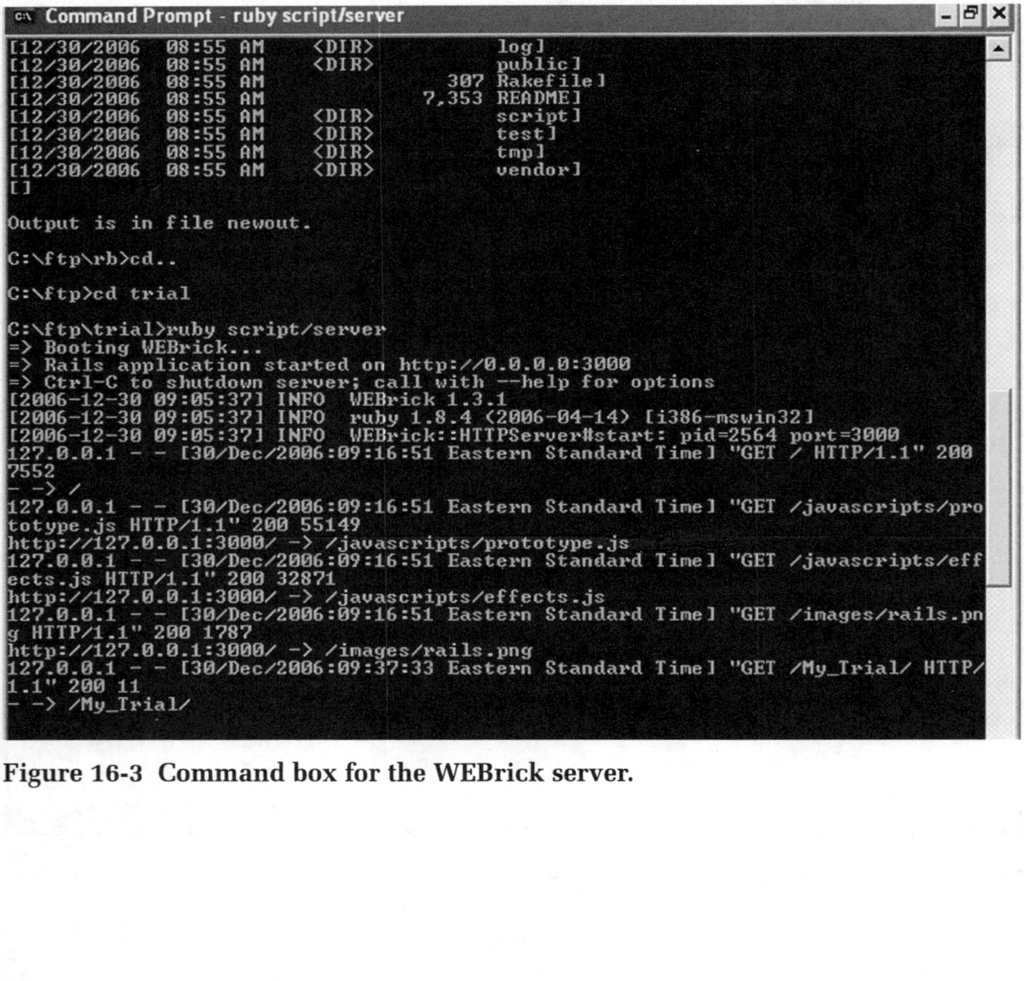

Figure 16-3 Command box for the WEBrick server.

CHAPTER 17

The Bioinformatics Library, Bio and Bioruby (Level 3)

17.1. BACKGROUND

Definitions abound for the field of bioinformatics. The most general definition of bioinformatics is the application of computers and computational methods to any biological and medical data. This broad definition would include modern epidemiology, biostatistics, medical informatics, computational and systems biology, biological modeling, hospital information systems, much of modern bioengineering science and a host of related pursuits. Most people do not think of these fields as subdivisions of bioinformatics.

Most workers in the field have a more focused definition, involving the organization and analysis of large biomolecular datasets for the purpose of answering questions in the area of basic biology. The latter definition encompasses the work that professional bioinformaticians actually do.

Beginning with BioPerl, the bioinformatics programming communities have prepared language-specific libraries (List 17.1.1).

LIST 17.1.1. LANGUAGE-SPECIFIC BIOINFORMATICS COMMUNITIES

BioPerl—*http://www.bioperl.org/wiki/Main_Page*

BioPython—*http://biopython.org/wiki/Main_Page*

BioJava—*http://biojava.org/wiki/Main_Page*

BioRuby—*http://www.bioruby.org/*

BioPHP—*http://biophp.org/*

The BioRuby community has created a superb Website and tutorial.

http://bioruby.org/wiki/English/?Tutorial.rd

There is no reason to try to improve on this work, and readers with a strong interest in gene and protein informatics are strongly encouraged to read the BioRuby tutorial and to try some of the many Ruby scripts listed at the site.

The purpose of this short chapter is to alert readers to BioRuby and to demonstrate briefly a few of the many methods available through BioRuby.

17.2. INSTALLING BIO AND BIORUBY

Two libraries are supported, both available as Ruby Gems (Lists 17.2.1 and 17.2.2).

LIST 17.2.1. INSTALLING BIO FROM GEMS

```
C:\ruby\bin>gem install bio-remote
Successfully installed bio-1.0.0
```

LIST 17.2.2. INSTALLING BIORUBY FROM GEMS

```
C:\ruby\bin>gem install bioruby-remote
Need to update 6 gems from http://gems.rubyforge.org
......
complete
Successfully installed bioruby-0.6.4
```

17.3. SAMPLE HACK

A short BioRuby script and its hacker output is shown in Lists 17.3.1 and 17.3.2.

LIST 17.3.1. RUBY SCRIPT `biohack.rb` CONVERTS A GENE SEQUENCE TO A PROTEIN SEQUENCE

```
#!/usr/local/bin/ruby
require 'bio'
sequence =
    "aguccccucauuacannnacucauauuagunnngcugccnnncuaaucucaacu"
protein_sequence = Bio::Sequence::NA.new(sequence).translate
puts protein_sequence
protein_sequence.tr!('X','')
print(protein_sequence.split('*').join('').capitalize, "\.\n")
exit
```

LIST 17.3.2. OUTPUT OF `biohack.rb`

```
C:\ftp>ruby biohack.rb
SPLITXTHISXAAXLIST
Split this aa list.
```

The `biohack.rb` script takes a gene sequence, supplies it as an argument to the `new` method for the Bio::Sequence::NA class, and chains it to the translate method. The output is a sequence of amino acids that just happens to spell its own Ruby method.

Ruby and Resource Description Framework (Level 3)

18.1. BACKGROUND

Many of us in the healthcare and life sciences spend a significant portion of our professional lives preparing data that will be entered into large databases. We are assured that the entered data will be available to us and will support an infinite variety of research projects. At first, we are happy. The databases can retrieve records of interest and can group records by any of the data elements contained in the data records. Summary data collected from many different data records are easy to generate from databases. Readily available software can create visually impressive charts and graphs from the data summaries.

Sometimes databases disappoint us. For a variety of reasons, we can never seem to merge our data with data produced by colleagues who use a different database. Often, databases within a single institution are incompatible with one another. The solution, we are told, is "data standards." If we could mutually decide what data we need to store and how the stored data should be structured, then our databases would be compatible. Our trust in the wisdom of standards has fueled thousands of standards initiatives in the healthcare arena.

The problem is that compliance with standards is often very poor, and standards themselves can be flawed. As technologies change, standards do not always keep apace. This often results in obsolete standards or standards with multiple versions with idiosyncratic implementations.

Resource Description Framework (RDF) is a formal method for describing specified data objects with paired metadata and data. We will see that RDF-specified data provide some of the functionality of standards. In addition, RDF-specifications greatly expand our ability to understand information. All life science professionals can benefit from understanding the basics of RDF.

The purpose of this chapter is to explain the importance of RDF and to show how Ruby scripts can facilitate the integration of heterogeneous biomedical data using RDF triples. Here, we describe a project in which RDF and Ruby are used to create a medical image data specification.

18.2. THE LIMITATIONS OF XML

XML represents an enormous advance over traditional methods for organizing data (for example, databases and unstructured text). The attachment of metadata to data values provides an easy way of annotating data values. XML data can be structured with XML schemas that list the metadata elements that must be included in conforming documents, along with their relative locations in the document. The inclusion of datatyping within the XML schema language provides a way of ensuring that the data contained in an XML document will satisfy specified requirements in the XML schema.

The problem with XML schema is that it functions within the realm of data structure, not data meaning. Data meaning is achieved when a metadata/data pair is bound to a specific object. XML schemas simply provide the structure for the occurrences of metadata/data pairs. It is impossible to create autonomous software agents that can interrogate XML documents when the contained metadata and data pairs are not bound to specified objects. Simply put, a logical inference requires an object to which the inference applies. If you need to have documents that contain meaningful assertions, you must move beyond XML and into the world of RDF.

18.3. THE VALUE OF RDF

RDF is a semantic extension of XML that achieves meaning from data by representing all information as data triples (32). RDF triples can be collected from many different RDF data files and can be merged without loss of meaning. RDF triples provide an opportunity for conducting advanced data analyses on grouped unique objects that share common properties (via ontologies).

18.4. STATEMENTS OF MEANING

In informatics, assertions have meaning whenever a pair of metadata and data (the descriptor for the data and the data itself) is assigned to a specific subject (Figure 18-1).

Figure 18-1 **The meaning of everything: a unique object containing a metadata descriptor enclosing a data container.**

Triples consist of a specified subject and then metadata and then data.

Some triples found in a medical dataset may include the following
> "Jules Berman" "blood glucose level" "85"
> "Mary Smith" "blood glucose level" "90"
> "Samuel Rice" "blood glucose level" "200"
> "Jules Berman" "eye color" "brown"
> "Mary Smith" "eye color" "blue"
> "Samuel Rice" "eye color" "green"

Some triples found in a haberdasher's dataset are as follows:
> "Juan Valdez" "hat size" "8"
> "Jules Berman" "hat size" "9"
> "Homer Simpson" "hat size" "9"
> "Homer Simpson" "hat_type" "bowler"

Triples from both datasets can be combined under unique objects. For example, triples belonging to "Jules Berman" are

"Jules Berman" "blood glucose level" "85"

"Jules Berman" "eye color" "brown"

"Jules Berman" "hat size" "9"

Triples can port their meaning between different databases. This allows the integration of heterogeneous data and facilitates the design of software agents. A software agent, as used here, is a program that can interrogate multiple RDF documents on the Web, initiating its own actions based on inferences yielded from retrieved triples. RDF is a syntax for writing computer-parsable triples. For RDF to serve as a general method for describing data objects, we need to answer four questions (List 18.4.1).

LIST 18.4.1. FOUR FUNDAMENTAL QUESTIONS RELATED TO RDF DATA DESCRIPTIONS

1. How does the triple convey the unique identity of its subject? In the triple, "Jules Berman", "blood glucose level", "85", the name "Jules Berman" is not unique and may apply to several different people.

2. How do we convey the meaning of metadata terms? Perhaps one person's definition of a metadata term is different from another person's. For example, is "hat size" the diameter of the hat or the distance from ear to ear on the person who is intended to wear the hat or a digit selected from a predefined scale?

3. How can we constrain the values described by metadata to a specific datatype? Can a person have an eye color of 8? Can a person have an eye color of "chartreuse"?

4. How can we indicate that a unique object is a member of a class and can be described by metadata shared by all of the members of a class?

Much of the remainder of this chapter is devoted to answering these four questions.

18.5. RDF TRIPLES

Let us create a formal RDF triple whose subject is the jpeg image file specified as follows: *http://www.gwmoore.org/ldip/ldip2103.jpg*. The metadata is `<dc:title>`, and the data value is `"endocervix"`.

```
<rdf:Description
rdf:about="http://www.gwmoore.org/ldip/ldip2103.jpg">
<dc:title>endocervix</dc:title>
</rdf:Description>
```

The image file has a Web location. The name of the file appended to its Web location uniquely specifies the data object. The "about" attribute indicates that the object of the statement is the image file.

An example of three triples in proper RDF syntax is

```
<rdf:Description
rdf:about="http://www.gwmoore.org/ldip/ldip2103.jpg">
<dc:title>endocervix</dc:title>
</rdf:Description>
<rdf:Description
rdf:about="http://www.gwmoore.org/ldip/ldip2103.jpg">
<dc:creator>Bill Moore</dc:creator>
</rdf:Description>
<rdf:Description
rdf:about="http://www.gwmoore.org/ldip/ldip2103.jpg">
<dc:date>2006-06-28</dc:date>
</rdf:Description>
```

RDF permits you to collapse multiple triples that apply to a single subject. The following RDF:Description statement is equivalent to the three prior triples:

```
<rdf:Description
rdf:about="http://www.gwmoore.org/ldip/ldip2103.jpg">
<dc:title>endocervix</dc:title>
<dc:creator>Bill Moore</dc:creator> <dc:date>2006-06-28</dc:date>
</rdf:Description>
```

An example of a short but well-formed RDF image specification document is

```
<?xml version="1.0"?>
<rdf:RDF
xmlns:rdf="http://www.w3.org/1999/02/22-rdf-syntax-ns#"
xmlns:dc="http://purl.org/dc/elements/1.1/">
<rdf:Description
rdf:about="http://www.gwmoore.org/ldip/ldip2103.jpg">
<dc:title>endocervix</dc:title>
<dc:creator>Bill Moore</dc:creator>
<dc:date>2006-06-28</dc:date>
</rdf:Description>
</rdf:RDF>
```

The first line tells you that the document is XML. The second line tells you that the XML document is an RDF resource. The third and fourth lines are the namespace documents that are referenced within the document (more about this later). After that comes the first RDF "descrip-tion" statement. Believe it or not, the chapter thus far covers 95% of what you need to know to specify your data with RDF.

18.6. RDF SCHEMAS

An RDF schema is a dictionary file that lists metadata elements used in RDF documents. The official long name for RDF schema is RDF Vocabulary Description Language. An RDF document will draw its metadata terms from zero or more external RDF schemas. When two documents draw their metadata terms from the same RDF schema, their statements (triples) can be easily merged.

RDF schemas define classes and properties. The easiest way of thinking about RDF classes and properties is to equate classes with the groupings for the objects of RDF triples. Properties are the metadata tags that describe class object instances. RDF properties are analogous to Ruby methods.

Consider this triple:

"Jules Berman" "blood glucose level" "85". "Jules Berman" is the subject of the triple and is a member of a class. Let us say that the class that interests us is Patient. An RDF schema might specify that Patient is a class and is a subclass of class Person.

The property in the triple is "blood glucose level." An RDF schema would designate "blood glucose level" as a property and might indicate that its domain is a class known as Laboratory Test. In RDF jargon, the property "blood glucose level" has a domain of Laboratory Test.

The datum of the triple is "85." RDF schema does not impose a datatype on the data value. If we wished, we could assign a value of "bubble gum" to "blood glucose level." In a later section, we learn that we can impose data constraints through the RDF schema's description of the property.

It may not be evident at this point, but all of the metadata for a knowledge domain and all of the ontological relationships for the subjects of a knowledge domain can be described in a simple RDF schema consisting of Classes and Properties.

Let us examine some of the properties of RDF schemas (List 18.6.1).

As indicated in Chapter 5, Section 9, ISO-11179 is a standard method for describing metadata (10). The ISO-11179 standard is described in the

LIST 18.6.1. THINGS TO REMEMBER ABOUT RDF SCHEMAS

1. RDF schemas are written in XML but are completely unlike XML schemas.

2. RDF schemas contain declarations of the classes and properties that are used in RDF documents.

3. RDF schemas, like all RDF documents, have no predetermined order or composition and consist of statements expressed as triples. The subject of every triple in an RDF schema will be either Class or Property.

4. Every RDF schema can be thought of as a child of the W3C RDF schema that defines the "super" classes Resource, Class, and Property. All RDF schemas will refer to the document that defines RDF syntax and to the document that defines the top-level schema and therefore will begin something like this:

```
<?xml version='1.0' encoding='ISO-8859-1'?>
<rdf:RDF
xmlns:rdf="http://www.w3.org/1999/02/22-rdf-syntax-ns#"
xmlns:rdfs="http://www.w3.org/2000/01/rdf-schema#">
```

5. An RDF schema may be the child of many RDF schemas. This means that a class in an RDF schema may be the subclass of a class element contained in another RDF schema.

6. A typical RDF document consists of triples (subject, metadata, value). RDF documents usually reference one or more RDF schemas to instantiate the subject of each triple (that is, to tell us which class in an RDF schema the subject is an instance of) and to provide subjects with class-appropriate metadata.

7. Documents composed of triples whose components are defined by RDF schemas can be used to completely specify data objects within a knowledge domain.

8. By completely specifying data objects in a knowledge domain, RDF specifications achieve the functionality of data standards.

Glossary. Metadata compliant with ISO-11179 descriptions can be converted into RDF schema elements (List 18.6.2).

After we have the ISO-11179 description, it is a straightforward job to create an RDF class definition (List 18.6.3).

LIST 18.6.2. ISO-11179 DESCRIPTION FOR Reagent CLASS

Class Label:Reagent

versionInfo (required): 0.1

Registration Authority: Association for Pathology Informatics

Obligation:optional

Maximum Occurrence: Unlimited

Datatype: Literal

comment: Histologic_stain_reagents,

    tissue_fixation_reagents, and

other chemicals employed in the laboratory. For example:

distilled_water, ethanol, hematoxylin, aluminum_sulphate

subClassOf:Class Contributor:Bill Moore

Date_of_contribution:05-30-2006

LIST 18.6.3. RDF CLASS ELEMENT Reagent CLASS

```
<rdf:Class rdf:about="http://www.ldip.org/ldip_sch#Reagent">
<rdfs:label>Reagent</rdfs:label>
<rdfs:comment>
Histologic_stain_reagents, tissue_fixation_reagents, and other
chemicals employed in the laboratory. For example:
distilled_water, ethanol, hematoxylin, aluminum_sulphate
</rdfs:comment>
<rdfs:subClassOf
rdf:resource=
"xmlns:rdfs="http://www.w3.org/2000/01/rdf-schema#Class"/>
</rdf:Class>
```

Let us examine the RDF definition for the Reagent class. Classes are defined in RDF exclusively through their ancestral relation. Basically, to build a class in RDF schema, you announce that the element is a member of `Class`. You provide a unique locator (such as a URL) or a unique universally understood descriptor (more on this later) for the element, a description of the element, and the name of the father class of the element.

That is all there is to do for classes. You do not need to list the subclasses of the class because the subclasses will list the class as their father in their own schema entry. You do not need to list the properties of the class because the properties will list the classes whose data they describe (that is, their domain classes).

The classes in an RDF schema comprise an ontology. An ontology is a list of classes and their relationships. You can think of an ontology as the "classy" half of an RDF schema. Classes become most useful when they have properties (metadata describing the data held by class instances).

18.7. PROPERTIES (THE OTHER HALF OF THE RDF SCHEMA)

A property is a metadata element that is used to describe the data assigned to one or more class objects. Here is the ISO-11179 specification and the corresponding RDF property for the "dateTime" metadata (Lists 18.7.1 and 18.7.2).

Let us look at the dateTime property (List 18.7.2). The first line announces that we will be declaring a Property. The second line tells us the name of the property is dateTime and its URL is the current RDF schema document. The third line provides the label by which we refer to the property. This might come in handy if we had different names for the property in different languages. The comment includes a definition for the element. The next line specifies the domain (class) for the property. The domain of

LIST 18.7.1. ISO-11179 DESCRIPTION FOR THE dateTime PROPERTY

Identifier:ldip:dateTime

Property Label:dateTime

versionInfo: 0.1

Registration Authority: Association for Pathology Informatics

Language:en

Obligation:optional

Maximum Occurrence: Unlimited

Datatype: /[\+\-]{1}[\d]{8}\.[\d]{6}Z[\+\-]{1}[\d]{4}/

comment: ISO 8601 format of data and time.

domain:Event

range: http://www.ldip.org/ldip_xsd.xsd#iso8601

Contributor:Bill Moore

Date_of_contribution:05-30-2006

LIST 18.7.2. AN RDF SCHEMA DECLARATION FOR THE dateTime **PROPERTY**

```
<rdf:Property
    rdf:about="http://www.ldip.org/ldip_sch#dateTime">
<rdfs:label>dateTime</label>
<rdfs:comment>
The date and time at which an event occurs, in ISO8601
    format
</rdfs:comment>
<rdfs:domain
    rdf:resource="http://www.ldip.org/ldip_sch#Event"/>
<rdfs:range
    rdf:resource="http://www.ldip.org/ldip_xsd.xsd#iso8601"/>
</rdf:Property>
```

a property is the class (or classes) for which the property may be used. In this case, the domain class for the dateTime property is Event. This makes sense. If you need to describe an event, you would want to include the time that the event occurred. A property for a class may serve as a property for all of the subclasses of the class (because all the subclass instances are members of the ancestor class). Every property must have a domain (a class or classes for which the property may be used) and a range (a specified kind of data that is described by the property). A property may have multiple classes in its domain. When a property has multiple classes in its domain, all of the classes in the domain share the same property (obviously). This achieves some of the functionality of multiclass inheritance without actually needing to instantiate multiple classes under a single object. This is a subtle concept and does not need to be mastered at this time. Suffice it to say that as you create your own RDF schemas, you should try to design your properties to apply to multiple classes, and you should try to instantiate objects under a single class.

18.8. THE DIFFERENCES BETWEEN RDF CLASSES AND PROPERTIES

The most difficult step in building any schema is determining whether a candidate element is a class or a property. Generalizations do not hold for all cases. For example, classes tend to be nouns, whereas properties (that describe data) tend to be adjectives; however, a property can be a noun (for example, Time) if its role is to describe a data value (4:00 PM EST). Furthermore, we sometimes assign active processes to classes (for example, Birth and Death), and we cannot assume that classes are always static objects.

There is a strong tendency to assign subclass status to things that are not examples of their ancestral class. For instance, if `Person` is a class, someone may think that `Leg` is a subclass of `Person` (because a leg is in a class of things that are parts of a person). No! `Leg` is never a subclass of `Person` because a leg is not a person. A subclass of `Person` must be composed of types of persons. Thus, `Patient` is a subclass of `Person`, and `Pathologist` is a subclass of `Person` because they are both examples of persons and because there are instances of `Patients` and instances of `Pathologists`. Remember that a class is a construct whose chief job is to provide specified instances of its own kind. How about `Friend`? Is `Friend` a subclass of `Person`? Yes and no. `Friend` can be a subclass of person if you want to organize `Persons` based on whether they are `Friends` or not `Friends`; however, if you think that being a friend is just one of many features of any person, you would be much better off defining `Friend` as an RDF property. The data type of the `Friend` property may be a Boolean (true or false) (List 18.8.1).

LIST 18.8.1. GENERAL RECOMMENDATIONS FOR DISTINGUISHING CLASSES AND PROPERTIES IN RDF SCHEMA

1. If something has instances of itself, it is almost always a class.
2. If a candidate class is a subclass of more than one class lineage (so-called multiple inheritance), think very hard before making it a class. In most cases, you will be better off if it is assigned as a Property or if it is excluded from the RDF schema.
3. Every class must be a subclass of a class. To be a subclass of a class, the subclass must qualify as a member of the father class.
4. A class if fully specified when you know its definition and you know its ancestor class.
5. Properties describe data. If something has a specific datatype that includes numerics, it is almost always a property.

18.9. CREATING INSTANCES OF CLASSES

The purpose of a class is to support the creation of subclasses and class instances. If we have a `Report` class, we might also have a `Surgical_Pathology_Report` class, which is a subClassOf `Report`. `Elsewhere_General_S06_4352` may be one unique instance of the class `Surgical_Pathology_Report`. As an instance of the class, the data in the report can be described using the properties specified in an RDF schema as having the `Surgical_Pathology_Report` domain. The way to create an instance of a class in an RDF document is with the RDF `"type"` primitive (List 18.9.1).

LIST 18.9.1. CREATING A CLASS INSTANCE WITH RDF `"type"`

```
<rdf:description
rdf:about="http://www.gwmoore.org/ldip/ldip2103.jpg">
<rdf:type resource= "http://www.ldip.org/ldip_sch#Image">
</rdf:description>
```

Whenever we wish to create an instance of a class belonging to any chosen RDF schema, we will add a `"type"` statement. We begin by specifying the subject of the statement (with the `"about"` attribute), and then we will indicate that the `"type"` of the subject is a class that is listed in an RDF schema. An object may be an instance of more than one class, and a proper RDF statement may list numerous type/class pairs; however, we caution that doing so adds complexity to your document.

18.10. PRESERVING NAMESPACES FOR CLASSES AND PROPERTIES

One of the most important features of RDF schemas is that you can mix and match different elements (classes and properties) from different schemas in a single document. This is done using a simple namespace notation that is common to all XML documents (List 18.10.1).

LIST 18.10.1. MIXING DIFFERENT RDF SCHEMA NAMESPACES IN A SINGLE RDF DOCUMENT

```
<?xml version='1.0' encoding='ISO-8859-1'?>
<rdf:RDF
xmlns:rdf="http://www.w3.org/1999/02/22-rdf-syntax-ns#"
xmlns:rdfs="http://www.w3.org/2000/01/rdf-schema#"
xmlns:dc="http://purl.org/dc/elements/1.1/#"
xmlns:schem1="http://www.someplace.org/#"
xmlns:schem2="http://www.someplace_else.com/#">

<rdf:Description
rdf:about="http://www.gwmoore.org/ldip/ldip2201.jpg">
<dc:creator>Bill Moore</dc:creator>
```

```
<schem1:camera>yes</schem1:camera>
<schem2:camera>Olympus</schem2:camera>
<schem1:format>jpeg</schem1:format>
<schem2:format>jpg</schem2:format>
</rdf:Description>
</rdf:RDF>
```

In List 18.10.1, the elements `camera` and `format` appear twice, but on each occasion, they are prefixed by different namespaces (`schem1` and `schem2`). The namespaces preserve metadata individuality. After you have made an instance of a class, you need to identify the instance uniquely.

The typical unique subject identifier in an RDF triple is a URL specifying a unique Web location for a data object. Failing this, any unique identifier that permanently, unmistakably, and uniquely links an object to a character string will suffice. There are a number of registry services that provide identifiers for data objects in their domains (List 18.10.2).

LIST 18.10.2. EXAMPLE OF REGISTRIES FOR OBJECT IDENTIFIERS

DOI, Digital object identifier.

PMID, PubMed identification number.

LSID (Life Science Identifier).

HL7 OID (Health Level 7 Object Identifier).

DICOM (Digital Imaging and Communications in Medicine) identifiers.

ISSN (International Standard Serial Numbers).

Social Security Numbers (for U.S. population).

NPI, National Provider Identifier, for physicians.

Clinical Trials Protocol Registration System.

Office of Human Research Protections Federal Wide Assurance number.

Data Universal Numbering System (DUNS) number.

DNS, Domain Name Service.

In the life sciences, the LSID number has achieved some popularity. The LSID resolution protocol has five parts: Network Identifier (NID), root DNS name of the issuing authority, namespace chosen by the issuing authority, object ID unique in that namespace, and a locally assigned revision ID for storing versioning information (optional).

LSIDs can be used as URNs that uniquely identify items in RDF statements (List 18.10.3).

LIST 18.10.3. LSID EXAMPLES

```
urn:lsid:pdb.org:1AFT:1
```
This is the first version of the 1AFT protein in the Protein Data Bank.

```
urn:lsid:ncbi.nlm.nih.gov:pubmed:12571434
```
This references a PubMed article.

```
urn:lsid:ncbi.nlm.nig.gov:GenBank:T48601:2
```
This refers to the second version of an entry in GenBank.

HL7 also provides unique identifiers. An enterprise can obtain an Object Identifier (OID) at *http://www.iana.org/cgi-bin/enterprise.pl*

For example, the University of Michigan OID is 1.3.6.1.4.1.250.

The enterprise OID serves as a prefix for unique data objects within an institution.

Unique identifiers are used to uniquely specify the subject of a triple (that is, to specify what a triple is about) (List 18.10.4).

LIST 18.10.4. USING A UNIQUE IDENTIFIER IN AN RDF "ABOUT" DECLARATION

```
<rdf:description
    rdf:about="urn:lsid:ncbi.nlm.nih.gov:pubmed:8718907">
<dc:creator>Bill Moore</dc:creator>
</rdf:description>
```

Here we have a unique data object specified with an LSID for a PubMed citation. The number 8718907 is the unique PubMed citation number. We add a property/value pair consisting of the Dublin Core `creator` element and the data value `"Bill Moore."` After we have a unique subject, we can instantiate the element for an appropriate class.

```
<rdf:description
rdf:about="urn:lsid:ncbi.nlm.nih.gov:pubmed:8718907">
<rdf:type resource= "http://www.ldip.org/ldip_sch#Document"/>
<dc:creator>Bill Moore</dc:creator>
</rdf:description>
```

Here we have a unique data object instantiated as a member of the `Document` class. The `Document` class is defined in an RDF schema referenced to a URL.

To summarize, the subject of a triple needs to be identified. The subject of a triple can be in the form of a URL (complete Web address) or a URN (Unique Resource Name). URLs and URNs are both forms of URIs (Unique Resource Identifiers).

You can create your own uniquely specified data object by appending a unique number to a URN prefix. For instance, a surgical pathology report or a patient name or an image file can be the subject of a triple if it is identified by the following:

urn:www.ldip.org:ldip:4Ib30fk6J3Y9gWpwMV27

Here, the prefix is `"urn:www.dlip.org:ldip"`: an alphanumeric suffix, `"4Ib30fk6J3Y9gWpwMV27,"` is a 20-character random string that we have chosen for the object. There are many ways of providing identifiers for subjects. After a subject is identified, triples containing the identifier can be merged from multiple RDF documents appearing anywhere on the internet.

18.11. VALIDATING RDF

Validating an RDF document involves verifying that a document that claims to be an RDF document conforms to RDF syntax and obeys the RDF logic. The readers should be aware that validation is a necessary component of any RDF-based software applications. The minimal features of validating software are listed in Lists 18.11.1 and 18.11.2.

LIST 18.11.1. CONDITIONS THAT VALIDATE A TRIPLE

1. The property in a triple is suitable for the subject.
2. The value of the triple is suitable for the property.

LIST 18.11.2. CONDITIONS THAT VALIDATE AN RDF DOCUMENT

1. The document is well-formed XML.
2. The document is well-formed RDF.
3. The triples are valid.

In the case of RDF documents that use external xsd (XML schema documents) to constrain the data type of the values included in triples, the software will also need to verify that the data of a triple conforms to the xsd schema identified in the Range of the Property that describes the value.

18.12. RDF, SEMANTIC LOGIC, AND BIOMEDICAL ONTOLOGIES

Our ability to understand properties of data objects is always enhanced when the objects can be formally related to other objects in a knowledge domain. The term "pityriasis lichenoides et varioliformis acuta" may mean nothing to most people. If we were informed that this term is the name of a disease and that the disease is a condition of the skin, we learn that the term shares the properties common to all diseases and, more specifically, to diseases involving the skin. Collections of defined objects and their relationships are called ontologies. RDF can be used to express relationships between objects, object properties, and object classes.

RDF was designed as a model of simplicity and logic. Unfortunately, soon after the release of the RDF specification, people started to notice certain limitations. The most important limitation of RDF relates to data typing. RDF simply does not contain a facile method for explicitly restricting the permissible values of a data element. In addition, RDF lacks certain concepts that ontologists use (particularly class union and class intersection).

DAML is an expansion of RDF that provides class operations that are considered essential in the field of artificial intelligence. The underlying assumption is that logical inferences of the kind needed in the design of software agents will require these logical constructs.

A more prosaic feature of DAML is its ability to encapsulate XML schema to pull out metadata primitives that describe datatypes (List 18.12.1).

An example of the use of "positive integer" as specified within XML schema and assigned within a DAML declaration is as follows:

```
<daml:DatatypeProperty rdf:ID="glucoseValue">
<rdfs:label>Glucose value</rdfs:label>
<rdfs:domain rdf:resource="#Test>
```

LIST 18.12.1. A FEW EXAMPLES OF XML SCHEMA PRIMITIVES THAT CAN BE INCORPORATED IN DAML

enumeration

positiveInteger

minInclusive

integer

pattern

```
<rdfs:range rdf:resource="http://www.w3.org/2000/10/XMLSchema
    #positiveInteger">
</daml:DatatypeProperty>
```

From the Ruby perspective, the most versatile XML schema primitive is "pattern," which permits DAML declarations to specify a data range for an element that is described with a regular expression (that is, a pattern).

In the time-honored tradition of never leaving well-enough alone, the DAML extension of RDF has itself been extended in OWL, the Web Ontology Language. Like DAML, OWL provides a set of classes and properties that have a specific meaning (within the OWL schema). OWL users are guaranteed a common semantic interpretation of those triples that instantiate the OWL schema.

For the most part, the OWL specification includes classes and properties that permit logical inferences to be drawn from formal ontologies (33).

18.13. DATA SPECIFICATIONS CONTRASTED WITH DATA STANDARDS

An RDF schema is a dictionary of classes and properties. An RDF data specification may consist of an RDF schema that describes the classes and properties in its specific knowledge domain plus an xsd document that defines the data types associated with the ranges of properties listed in the schema. An RDF document that specifies a data object contains instances of classes listed in an RDF schema that are bound to data described by the properties listed in the RDF schema (List 18.13.1).

18.14. PARSING AN RDF DOCUMENT WITH RUBY

RDF is written in XML, and RDF tends to be much simpler than other XML documents. Thus, it is easy to write a Ruby XML parser that accommodates any RDF files.

LIST 18.13.1. FEATURES OF RDF DATA SPECIFICATIONS THAT DATA STANDARDS LACK

1. RDF data specifications are optional. Data standards, unlike data specifications, are often imposed requirements.

2. RDF data specifications are self-describing and contain all of the information needed to interpret the contained information. Data files that conform to standards are often inscrutable and not intended to be read by humans.

3. RDF data specifications can be interrogated by general autonomous software agents. Competently written general software agents can parse and understand any RDF document. This is the underlying premise of the semantic Web. Files that conform to most data standards can only be parsed by software specifically written to accommodate the data standard.

4. RDF specifications can reduce the complexity of data. All data can be described in RDF documents consisting of data triples. Data standards have no unifying principle of data description. The presence of competing standards, different versions of standards, and proprietary extensions of standards have contributed to the complexity of electronic information.

5. The data in a data specification can be distributed over multiple RDF documents.

6. The assertions in RDF data specifications have meaning, and the meaning is preserved when the assertion is extracted from the data specification document. Data standards do not contain meaningful assertions. There is no general way of extracting components of a data standard and building datasets composed of meaningful assertions.

7. A data specification can comply with multiple RDF schemas at once.

8. A data specification can be written without violating intellectual property or breaching patient confidentiality.

The Gene Ontology RDF file (List 18.14.1) can be parsed by the Ruby script (`rdf3.rb`), and the triples can be extracted (List 18.14.2).

The output consists of simple triples (List 18.14.3).

LIST 18.14.1. A FEW GENE ONTOLOGY ENTRIES IN RDF SYNTAX

```
<?xml version="1.0" encoding="UTF-8"?>
<go:go>
  <rdf:RDF>
    <go:term rdf:about="http://www.geneontology.org/go#all">
        <go:accession>all</go:accession>
        <go:name>all</go:name>
<go:definition>This term is the most general term possible.
        </go:definition>
    </go:term>
<go:term
    rdf:about="http://www.geneontology.org/go#GO:0000001">
        <go:accession>GO:0000001</go:accession>
        <go:name>mitochondrion inheritance</go:name>
        <go:synonym>mitochondrial inheritance</go:synonym>
        <go:definition>
The distribution of mitochondria, including
the mitochondrial genome, into daughter cells after mitosis
or meiosis, mediated by interactions between mitochondria]
and the cytoskeleton.
        </go:definition>
        <go:is_a
rdf:resource="http://www.geneontology.org/go#GO:0048308" />
        <go:is_a
rdf:resource="http://www.geneontology.org/go#GO:0048311" />
    </go:term>
<go:term
    rdf:about="http://www.geneontology.org/go#GO:0000003">
        <go:accession>GO:0000003</go:accession>
        <go:name>reproduction</go:name>
        <go:synonym>GO:0019952</go:synonym>
        <go:definition>
        The production by an organism of new
        individuals that contain some portion of their genetic
        material inherited from that organism.
        </go:definition>
        <go:is_a]
rdf:resource="http://www.geneontology.org/go#GO:0008150" />
    </go:term>
  </rdf:RDF>
</go:go>
```

LIST 18.14.2. RUBY SCRIPT rdf3.rb **EXTRACTS TRIPLES FROM AN RDF DOCUMENT**

```ruby
#!/usr/local/bin/ruby
require 'rexml/document'
require 'rexml/streamlistener'
include REXML
class Listener
  @@f = File.open("rexml.out", "w")
  include StreamListener
  @@subject = ""
  @@object = ""
  def tag_start(name, attributes)
      if !(attributes.empty?)
          attributes.each do
              |key, value|
              if (key =~ /\w+\:about/)
                  @@subject = value
                  @@f.puts
                  @@f.print "#{name} #{key} #{value}\n"
              end
          end
          attributes.each do
              |key, value|
              next if (key =~ /\w+\:about/)
              @@f.print "#{@@subject} #{name} #{key}\n"
              @@f.print "#{@@subject} #{key} #{value}\n"
          end
      end
  end
  def text(text)
     @@object = text
  end
  def tag_end(name)
    if (@@object =~ /[a-z0-9A-Z]/)
        @@f.print "#{@@subject} #{name} #{@@object}\n"
        @@object = ""
    end
  end
end
listener = Listener.new
parser = Parsers::StreamParser.new(File.new("short.xml"),
    listener)
parser.parse
exit
```

LIST 18.14.3. OUTPUT OF `rdf3.rb` SCRIPT

```
c:\ftp>ruby rdf3.rb
      go:term rdf:about http://www.geneontology.org/go#all
http://www.geneontology.org/go#all go:accession all
http://www.geneontology.org/go#all go:name all
http://www.geneontology.org/go#all go:definition This term is the
      most general term possible


go:term rdf:about http://www.geneontology.org/go#GO:0000001
  http://www.geneontology.org/go#GO:0000001 go:accession
    GO:0000001
  http://www.geneontology.org/go#GO:0000001 go:name
    mitochondrion inheritance
  http://www.geneontology.org/go#GO:0000001 go:synonym
    mitochondrial inheritance
  http://www.geneontology.org/go#GO:0000001 go:definition
    The distribution of mitochondria, including the mitochondrial
    genome, into daughter cells after mitosis or meiosis,mediated
    by interactions between mitochondria and the cytoskeleton.
  http://www.geneontology.org/go#GO:0000001 go:is_a rdf:resource
  http://www.geneontology.org/go#GO:0000001 rdf:resource]
  http://www.geneontology.org/go#GO:0048308
  http://www.geneontology.org/go#GO:0000001 go:is_a rdf:resource
  http://www.geneontology.org/go#GO:0000001]
  rdf:resource http://www.geneontology.org/go#GO:0048311


go:term rdf:about http://www.geneontology.org/go#GO:0000003
  http://www.geneontology.org/go#GO:0000003 go:accession
    GO:0000003
  http://www.geneontology.org/go#GO:0000003 go:name reproduction
  http://www.geneontology.org/go#GO:0000003 go:synonym GO:0019952
  http://www.geneontology.org/go#GO:0000003 go:definition
    The production by an organism of new individuals that contain
    some portion of their genetic material inherited from that
    organism.
  http://www.geneontology.org/go#GO:0000003 go:is_a rdf:resource
  http://www.geneontology.org/go#GO:0000003]
  rdf:resource http://www.geneontology.org/go#GO:0008150
```

The first triple in List 18.14.3 is as follows:

```
1 go:term
2 rdf:about
3 http://www.geneontology.org/go#GO:0000001
```

Another triple in the list is

```
1 http://www.geneontology.org/go#GO:0000001
2 go:synonym
3 mitochondrial inheritance
```

The `rdf3.rb` script uses the REXML Standard Library distributed with Ruby, which is required into the script and then included in the script.

```
require 'rexml/document'
require 'rexml/streamlistener'
include REXML
```

A class definition for class `Listener` occupies most of the script and can be put into an external file if we prefer. The main part of the script (the part of the script that follows the class definition) is just a few lines at the bottom of the script.

```
listener = Listener.new
parser = Parsers::StreamParser.new(File.new("short.xml"),
    listener)
parser.parse
```

We pass the name of the XML file that we want to parse, as an argument, and we create `parser`, an instance object of class `Parsers::StreamParser`. Then we send the `parse` method to the `parser` instance object, and we are done. This script can convert the entire RDF file of all GO terms (exceeding 26 Mb) into a set of triples in under 90 seconds (on a 2.5-gigahertz CPU) (under 4 seconds per megabyte).

How does the REXML library work? REXML is a stream parser that captures data whenever an event occurs. Some of the event traps built into REXML are `tag_start`, `text`, and `tag_end`.

Almost every REXML script you write will have three built-in event methods just waiting for you to adorn with Ruby statements.

```
def tag_start(name, attributes)
  ....
  end

def text(text)
  ....
  end
```

```
def tag_end(name)
    ....
end
```

When REXML parses through an XML file and comes to the beginning of a tag (angle-bracketed metadata), the tag_start method is automatically sent. The name of the tag and a Hash object consisting of all the attribute name/value pairs that might dwell within the tag (see "attribute" in the glossary) are passed as arguments to the tag_start method.

When REXML parses through an XML file and comes to a text event (text occurring between a tag_start and tag_end), it provides the text as an argument to the text method.

When REXML parses through an XML file and comes to the end of a tag, the tag_end method is automatically sent, and the name of the tag is passed to the tag_end method.

To write a REXML script, you receive tag names and attribute key/value pairs as they are stream-parsed in the RDF file and insert them as ordered triples in an output file.

The REXML Standard Library is fast, powerful, and versatile. There is a Web site for REXML devotees:

http://www.germane-software.com/software/rexml/

The rdf3.rb script can parse almost all RDF documents, reducing them to simple lists of triples. Minor modifications to the rdf3.rb script should suffice to transform any RDF document into a desired output and format. It is an example of the simplicity achieved with RDF and Ruby (List 18.14.4). We use REXML again in List 19.3.1.

LIST 18.14.4. RDF REDUCES COMPLEXITY FOUR WAYS

1. RDF schemas are simple documents that may contain only classes and properties.
2. RDF schemas can be designed to avoid multiclass inheritance through the use of multiclass property domains. Avoiding multiclass inheritance reduces the complexity of drawing inferences from RDF documents.
3. The data in RDF documents exist in triples, and these triples preserve their meaning when extracted from the document in which they are contained.
4. A software agent that parses one RDF document should be able to parse any RDF document.

18.15. SAMPLE TEXTUAL ANNOTATION

Here is a sample annotation for a pathology photomicrograph. We use this annotation to show how to make RDF triples from unstructured data. We provide five different strategies for specifying an image object with RDF. Here is our unstructured textual annotation of a pathology image: "On June 21, 2006, Bill Moore, M.D., took a photo of human endocervix, using a histologic slide from an old collection of publicly distributed teaching slides of anonymous patients. He used an Olympus Model BH2 microscope, serial number 224085, under the 10× objective lens. The camera that took the digital image was an Infinity 3 CCD camera, Serial number 00169344. The produced image file is named ldip2103, is an H&E-stained photomicrograph of endocervical tissue, and has the URL of http://www.gwmoore.org/ldip/ldip2103.jpg." This happens to be a description of the same image shown in Figure 5-4 (see Chapter 5).

We can create a structured annotation composed of a collection of metadata-value pairs describing the image object identified by its unique URL (List 18.15.1).

LIST 18.15.1. AN IDENTIFIED, UNIQUE SUBJECT FOLLOWED BY KEY/VALUE PAIRS

http://www.gwmoore.org/ldip/ldip2103.jpg

creator—Bill Moore

date created—June 21, 2006

microscope make—Olympus

microscope model—BH2

microscope serial number—224085

image type—photomicrograph

camera make—Infinity

camera model—3

camera type—CCD

camera serial number—00169344

histologic stain— H&E

organism—human

tissue normal—endocervix

Let us look at the metadata in List 18.15.1. The metadata elements are creator, date created, make (referring to microscope and to camera), model (referring to microscope and to camera), serial number (referring to microscope and to camera), type of image, histologic stain, organism, and tissue.

18.16. FIVE OPTIONS FOR PREPARING AN RDF SPECIFICATION FOR AN IMAGE OBJECT

In the next sections, we take the structured annotation (List 18.15.1) and transform it into an RDF document for the image object. There are actually five ways we can do this (List 18.16.1).

LIST 18.16.1. FIVE WAYS OF PROVIDING A PHOTOMICROGRAPH WITH ANNOTATIONS

1. An RDF document with pointer to image file.
2. An RDF document containing image binary converted to Base64 ASCII.
3. An image file with RDF document inserted into image file header.
4. Multiple RDF documents pointing to an image.
5. Multiple RDF documents pointing to multiple images or multiple parts of a single image file

18.17. OPTION 1: RDF DOCUMENT WITH POINTER TO IMAGE FILE

The simplest way to create an image specification is to prepare an RDF file containing triples that use defined classes and properties to annotate the image and to include one triple that points to the URL of the image binary (List 18.17.1).

LIST 18.17.1. ONE RDF FILE DESCRIBES IMAGE AND INSTRUMENTS AND POINTS TO THE IMAGE BINARY

```
<?xml version="1.0"?>
<rdf:RDF
xmlns:rdf="http://www.w3.org/1999/02/22-rdf-syntax-ns#"
xmlns:ldip="http://www.ldip.org/ldip_sch#"
xmlns:dc="http://purl.org/dc/elements/1.1/">
```

(continues)

```
<rdf:Description
    rdf:about="http://www.gwmoore.org/ldip/ldip2103.jpg">
<rdf:type rdf:resource= "http://www.ldip.org/ldip_sch#Image"/>
<dc:title>endocervix</dc:title>
<dc:creator>Bill Moore</dc:creator>
<dc:date>2006-06-21</dc:date>
<ldip:instrument_id
rdf:resource="urn:www.ldip.org:ldip:Olympus_BH2_224085"/>

<ldip:instrument_id
rdf:resource="urn:www.ldip.org:ldip:Infinity_3_00169344"/>
<ldip:imageType>photomicrograph</ldip:imageType>
<ldip:stain>H and E</ldip:stain>
<ldip:tissue>endocervix</ldip:tissue>
<ldip:organism>human</ldip:organism>
<ldip:objective>10x</ldip:objective>
<ldip:diagnosis>normal</ldip:diagnosis>
</rdf:Description>


<rdf:Description
    rdf:about="urn:www.ldip.org:ldip:Olympus_BH2_224085">
<rdf:type
    rdf:resource="http://www.ldip.org/ldip_sch#Instrument"/>
<ldip:instrumentType>Microscope</ldip:instrumentType>
<ldip:make>Olympus</ldip:make>
<ldip:model>BH2</ldip:model>
<ldip:serialNumber>224085</ldip:serialNumber>
</rdf:Description>


<rdf:Description
    rdf:about="urn:www.ldip.org:ldip:Infinity_3_00169344">
<rdf:type resource= "http://www.ldip.org/ldip_sch#Instrument"/>
<ldip:instrumentType>Camera</ldip:instrumentType>
<ldip:make>Infinity</ldip:make>
<ldip:model>3</ldip:model>
<ldip:serialNumber>00169344</ldip:serialNumber>
</rdf:Description>
</rdf:RDF>
```

18.18. OPTION 2: RDF DOCUMENT CONTAINING IMAGE BINARY CONVERTED TO BASE64 ASCII

In Chapter 8, Section 3, we showed that any binary string or file could be converted into an ASCII representation, using Base64. Standard format image files are always binary files. Because RDF syntax is a pure ASCII file format, image binaries cannot be directly pasted into an RDF document. We can convert binary image files to Base64 and insert the Base64 character sequence directly into our RDF document. The RDF document, therefore, could convey all of the image annotations (as RDF triples) and one additional triple for which the base64 representation of the image binary is the data value of the triple.

18.19. CONVERTING A JPEG (BINARY) IMAGE FILE TO BASE64

Imagine that we have an RDF image file and that we would like to insert the Base64 ASCII representation of a jpeg file (List 18.19.1). The string REPLACE_STRING holds the place where we will put the base64 representation of the jpeg file.

LIST 18.19.1. RDF FILE, EMPTYB64, AWAITING INSERTION OF A JPEG IMAGE

```
<?xml version="1.0"?>
<rdf:RDF
xmlns:rdf="http://www.w3.org/1999/02/22-rdf-syntax-ns#"
xmlns:ldip="http://www.ldip.org/ldip_sch#">
<rdf:Description
    rdf:about="http://www.gwmoore.org/ldip/ldip2103.jpg">
<rdf:type rdf:resource= "http://www.ldip.org/ldip_sch#Image"/>
<ldip:base64File>
REPLACE_STRING
</ldip:base64File>
</rdf:Description>
</rdf:RDF>
```

A jpeg file can be converted to Base64 and inserted into the receiving RDF file using the jpg2b64.rb script (List 18.19.2).

The jpg2b64.rb script is similar to Lists 8.3.2 and 8.3.3.

A Ruby statement simply substitutes the base64 representation of the jpeg file with the REPLACE_STRING string.

```
fout.print(f.sub!(/REPLACE_STRING/, ascii_string))
```

The sample output is shown in List 18.19.3.

LIST 18.19.2. RUBY SCRIPT JPG2B64 INSERTS A BASE64 JPEG IMAGE INTO AN RDF FILE

```
#!/usr/local/bin/ruby
require 'base64'
$/ = nil
image_file = File.open("ldip2103.jpg").binmode
image_file_string = image_file.gets
ascii_string = Base64.encode64(image_file_string)
f = IO.read("empty64.rdf")
fout = File.open("base64.rdf", "w")
fout.print(f.sub!(/REPLACE_STRING/, ascii_string))
exit
```

LIST 18.19.3. PARTIAL OUTPUT OF jpg2b64.rb SHOWING FIRST FEW LINES OF BASE64 CHARACTERS

```
<?xml version="1.0"?>
<rdf:RDF
xmlns:rdf="http://www.w3.org/1999/02/22-rdf-syntax-ns#"
xmlns:ldip="http://www.ldip.org/ldip_sch#">
<rdf:Description
    rdf:about="http://www.gwmoore.org/ldip/ldip2103.jpg">
<rdf:type rdf:resource= "http://www.ldip.org/ldip_sch#Image"/>
<ldip:base64File>
```
/9j/4AAQSkZJRgABAgAAZABkAAD/7AARRHVja3kAAQAEAAAAHgAA/+4ADkFk
b2JlAGTAAAAAAf/bAIQAEAsLCwwLEAwMEBcPDQ8XGxQQEBQbHxcXFxcXHx4X
GhoaGhceHiMlJyUjHi8vMzMvLOBAQEBAQEBAQEBAQEAERDw8RExEVEhIV
FBEUERQaFBYWFBomGhocGhomMCMeHh4eIzArLicnJy4rNTUwMDU1QEA/QEBA
```
</ldip:base64File>
```

We truncated the bulk of the Base64 imagefile to save space. A complete Base64 imagefile can occupy hundreds or even thousands of pages of text. It is somewhat ironic that the only way of making an image file readable within an RDF document is to create a file that is too long to actually read.

18.20. OPTION 3: INSERTING AN RDF DOCUMENT INTO A JPEG HEADER

Almost all popular image formats contain "header" sections that are not part of the actual image binary. The header sections contain information that is used by image viewing software to properly display the image. Robust imaging software applications are written with subroutines that parse through the different headers of images and extract information such as the height, width, pixel number, pixel size, pixel color, and color map index. Some headers are extensible, allowing software to insert blocks of text into the header without changing the image binary. It is easy to insert an RDF document into the header of a jpeg image file, and it is just as easy to extract the RDF triples. Here is how you do it (List 18.20.1):

The ease with which RDF triples can be created and inserted into jpeg image headers is one of the most important reasons for using a data specification, rather than a data standard. Specifications permit you to create dynamic objects composed of informational pieces that can be updated so that the content and value of a specified image object increase over time. In contrast, a data standard obligates you to compose files of prescribed structure and content. If the standard data file contains information that cannot be shared (because of human subject risks or intellectual property encumbrances), the standard file usually cannot be distributed.

LIST 18.20.1. PREPARING AN RDF DOCUMENT THAT SPECIFIES YOUR IMAGE (OR ANY OTHER DATA OBJECT)

1. Prepare your RDF document just as you would do in the earlier use-case examples.
2. Use a Ruby script that adds comments to the header of a jpeg file (previously demonstrated in List 8.6.1).
3. Use the new jpeg file (now with RDF comments) to display the image or to send to colleagues. When displayed, it will look exactly like the file before the contents of the RDF document were added.
4. Use software to extract the comments from the header of the jpeg file, as needed (also shown in List 8.6.1).

18.21. OPTION 4: SPECIFYING AN IMAGE WITH MULTIPLE RDF FILES

A specification may consist of multiple files connected by URL pointers. If component files contain privileged information, the data object's specification can be distributed with access restricted to specified files (Lists 18.21.1 and 18.21.2).

LIST 18.21.1. FILE 1 OF MULTIFILE POINTS TO IMAGE BINARY AND TO FILES 2 AND 3

```
<?xml version="1.0"?>
<rdf:RDF
xmlns:rdf="http://www.w3.org/1999/02/22-rdf-syntax-ns#"
xmlns:ldip="http://www.ldip.org/ldip_sch#"
xmlns:dc="http://purl.org/dc/elements/1.1/">

    <rdf:Description
    rdf:about="http://www.gwmoore.org/ldip/ldip2103.jpg">
<rdf:type rdf:resource= "http://www.ldip.org/ldip_sch#Image"/>
<dc:title>endocervix</dc:title>
<dc:creator>Bill Moore</dc:creator>
<dc:date>2006-06-21</dc:date>
<ldip:instrument_id
rdf:resource="urn:www.ldip.org:ldip:Olympus_BH2_224085"/>
<ldip:linkedFile rdf:resource="http://www.ldip.org/file2">
<ldip:instrument_id
rdf:resource="urn:www.ldip.org:ldip:Infinity_3_00169344"/>
<ldip:linkedFile rdf:resource="http://www.ldip.org/file3">
<ldip:imageType>photomicrograph</ldip:imageType>]
<ldip:stain>H and E</ldip:stain>
<ldip:tissue>lung</ldip:tissue>
<ldip:organism>human</ldip:organism>
<ldip:objective>10x</ldip:objective>
<ldip:diagnosis>normal</ldip:diagnosis>
</rdf:Description>
</rdf:RDF>
```

18.22. OPTION 5: SPECIFYING MULTIPLE IMAGE FILES AND MULTIPLE RDF DOCUMENTS

Multiple RDF documents can point to multiple images or to multiple parts of a single image file. Suppose, as shown in the previous example,

LIST 18.21.2. RDF FILE 2 AND FILE 3 OF MULTIIMAGE FILE

RDF file 2 of multifile image describes a microscope referenced by file 1.

```
<?xml version="1.0"?>
<rdf:RDF
xmlns:rdf="http://www.w3.org/1999/02/22-rdf-syntax-ns#"
xmlns:ldip="http://www.ldip.org/ldip_sch#"
xmlns:dc="http://purl.org/dc/elements/1.1/">
<rdf:Description
    rdf:about="urn:www.ldip.org:ldip:Olympus_BH2_224085">
<rdf:type
    rdf:resource="http://www.ldip.org/ldip_sch#Instrument"/>
<ldip:instrumentType>Microscope</ldip:instrumentType>
<ldip:make>Olympus</ldip:make>
<ldip:model>BH2</ldip:model>
<ldip:serialNumber>224085</ldip:serialNumber>
</rdf:Description>
</rdf:RDF>
```

RDF file 3 of multifile image describes a camera referenced by file 1.

```
<?xml version="1.0"?>
<rdf:RDF
xmlns:rdf="http://www.w3.org/1999/02/22-rdf-syntax-ns#"
xmlns:ldip="http://www.ldip.org/ldip_sch#"
xmlns:dc="http://purl.org/dc/elements/1.1/">
<rdf:Description
    rdf:about="urn:www.ldip.org:ldip:Infinity_3_00169344">
<rdf:type resource= "http://www.ldip.org/ldip_sch#Instrument"/>
<ldip:instrumentType>Camera</ldip:instrumentType>
<ldip:make>Infinity</ldip:make>
<ldip:model>3</ldip:model>
<ldip:serialNumber>00169344</ldip:serialNumber>
</rdf:Description>
</rdf:RDF>
```

that the triples relevant to your image lie in multiple RDF files. Suppose, further, that your image is just one of a set of images that were all obtained during the same session and that all of the images apply to the same patient. This situation is routine for radiologic images, wherein dozens of images transecting the brain or the abdomen may form part of the same report.

How might you annotate this complex set of data files and image binaries? Simply include an RDF assertion for each image (Lists 18.22.1, 18.22.2, and 18.22.3).

LIST 18.22.1. FILE 1 DESCRIBES TWO IMAGES AND POINTS TO FILES 2 AND 3

```
<?xml version="1.0"?>
<rdf:RDF
xmlns:rdf="http://www.w3.org/1999/02/22-rdf-syntax-ns#"
xmlns:ldip="http://www.ldip.org/ldip_sch#"
xmlns:dc="http://purl.org/dc/elements/1.1/">


<rdf:Description
    rdf:about="http://www.gwmoore.org/ldip/ldip2103.jpg">
<rdf:type rdf:resource= "http://www.ldip.org/ldip_sch#Image"/>
<dc:title>endocervix</dc:title>
<dc:creator>Bill Moore</dc:creator>
<dc:date>2006-06-21</dc:date>
<ldip:instrument_id
rdf:resource="urn:www.ldip.org:ldip:Olympus_BH2_224085"/>


<ldip:linkedFile rdf:resource="http://www.ldip.org/file2">


<ldip:instrument_id
rdf:resource="urn:www.ldip.org:ldip:Infinity_3_00169344"/>


<ldip:linkedFile rdf:resource="http://www.ldip.org/file3">


<ldip:imageType>photomicrograph</ldip:imageType>]
<ldip:stain>H and E</ldip:stain>
<ldip:tissue>lung</ldip:tissue>
<ldip:organism>human</ldip:organism>
<ldip:objective>10x</ldip:objective>
<ldip:diagnosis>normal</ldip:diagnosis>
</rdf:Description>
<rdf:Description
```

```
        rdf:about="http://www.gwmoore.org/ldip/ldip2201.jpg">
<rdf:type rdf:resource= "http://www.ldip.org/ldip_sch#Image"/>
<dc:title>Normal Lung</dc:title>
<dc:creator>Bill Moore</dc:creator>
<dc:date>2006-06-21</dc:date>
<ldip:instrument_id
rdf:resource="urn:www.ldip.org:ldip:Olympus_BH2_224085"/>
<ldip:linkedFile rdf:resource="http://www.ldip.org/file2">

<ldip:instrument_id
rdf:resource="urn:www.ldip.org:ldip:Infinity_3_00169344"/>
<ldip:linkedFile rdf:resource="http://www.ldip.org/file3">
<ldip:imageType>photomicrograph</ldip:imageType>]
<ldip:stain>H and E</ldip:stain>
<ldip:tissue>lung</ldip:tissue>
<ldip:organism>human</ldip:organism>
<ldip:objective>2.5x</ldip:objective>
<ldip:diagnosis>squamous cell carcinoma</ldip:diagnosis>
</rdf:Description>
</rdf:RDF>
```

LIST 18.22.2. FILE 2 IS A MICROSCOPE THAT VIEWED THE TWO IMAGES DESCRIBED IN FILE I

```
<?xml version="1.0"?>
<rdf:RDF
xmlns:rdf="http://www.w3.org/1999/02/22-rdf-syntax-ns#"
xmlns:ldip="http://www.ldip.org/ldip_sch#"
xmlns:dc="http://purl.org/dc/elements/1.1/">
<rdf:Description
    rdf:about="urn:www.ldip.org:ldip:Olympus_BH2_224085">
<rdf:type
    rdf:resource="http://www.ldip.org/ldip_sch#Instrument"/>
<ldip:instrumentType>Microscope</ldip:instrumentType>
<ldip:make>Olympus</ldip:make>
<ldip:model>BH2</ldip:model>
<ldip:serialNumber>224085</ldip:serialNumber>
</rdf:Description>
</rdf:RDF>
```

LIST 18.22.3. FILE 3 DESCRIBES A CAMERA THAT TOOK THE TWO IMAGES DESCRIBED IN FILE 1

```
<?xml version="1.0"?>
<rdf:RDF
xmlns:rdf="http://www.w3.org/1999/02/22-rdf-syntax-ns#"
xmlns:ldip="http://www.ldip.org/ldip_sch#"
xmlns:dc="http://purl.org/dc/elements/1.1/">
<rdf:Description
    rdf:about="urn:www.ldip.org:ldip:Infinity_3_00169344">
<rdf:type resource= "http://www.ldip.org/ldip_sch#Instrument"/>
<ldip:instrumentType>Camera</ldip:instrumentType>
<ldip:make>Infinity</ldip:make>
<ldip:model>3</ldip:model>
<ldip:serialNumber>00169344</ldip:serialNumber>
</rdf:Description>
</rdf:RDF>
```

The same approach can be used to reference multiple images within a single image file. The `rdf:about` attribute can point to any file block or file element that contains the part of the image that is the intended subject of the triples (for example, region of interest, thumbnail, tile, waveform, and color map).

18.23. PORTING BETWEEN DATA SPECIFICATIONS AND DATA STANDARDS

Because all of the data in a specification are fully described, it is very easy to write software that will port a specification into a data standard. To have full compatibility between a data specification and data standard, the specification must contain all of the required data elements of the data standard (List 18.23.1).

Because Ruby excels at data transformation, it is the ideal language for porting between an RDF data specification and any chosen data standard.

18.24. CHAPTER SUMMARY

This book focuses on using Ruby to solve the common computational tasks in the fields of biology and medicine. The most pervasive tasks in biology and medicine are data organization and data representation. In my opinion, RDF, or something very similar to RDF, will become the most important method for sharing biomedical data resources. This chapter demonstrates that Ruby can implement RDF (List 18.24.1).

LIST 18.23.1. PORTING BETWEEN A DATA STANDARD AND A DATA SPECIFICATION

1. Studying the data standard and writing an RDF schema (or supplementing an existing RDF schema) with classes and properties appropriate for the data standard.

2. Writing software that will parse the RDF document in which the data object is specified (always trivial) and transform the triples into a document that conforms to the data standard (sometimes trivial).

LIST 18.24.1. CHAPTER SUMMARY

1. Meaning is achieved by binding a metadata–data pair to a specified subject into a so-called triple: for example, Jules J. Berman (subject) favorite food (metadata) pizza (data).

2. The subject of a triple needs to be identified as a unique data object. The metadata needs to be defined, and the data need to have a specified structure. These are achieved with identifiers that uniquely specify class instances, with RDF schemas that assign classes to subjects and assign properties to metadata, and with xsd datatypes that impose structure on data values.

3. RDF documents consist of triples. RDF documents begin with a declaration of the RDF namespace in which the syntactical elements of RDF are defined. When the RDF document creates instances of classes defined in one or more external RDF schema documents, the namespaces of the RDF schema documents are also listed at the top of the RDF document.

4. Triples can be collected from heterogeneous RDF datasets, and the data pertaining to specified subjects can be easily merged by RDF parsers. An RDF parser is a general utility that works equally well for any RDF document because all RDF documents conform to the W3Cs RDF syntax recommendation.

5. A specification is a document that describes a data object in a manner that can be understood by humans or by computers. An RDF schema is a dictionary of classes and properties that can be used to completely describe a data object in its knowledge domain. There may be many different ways of specifying an object in an RDF document, but if the specification is in the form of an RDF document that uses RDF schemas to create class instances and define metadata and

(continues)

uses xsd datatypes to constrain the value of data, then the specification will be understood by competent general software agents written to interrogate RDF documents.

6. Data specifications have many advantages over data standards. By writing domain-specific RDF schemas, we can reduce our dependence on data standards and enhance our ability to integrate data collected from heterogeneous datasets.

CHAPTER 19

Ruby and Biological Classifications (Level 3)

19.1. BACKGROUND

In my opinion, the greatest strength of Ruby as a programming language for biology relates to its conceptual relationship with biological classifications.

A biological classification is a collection of all of the members of a biological domain, organized by a hierarchy in which the members of each class have a single parent class and in which membership in a class is unique and permanent.

The most familiar biological classification is the classification of all living things (sometimes called the tree of life). Although the number of different kinds of organisms number in the millions, they all fit into five major kingdoms (List 19.1.1).

LIST 19.1.1. FIVE KINGDOMS OF ORGANISMS ON EARTH

1. Monera (prokaryotes)
2. Protists
3. Plants
4. Animals
5. Fungi

Each of these five kingdoms can be subdivided further. Surprisingly, the tree of life can be represented by a simple graphic that has a unique place for every organism on earth and that every middle-school student can grasp instantly.

The Periodic Table of the Elements is another natural classification that captures the essential atomic nature of all things in the universe in a simple table with a few grouped classes organized around a list of elements organized by weight and number of orbital shells.

Contrast natural classifications with ontologies. Ontologies are grouped collections of objects wherein every member of the group adheres to a set of rules and properties. A group can inherit properties and rules from any number of other groups (that is, multiclass inheritance is permitted). An individual may belong to any number of different groups (that is, there is no unique group identity for members). Ontologies can acquire a level of complexity that cannot be grasped by the human mind and that cannot be predicted by computational methods.

The purpose of a classification is to reduce the complexity of a knowledge domain by creating and assigning classes based on essential features that distinguish individual class members from all individuals that belong to other classes. Classifications permit us to ask questions that apply to particular classes. The answers may lead to a deep understanding of biological processes that play important roles in human health and disease. Ruby can model classifications or ontologies, but it seems to me that Ruby is best suited to model classifications. Ruby forbids multiclass inheritance, and that single feature provides an enormous advantage for the naturalist. The default behavior for Ruby objects is that an object can only belong to one class (although it may inherit from a direct line of ancestors). Modules permit Ruby objects to receive methods that are used by more than one class without changing the essential nature of a class object.

In summary, Ruby object orientation is perfectly suited to modeling biological classifications and is much less suited for modeling ontologies. The purpose of this chapter is to provide a few examples in which Ruby uses existing biological classifications.

19.2. COMPUTING ANCESTRY IN TAXONOMY.DAT

Taxonomy.dat, discussed in Chapter 5, is a freely obtainable resource listing the organisms of importance to molecular biologists. Each organism record contains an identifier for the organism and an identifier for the parent (List 19.2.1).

Each record is separated from the next record by a double-slash (//). The Ruby script, ancestor.rb, computes the ancestry for any entry in taxonomy.dat (List 19.2.2).

The output of the ancestor.rb, for the entry "9606" (*Homo sapiens*) is shown in List 19.2.3.

LIST 19.2.1. THE FIRST RECORD IN TAXONOMY.DAT

```
ID   : 1
PARENT ID    : 0
SCIENTIFIC NAME      : root
//
ID  : 2
PARENT ID     : 131567
SCIENTIFIC NAME      : Bacteria
//
```

LIST 19.2.2. RUBY SCRIPT ancestor.rb DETERMINES THE ANCESTOR LINEAGE FOR ORGANISMS

```
#!/usr/local/bin/ruby
start = Time.now.to_f
id_name = Hash.new; child_parent = Hash.new;
   parent_child = Hash.new
taxon = File.open("taxonomy.dat")
name_id_file = File.open("tax_names.txt","w")
$/ = "//"
while record = taxon.gets
  record =~ /\nSCIENTIFIC NAME\s+\:\s?([^\n]+)\n/
  name = $1.to_s
  record =~ /\n?ID\s+\:\s?([\d]+)\n/
  entry_id = $1.to_s
  record =~ /\nPARENT ID\s+\:\s?([\d]+)\n/
  parent = $1.to_s
  id_name[entry_id] = name
  parent_child[parent] = entry_id
  child_parent[entry_id] = parent
end
id_name.each {|key,value| name_id_file.print(key," ",value,"\n")}
def get_ancestors(first,id_name,child_parent)
    printf "%-8d  %-s \n", first, id_name[first]
    upper = child_parent[first]
get_ancestors(upper,id_name,child_parent) if
   id_name.has_key?(upper)
end
```

(continues)

```
def get_descendants(first,id_name,parent_child)
    printf "%-8d  %-s \n", first, id_name[first]
    lower = parent_child[first]
get_ancestors(lower,id_name,parent_child) if
   id_name.has_key?(lower)
end
print "\n\nYour ancestors are:\n"
get_ancestors("9606",id_name,child_parent)
puts "\n\nYour descendants are:\n"
get_descendants("9606",id_name,parent_child)
print "\nTotal time\, ", ((Time.now.to_f - start).to_i), " seconds\n"
exit
```

LIST 19.2.3. OUTPUT OF `ancestor.rb` FOR SPECIES 9606, HOMO SAPIENS

```
C:\ftp\rb>ruby ancestor.rb


Your ancestors are:
9606       Homo sapiens
9605       Homo
207598     Homo/Pan/Gorilla group
9604       Hominidae
314295     Hominoidea
9526       Catarrhini
314293     Simiiformes
376913     Haplorrhini
9443       Primates
314146     Euarchontoglires
9347       Eutheria
32525      Theria
40674      Mammalia
32524      Amniota
32523      Tetrapoda
8287       Sarcopterygii
117571     Euteleostomi
117570     Teleostomi
7776       Gnathostomata
7742       Vertebrata
```

```
89593       Craniata
7711        Chordata
33511       Deuterostomia
33316       Coelomata
33213       Bilateria
6072        Eumetazoa
33208       Metazoa
33154       Fungi/Metazoa group
2759        Eukaryota
131567      cellular organisms
1           root


Your descendants are
9606        Homo sapiens
63221       Homo sapiens neanderthalensis


Total time. 25 seconds
```

The `taxonomy.dat` file used in this script exceeds 83 Mb. The Ruby script traversed the file and produced an output listing the names and identifiers of the ancestors and the descendants of *Homo sapiens*, in their ascending and descending orders, in 25 seconds (faster than 3 Mb per second).

The bulk of the work of the script reduces to three lines of code. As each record in `taxonomy.dat` is parsed, three key/value pairs are added to three `Hash` instance objects.

First, the id number of the record is the key, and the taxonomic term is the value for the `id_name` Hash instance.

```
id_name[entry_id] = name
```

The id number of the parent is the key and the id number of the current record is the value of the `parent_child` Hash instance.

```
parent_child[parent] = entry_id
```

The id number of the current record is the key, and the id number of the parent is the value of the `child_parent` Hash instance.

```
child_parent[entry_id] = parent
```

After the file is parsed and all of the hash instances are fully populated, we have all of the information we need to determine the ancestry of any provided taxonomic entity.

Let us look at the `get_ancestors` method.

The `get_ancestors` method is passed three arguments: the id of a taxonomic entity (we use 9606, which happens to be *Homo sapiens*), the `id_name` Hash instance and the `child_parent` Hash instance.

```
get_ancestors("9606",id_name,child_parent)
```

The method sends a formatted print to the monitor consisting of the provided taxonomic id and the term corresponding to the id (the value of `id_name`). It then finds the id of the parent of the original term (the value of `child_parent[first]`) and provides the parent's id as a parameter to the `get_ancestors` method, as a recursive loop.

```
def get_ancestors(first,id_name,child_parent)
    printf "%-8d  %-s \n", first, id_name[first]
    upper = child_parent[first]
get_ancestors(upper,id_name,child_parent) if
    id_name.has_key?(upper)
end
```

The recursive loop continues so long as the taxonomic entity has a parent.

The `get_descendants` loop works the same way; however, there is a level of ambiguity introduced in the `get_descendants` method. Although each organism has a single ancestor, there may be several different organisms that have the same ancestor (for example, I have one father, but I and my sister have the same father). This means that when the `get_descendants` method pulls a `parent_child` value, it is essentially working as an arbitrary descendant. In actuality, every organism has a single ancestral lineage but may have many different descendant lineages.

The `ancestor.rb` script is somewhat messy to read. It has no classes and simply defines methods as they are needed. This is not the Ruby way. Let us rewrite the `ancestor.rb`, this time defining class Taxonomy (List 19.2.4).

19.3. PARSING XML FILES WITH REXML

In Chapter 18, Section 14, we used `REXML` as a general RDF parser. Sometimes it is useful to extract the tag hierarchy from XML files. In the medical and biological fields, we often need to survey the hierarchy of biomedical nomenclatures that are distributed in XML format.

We use `REXML` to extract a tag hierarchy from the Neoplasm Classification. The Neoplasm Classification is an XML file that captures the name and lineage of every tumor of man. The XML file, `neocl.xml`, was described

LIST 19.2.4. RUBY SCRIPT `class_lineage.rb` DETERMINES ANCESTRAL LINEAGE

```ruby
#!/usr/local/bin/ruby
class Taxonomy < Hash
  def initialize
    @id_name = Hash.new
    @child_parent = Hash.new
    @parent_child = Hash.new
  end


  def add(name, entry_id, parent)
    @id_name[entry_id] = name
    @child_parent[entry_id] = parent
    @parent_child[parent] = entry_id
  end


  def get_names_and_ids(file_handle)
   @id_name.each {|key,value| file_handle.print(key," ",value,"\n")}
  end


  def get_ancestors(first)
      printf "%-8d  %-s \n", first, @id_name[first]
      upper = @child_parent[first]
      get_ancestors(upper) if @id_name.has_key?(upper)
  end
  def get_descendants(first)
      printf "%-8d  %-s \n", first, @id_name[first]
      lower = @parent_child[first]
      get_descendants(lower) if @id_name.has_key?(lower)
  end
end


start = Time.now.to_f
class_finder = Taxonomy.new
taxon = File.open("taxonomy.dat")
name_id_file = File.open("taxnames.txt","w")
$/ = "//"
while record = taxon.gets
```

(continues)

```
    record =~ /\nSCIENTIFIC NAME\s+\:\s?([^\n]+)\n/
    name = $1.to_s
    record =~ /\n?ID\s+\:\s?([\d]+)\n/
    entry_id = $1.to_s
    record =~ /\nPARENT ID\s+\:\s?([\d]+)\n/
    parent = $1.to_s
    class_finder.add(name, entry_id, parent)
end
class_finder.get_names_and_ids(name_id_file)
print "\n\nYour ancestors are:\n"
class_finder.get_ancestors("9606")
puts "\n\nYour descendants are:\n"
class_finder.get_descendants("9606")
print "\nTotal time\, ", ((Time.now.to_f - start).to_i), "
    seconds\n"
exit
```

in Chapter 5, Section 9. Terms in the Neoplasm Classification appear in the following form:

```
<name nci-code = "C3756000">teratocarcinoma</name>
```

Each term in the nomenclature has an ancestral lineage coded by the XML file as nested tags. We want to transform the Neoplasm Classification's XML file into a plain-text file in which each neoplasm term is listed along with its entire hierarchical lineage. We use the neoself.rb Ruby script to parse and transform the neocl.xml file (List 19.3.1).

The neoself.rb script requires about 57 seconds (on a 2.5-gigahertz CPU) to parse the 10-Mb Neoplasm Classification and to produce a 22-Mb output file listing 146,168 neoplastic entities and the complete ancestry of each entity (List 19.3.2).

The first tumor in List 19.3.2 is teratoma.

```
teratoma|3403000|totipotent_or_multipotent_
differentiating> primitive_differentiating>
primitive>embryonic>neoplasms>tumor_classification>
```

The teratoma term has a nomenclature code, "340300", and teratoma is an instance of the class of tumors called totipotent_or_multipo-tent_differentiating tumors. This class is a subclass of primitive_differentiating tumors, which is a subclass of primitive tumors, which is a subclass of embryonic tumors, which is a subclass of neoplasms, which is a subclass of the root class tumor_classification.

LIST 19.3.1. RUBY SCRIPT neoself.rb **PROVIDES TAG HIERARCHY FOR XML FILE**

```ruby
#!/usr/local/bin/ruby
start_time = Time.new.to_f
require 'rexml/document'
require 'rexml/streamlistener'
include REXML
class Listener
  include StreamListener
  @@out = File.open("neoruby.txt","w")
  @@count = 0
  @lastname = ""
  @neoplasm_name = ""
  @code = ""
  def tag_start(name, attributes)
      @code = "#{attributes}"
      @code = $& if (@code =~ /[0-9]{7}/)
@lastname = "#{name}\>#{@lastname}" if (@code !~ /[0-9]{7}/)
  end
  def text(text)
      @neoplasm_name = text
  end
  def tag_end(name)
    @@count = @@count+1
    if (name =~/name/)
@@out.puts("#{@@count}\|#{@neoplasm_name}\|#{@code}\|#{@lastname}")
    end
    @lastname.gsub!(/#{name}\>/, "")
  end
end


listener = Listener.new
parser = Parsers::StreamParser.new(File.new("neocl.xml"),
    listener)
parser.parse
end_time = Time.new.to_f
puts "Total time is #{end_time - start_time}"
exit
```

LIST 19.3.2. THE FIRST 10 OUTPUT RECORDS PRODUCED BY THE
`neoself.rb` **SCRIPT**

1 | teratoma | 3403000 | totipotent_or_multipotent_differentiating>
primitive_differentiating>primitive>embryonic>neoplasms>tumor_classification>

2 | embryonal ca | 3752000 | totipotent_or_multipotent_differentiating>
primitive_differentiating>primitive>embryonic>neoplasms>tumor_classification>]

3 | embryonalcancer | 3752000 | totipotent_or_multipotent_differentiating>
primitive_differentiating>primitive>embryonic>neoplasms>tumor_classification>

4 | embryonal carcinoma | 3752000 | totipotent_or_multipotent_differentiating>
primitive_differentiating>primitive>embryonic>neoplasms>tumor_classification>

5 | mixed embryonal carcinoma and teratoma | 3756000 | totipotent_or_
multipotent_differentiating>
primitive_differentiating>primitive>embryonic>neoplasms>tumor_classification>]

6 | teratocarcinoma | 3756000 | totipotent_or_multipotent_differentiating>
primitive_differentiating>primitive>embryonic>neoplasms>tumor_classification>

7 | ovary with dermoid cyst | 3856000 | totipotent_or_multipotent_differentiating>
primitive_differentiating>primitive>embryonic>neoplasms>tumor_classification>

8 | dermoid cyst arising in ovary | 3856000 | totipotent_or_multipotent_differentiating>
primitive_differentiating>primitive>embryonic>neoplasms>tumor_classification>

9 I dermoid cyst involving ovary I 3856000 I totipotent_or_multipotent_differentiating>
primitive_differentiating>primitive>embryonic>neoplasms>tumor_classification>

10 I dermoid cyst arising from ovary I 3856000 I totipotent_or_multipotent_
differentiating>
primitive_differentiating>primitive>embryonic>neoplasms>tumor_classification>

We used the REXML Standard Library previously in List 18.14.2. A few lines of neoself.rb account for the bulk of the script's work.

In the XML file, each tumor is embedded in its lineage through nested XML tags.

Each time the tag_start event occurs, the script adds the code to a string of the parent tags for the neoplasm term.

```
def tag_start(name, attributes)
    @code = "#{attributes}"
    @code = $& if (@code =~ /[0-9]{7}/)
    @lastname = "#{name}\>#{@lastname}" if (@code !~ /[0-9]{7}/)
  end
```

The @lastname instance variable is the lineage list for each neoplasm's tag.

```
@lastname = "#{name}\>#{@lastname}" if (@code !~ /[0-9]{7}/)
```

When the tag_end event is triggered, we remove the name of the current tag. This shortens the lineage list whenever the XML file moves back up the hierarchy to enter a new lineage branch.

```
def tag_end(name)
    @@count = @@count+1
    if (name =~/name/)
@@out.puts("#{@@count}\|#{@neoplasm_name}\|#{@code}\|#{@lastname}")
    end
    @lastname.gsub!(/#{name}\>/, "")
  end
```

We use the gsub! method to delete lineage tags as their tag_end event is encountered.

```
@lastname.gsub!(/#{name}\>/, "")
```

The scripts in this chapter illustrate how easily any classification can be transversed and interrogated using Ruby scripts.

Book Summary
(Level 3)

20.1. BACKGROUND

One of the touted advantages of object-oriented programming is that it reduces software complexity. Unfortunately, this is not always true. Too often, object-oriented programming simply hides the complexity of programs.

Like any other innovation, object orientation is a technique that can be abused. The biggest problem in software development today is complexity. It is too easy for programmers to produce software that operates at a level of complexity that is unmatched by any physical system and with behavior that is computationally unpredictable.

Object-oriented programs, with their reliance on polymorphism, inheritance, composition, and encapsulation, can sometimes defy human understanding.

The purpose of this chapter is to provide some guidelines to reduce the complexity of Ruby scripts. You may have specific requirements or preferences that would outweigh my recommendations, particularly if you are writing software that must conform to a prescribed structure or interface; however, many readers of this book are full-time biomedical professionals and sometime programmers who will write scripts that are used a few times and put aside until needed. These programmers or their colleagues will need to assess quickly how the script works and will need to modify the script and its class library to accommodate a different data format or a different computational goal or new interoperability requirements. Under these conditions, simplicity will be rewarded.

20.2. RECOMMENDATIONS FOR SIMPLE RUBY SCRIPTS

LIST 20.2.1. RECOMMENDED PROGRAMMING STRATEGIES TO REDUCE COMPLEXITY

- Short Ruby scripts solve common tasks. Avoid writing long scripts.

- Adding classes increases complexity. Do not create new object classes unless they reduce the complexity of your class library.

- Avoid creating polymorphic methods or overriding existing class methods.

- Never use Mixins as a work-around to multiclass inheritance. Mixins are properly used as a source of methods and constants protected by a namespace. Do not create classes within modules.

- Model Ruby classes along the same principles as biological classifications. Ruby classes should conform to natural laws of classification. When creating subclasses, use the same criteria for assigning subclasses as those used by naturalists to classify living organisms. All members of a subclass should be bona fide members of the ancestor class, not simply a class of objects that happen to share the instance methods available to the ancestor class.

- Whenever possible, rely on the built-in Ruby classes and modules in your scripts.

- Serialize persistent data structures with built-in Ruby methods (for example, YAML). Avoid using commercial databases to serialize persistent data structures.

- Use comment lines and RDoc to document your class libraries fully.

- Write command-line programs. Avoid writing graphic user interfaces for your scripts.

- Choose names that describe the object represented by the name. Avoid using names such as "Class1," "method5," and "foo."

- Write scripts that have a specific, well-described, and easily understood purpose. Avoid multipurpose scripts.

- Ensure that your scripts are sufficiently fast for their intended purposes.

- If possible, create new scripts from pre-existing working scripts.

20.3. SHORT RUBY SCRIPTS SOLVE COMMON TASKS

The longer the script, the less likely you or anyone else will understand its basic algorithm. If you are a biomedical professional, you may find it easier to think of your scripts as utilities rather than as programs. Utilities are short pieces of code that perform a specific, defined function and nothing else. Typically, utilities can be described with a single algorithm. You will find that utilities, as their name implies, are very useful and can almost always be written in a few dozen lines of code (or less).

20.4. ADDING CLASSES INCREASES COMPLEXITY

The built-in Ruby classes are incredibly versatile. You may never need to create your own classes if you take the time to learn the methods that Ruby provides. When you start building your own classes, you add complexity to your programs. Do not create new object classes unless they reduce the complexity of your class library.

20.5. AVOID CREATING POLYMORPHIC METHODS OR OVERRIDING EXISTING CLASS METHODS

In Ruby, every method can be polymorphic. A method sent to an object will result in a search up the object's class hierarchy until the method is found. There is no way of knowing in advance which method will actually dispatch.

Any Ruby method can be overridden at runtime. A Ruby script can take information (environment variables describing the user's operating system, user-provided input arguments, event data) and use this data to change the behavior of the script. Even class assignments can be overridden, as the following script demonstrates (Lists 20.5.1 and 20.5.2).

The same object name can be assigned to two different classes without raising an exception. Only when we send an instance method from the overridden class do we finally raise a `NoMethodError`.

It is very easy for a Ruby script to behave in a manner that only the programmer is likely to understand. It is also easy to create Ruby scripts that nobody, including the programmer, will ever understand.

If you want scripts that execute in a predictable manner, you should think twice before purposefully creating polymorphic methods or overriding existing methods.

LIST 20.5.1. RUBY SCRIPT `conflict.rb` OVERRIDES A CLASS ASSIGNMENT

```
#!/usr/local/bin/ruby
class HelloClass
    def hello
       puts "hello"
    end
end
class InterestClass
    def return_number(number)
        puts (number)
    end
end
me = HelloClass.new
puts me.class
puts me.object_id
me = InterestClass.new
puts
puts me.object_id
puts me.class
puts
me.return_number(1000)
me.hello
exit
```

LIST 20.5.2. OUTPUT OF `conflict.rb` SCRIPT

```
C:\ftp\rb>ruby conflict.rb
HelloClass
20933470

20933410
InterestClass

1000
public.rb:21: undefined method `hello' for
#<InterestClass:0x27ed644> (NoMethodError)
```

20.6. NEVER USE MIXINS AS A WORKAROUND TO MULTICLASS INHERITANCE

Mixins are properly used as a source of methods and constants protected by a namespace. Do not create classes within modules.

Ruby, unlike many other Programming languages, forbids multiclass inheritance. It is common knowledge that Mixins (the inclusion of modules in a class) overcome restrictions on multiclass inheritance by allowing any class to include the class methods derived outside of its single-lineage ancestry. This is technically true, but I would strongly argue that multiclass inheritance is never a good idea; thus, you should not use Mixins to overcome Ruby's single-class object hierarchy. Instead, you should limit class methods to constitutive operations appropriate for the objects of a class and all of its subclasses. Module Mixins should be employed to provide classless methods and constants (that is, methods and constants that are not constitutive for any one class) under a specified namespace.

20.7. MODEL RUBY CLASSES ALONG THE SAME PRINCIPLES AS BIOLOGICAL CLASSIFICATIONS

Imagine that you are using Ruby to model the classification of living organisms. You would certainly have a class Bird and a class Mammal and a class Insect. Would it be correct to define a method `flight` in class Bird? I would say no. Flight, although common among birds, is not a constitutive property of birds. There are several examples of extant flightless birds (penguin, ostrich, emu, rhea, and cassowary) as well as extinct flightless birds (auk, dodo, and moa). In that case, should you create two subclasses of birds (flying and flightless) and provide a `flight` method for the flying birds? No, that would be a bad idea for a number of reasons. First, flight is not exclusively found among birds. Thousands of different insect species can fly. If `flight` is a method for a subclass of birds, it will need to be a method for insects as well. Aside from that consideration, is it really wise to subclassify birds on the basis of whether a particular method (`flight`, in this case) might apply? Would subclassifying birds based on flight separate birds that have common, constitutive features (for example, a common ancestor) and unite birds that are dissimilar (for example, penguins and ostriches)? Would it be better for `flight` to be omitted from any particular class of animal and to be included as a generic method available through a module? Yes, as a module method, `flight` could be available across many different classes of animals. This would be a legitimate use of a module method to offer several distinct classes a single method that may apply to certain instances of their classes.

Ruby does not enforce good class organization. You can create sub-classes of classes that have no sensible relation to the parent class. You can add modules to your classes ad libitum. You can use delegation to forward method requests from one class to another. Many of these sub-terfuges can be done dynamically at runtime. The problem is that all of these methods can create a level of complexity unmatched by any real-world system. Strict classification rules, developed by biologists over millennia and listed in Chapter 19, should apply to Ruby scripts, just as they apply to all living things.

When creating subclasses, use the same criteria for assigning subclasses as those used by naturalists to classify living organisms. All members of a subclass should be bona fide members of the ancestor class, not sim-ply a class of objects that happen to share the instance methods avail-able to the ancestor class.

Object-oriented programming, within the realm of biology and medi-cine, is a software technique that extends the ancient practice of biolog-ical classification. The biologist/programmer must work from a class system wherein each class is a fully realized member of its parent class, distinguished by properties that clarify its unique identity. This means that facile techniques that circumvent single-class inheritance create a class structure that violates biological reality.

20.8. WHENEVER POSSIBLE, RELY ON BUILT-IN RUBY CLASSES AND METHODS IN YOUR SCRIPTS

In general, it is best to decrease interdependencies between your scripts and external applications. This is best done by using the built-in Ruby classes, modules, methods, and data structures.

For example, it might be better to achieve the functionality of an exter-nal database application with built-in or standard library extensions (such as SDBM and YAML). If you avoid using external databases to seri-alize persistent data structures, you reduce the interdependencies of your scripts and increase the likelihood that your scripts can be shared by your colleagues.

20.9. USE COMMENT LINES AND RDOC TO DOCUMENT YOUR CLASS LIBRARIES FULLY

Scripts seem obvious and self-explanatory the day they are written. As the days pass, the same script becomes less and less understandable, even to its creator. A year later, the script is inscrutable to everyone.

There is only one solution: documentation. Good practice includes writing a short but exact description of the purpose of the script. If it is a command-line script that expects command-line arguments, these should be listed and clarified. The lines of the script should be commented. When new variables are created, their purpose in the script should be described.

If you want to share your script, class library, or module with the world, it is a good idea to embed RDoc notation (see Chapter 4, Section 2).

20.10. WRITE COMMAND-LINE PROGRAMS

With few exceptions, graphic user interfaces (GUIs) are only needed for commercial software applications. I have seen elaborate GUIs for applications that could have been written with just a few lines of code. For projects that will only be used by yourself and maybe a few of your colleagues, it is usually best to create a command-line interface in which the script is invoked in the operating shell. Annotations within the script can provide usage advice (that is, command-line arguments and a description of the purpose of the script).

20.11. CHOOSE NAMES THAT DESCRIBE THE OBJECT REPRESENTED BY THE NAME

The Ruby language, like the Ruby gem, is known for its clarity. Unfortunately, good Ruby code can become very murky if you choose nondescriptive names for classes and objects. If you create a class for nurses, you might be better off calling it class Nurse, rather than class Clara (after Clara Barton, perhaps?). If you believe that you have already created a class Nurse, it might be appropriate to choose another name that adds information that distinguishes your new class from your prior class (for example, CaregiverNurse). Be consistent in the way you represent multiword names (Caregiver_Nurse, Caregiver_nurse, CareGiverNurse). As always, ask yourself whether you need to create another class when a small addition to an existing class will suffice.

Except as iterator variables, avoid using metasyntactic variables. These are variable names that import no specific meaning, such as x, n, and foo.

20.12. AVOID MULTIPURPOSE SCRIPTS

Scripts with many purposes tend to be unnecessarily complex. If you need to perform many different projects, it is often best to create multiple different well-defined scripts, with one function per script. If you need to wrap multiple processes in a single script, it might be preferable to write several class libraries, each with an understandable and abstracted purpose, and to `require` those libraries into your script as they are needed.

20.13. ENSURE THAT YOUR SCRIPTS ARE SUFFICENTLY FAST FOR THEIR INTENDED PURPOSES

This seems so obvious that it is hardly worth mentioning, but one of the most common errors in programming is to develop methods that only work for small input files or that will only accommodate a small number of users.

Object-oriented programming languages incur speed penalties as Ruby searches for class-appropriate code for each method call.

Consider the code from List 6.4.1. This Ruby script `snom_get.rb` parsed the 775+ Mb MRCONSO file, interrogating each line for the presence of English SNOMED-CT terms, and produced a 47-Mb file consisting of UMLS unique concept identifiers and terms. On a modest 2.8-gigahertz CPU desktop computer, the Ruby script executed in 390 seconds, a parsing speed of about 2 Mb per second.

How does this stack up against Perl? The Ruby script can easily be converted to a Perl script (List 20.13.1).

LIST 20.13.1. PERL EQUIVALENT TO `snom_get.rb`

```perl
#!/usr/bin/perl
$start = time();
open (TEXT,"c\:\\entrez\\mrconso");
$line = " ";
open (OUT,">snom.txt");
while ($line ne "")
   {
   $line = <TEXT>;
   @linearray = split(/\|/,$line);
   $cuinumber = $linearray[0];
   $language = $linearray[1];
   $vocabulary = $linearray[11];
   next if ("ENG" ne $language);
   next unless ($vocabulary eq SNOMEDCT);
   print OUT $cuinumber . " " . $linearray[14];
   }
$end = time();
print ($end - $start) . "\n";
exit;
```

This Perl script executed in 154 seconds on the same computer. This represents a speed more than twice that of the Ruby script. Although Ruby is an alluring language that will enthrall you with its performance, a beautiful language takes a little longer to "get ready," and you must be prepared to wait a little at each encounter. In this case, though Perl was more than twice as fast as Ruby, both scripts completed their task in a few minutes, and that is probably sufficient when parsing a 775-Mb file.

Sometimes, however, a script executes so slowly that it cannot be used for its intended purpose. Imagine a spell checker (a program that parses words, checking each word for its correct spelling) that operates at a speed of one word every 0.06 seconds. This sounds like a fast speed as each word would require the smallest fraction of a second to check for spelling errors; however, at this rate, it would take 9 million seconds to parse a 1-gigabyte file (which contains about 150 million words). For a 1-terabyte file (the typical weekly output of a large hospital system), the spell checker would require 9 billion seconds to parse the file. Aside from issues of accuracy and precision, the spell checker would be impractical for people with large files.

Often, the laziest approach produces the best and fastest scripts. Do not create or use classes that you do not need. In particular, do not use GUI libraries unless they are absolutely necessary to the functionality of your software. Look very carefully at all iterating loops and recursive routines. Are they necessary? If so, are they written efficiently?

Ruby provides several methods to determine the speed of execution of a script (see Chapter 4, Section 2).

20.14. IF POSSIBLE, CREATE NEW SCRIPTS FROM PRE-EXISTING WORKING SCRIPTS

I never create a Ruby script from a blank screen. Every Ruby script has some similarity to a prior Ruby script. I keep my Ruby scripts in a single directory, and when I want to write a new script, I scan the directory, looking for an old script that has a similar function or that uses the same class libraries that I need for the current script. I then copy the script and quickly delete the code lines that are irrelevant to my current project. Then I begin to modify lines.

Is this a sign that all of my scripts (except maybe the first) lack any originality? No, it is probably just another indication that everything in life is composed of familiar patterns. In software, common coding patterns have very precise syntax, and it is very easy to forget a quotation mark or a parenthesis or blocked iterator variable or to misspell a class or to use a lowercase character when only an uppercase character will suffice.

My collection of tested Ruby scripts is written with correct syntax and uses Ruby class libraries that function in a predictable manner all of the time. My productivity as a programmer is, in large part, determined by my recollection of classes and scripts written by a younger, and perhaps smarter, version of myself.

Epilogue

BACKGROUND

As a scientist, I have always been wary of writers who personalize their work. Basically, the sciences should speak for themselves, and the role of the science writer is to present a clearly written, objective explanation of the subject matter. Despite these convictions, I feel that the book would be incomplete without some discussion of perennial questions that arise, in one guise or another, whenever I discuss programming with clinical staff or with laboratory-based researchers.

IS IT REASONABLE TO EXPECT A HEALTHCARE PROFESSIONAL TO BE A PROGRAMMER?

I have come to believe that every scientist would greatly benefit from a few basic programming skills. Some tasks just cannot be done with commercial applications (for example, transforming a document or a dataset from one form of data presentation to another). These tasks can often be accomplished with a few lines of code from any of the popular scripting languages (Ruby, Perl, or Python).

Consider this scenario, which is loosely modeled on a true story. A group of funded investigators have created a dataset consisting of about 10,000 records of cancer tissue samples, each annotated with about 20 data elements (for example, diagnosis, age of patient at time of diagnosis, gender of patient, and stage of disease at time of biopsy). They want to make the data available to the public from a Web search engine. After several meetings, the investigators decide to contract the work to a software developing company. A formal request for proposals is prepared (requiring additional meetings, the assistance of a contract specialist, and about 40 hours of work). During the period when the request for proposals is open, several companies write proposals and bid for the contract. Another committee is created to review the received proposals. One contractor is selected to host a Website and to create a searchable database. The contract cost is $75,000. One person from the institution's contract office and one person from the group of investigators are assigned to oversee the contractor. Thus far, 6 months have passed. Three months and many meetings later, the contractor has completed the Website. One year later, the federal funding for the project lapses and the Website is closed.

Because the dataset for the project was available at the beginning of the project, by all rights, the entire effort could have been achieved by a single person in a single day.

Here are three alternate scenarios.

1. One of the members of the project knows a little programming and some basic HTML. She transforms the dataset to an HTML table (using a few lines of Ruby) and uploads the entire data collection onto one HTML page. She has the department Webmaster add the HTML page to the public HTML directory on the department's server. The Webmaster also adds a link from the department's home page to the new HTML page. The public can now open a page that contains 10,000 tabulated records. Using their Web browser's "find" box, they can search for records of interest. Total time for the project is 2.5 hours. The total cost is $0.00.

2. One of the members of the project knows a little CGI programming. She goes to the Website of a popular Internet service provider (ISP) that supports Ruby. She arranges to pay $4.99 per month to host a Web page. For this fee, she is given FTP access to her own directory in which she can deposit public HTML pages. She is given access to another directory (/cgi-bin) in which she will deposit her Ruby CGI script and her dataset file. Through her ISP, she registers a domain (Internet address) for her new Website (no extra cost).

   She prepares an HTML page that describes the database and provides an input box for users to enter a query term. This HTML page is deposited on her public HTML subdirectory. This is done with FTP, using an ftp address and password provided by the ISP. She writes a short CGI Ruby script to search the dataset and to return an HTML page to the client's browser. She deposits this script and the dataset onto the cgi-bin directory. She spends a few hours ensuring that the HTML pages are adequate and that the query requests are processed as desired. When she is finished, she sends an e-mail to a list of researchers, announcing that the database is available to the public. The total time is 8 hours. The total cost is $60.00 per year.

3. One of the investigators has her own server and is an experienced Ruby programmer. She already has Ruby on Rails and MySQL installed on her server. She loads the dataset into the MySQL database and prepares a client HTML page from a Rails template. The total time is 6 hours. The total cost is nothing additional beyond the pre-existing cost of owning and operating a Web server.

Within our lifetimes, biomedicine has transformed into a data-intensive field. A large portion of the work of biology and medicine is computational. Most of this work cannot be tasked to existing commercial software applications. As a society, the time is coming when we can no longer afford the luxury of contracting every minor computer-oriented task to professional programmers. All healthcare professionals will soon be expected to perform common programming tasks.

MY PERSONAL PATH TO RUBY

For years, I was a devoted Perl programmer. I love Perl because it lets me do almost anything I need to do. Most of my Perl scripts involve just a few lines of code, work flawlessly, and are written in a matter of a few minutes. I have a collection of hundreds of basic Perl scripts. When I need to write a new script, I look through my directory, find the Perl script that is most like the one that I need, and modify it to suit my current needs. Life with Perl has been very, very good.

Over the past decade, I have become intensely interested in organizing biological information. My interests switched from studying diseases (as a PhD and MD pathologist) to studying how to classify diseases and properly annotate information that describes diseases. These pursuits led to the larger problem of merging heterogeneous biological databases. Suddenly, my professional life became complex and inchoate. I wrote a number of scientific papers on disease classification, but I could not shake the feeling that the biomedical field had become too complex to yield useful analysis.

I thought that developing data standards would help. If everyone captured their biological data in the same format, it would be easier to share data. XML had emerged as a great innovation in data organization. Each datum would be flanked by metadata (corresponding to XML tags) that described the datum. Each metadata would be standardized. Perl had many freely available modules for parsing XML data. It looked like everything would work out okay for me and Perl.

A problem soon arose. I learned that simply organizing data in schematized XML documents was insufficient to provide any rational meaning to data. Out-of-the-box XML is simply a way of organizing data/metadata pairs according to an XML schema that specifies the content and structure of the document. RDF (Resource Description Framework) took XML one step further, requiring that each data/metadata pair bind to a specified object (the thing described by the data/metadata pair). In informatics, "meaning" is achieved when a property and a value are bound to a fully specified object, the so-called RDF triple (List Epilogue.1).

LIST EPILOGUE.1. THREE CONDITIONS FOR A MEANINGUL ASSERTION IN INFORMATICS

1. There is a specified object about which the statement is made.
2. There is data that pertains to the specified object.
3. There is metadata that describes the data (that pertains to the specified object.)

Once again, Perl was equal to the job of parsing RDF datasets. My path seemed straightforward. Henceforward, all biomedical data should be collected in RDF format, thus facilitating the task of merging heterogeneous databases! Unfortunately, there was a fundamental feature of RDF that changed my approach to the problem: RDF schema.

An RDF schema is a dictionary file that lists metadata elements used in RDF documents (see Chapter 18). When two documents draw their metadata terms from the same RDF schema, their statements (triples) can be easily merged. RDF schemas contain Classes and Properties. Classes in RDF schema are equivalent to classes in Ruby. RDF documents contain the instance objects of the classes defined in one or more RDF schemas. Within RDF documents, the instances are the objects of the triples (the thing that the metadata and data pair are "about"). An RDF property is the metadata that describes the data and, when applied to an instance object, is equivalent to a key in a Ruby Hash object. An RDF property can apply to different object classes, so the definitions of named properties are analogous to Ruby modules. The value described by the property of an object instance is equivalent to the values of the Hash object. RDF documents create object instances of classes with the "type" declaration, in the same way that the Ruby creates object instances of classes with the "new" method. RDF documents use the "xmlns:" declaration to call external namespaces into the document. This is equivalent to requiring an external class or library into a Ruby script (List Epilogue.2).

The equivalencies between Ruby and RDF are striking.

LIST EPILOGUE.2. ANALOGOUS ELEMENTS AND METHODS IN RDF AND RUBY

```
RDF Schema                    => Ruby Class definition
RDF Class                     => Ruby Class
RDF instance property         => Ruby Hash key
RDF "type" declaration        => Ruby "new" statement
RDF "xmlns:" declaration      => Ruby "require" statement
RDF schema property           => Ruby Module Mixin
RDF triple                    => Ruby Class instance +
                                 instance hash
RDF object metadata/data pairs => Ruby Hash instance object
RDF single class inheritance  => Ruby single class inheritance
RDF open world semantics      => Ruby class Nil
```

There are three features of RDF that, in my opinion, make Ruby a uniquely suitable programming language for implementing RDF and the semantic Web (List Epilogue.3).

LIST EPILOGUE.3. THREE ESSENTIAL FEATURES SHARED BY RDF AND RUBY

1. Single class inheritance
2. Multi-class properties
3. Nil inferencing

Single class inheritance means that a class can only have one direct ancestor. This feature is true for RDF, Ruby, and the natural world. A unique object can only have one essential identity within a classification (see Chapter 19). Within a classification, a unique object can share methods (properties) in common with objects from other classes, and this is done in Ruby with modules and in RDF schemas with properties. A human can fly like a bird and swim like a fish, but a human is neither a bird nor a fish. The "fly" property and the "swim" property range over multiple classes, whereas "Jules Berman," "Tweety-bird," and "Nemo" are uniclass objects. Ontologies that are built with multiclass inheritance, and programming languages that permit multiclass inheritance (Perl and Python) can create systems of a complexity that is unmatched in nature.

Nil inferencing is another subtle feature shared by Ruby and RDF. In Ruby, there are three possible descriptors for any statement: true, false, or nil. In

Perl and Python, every statement is either true or false, with all non-zero values considered "true" and "0" considered "false." Aside from the fact that this makes no sense, it leads to some very silly inferences.

If "likes pizza" is a property of all instances of class "pathologist," then how might we evaluate this statement:

"Jules Berman likes pizza."

Well, if Jules Berman has not been declared an instance object of class pathologist, then Perl and Python would return false, because any statement in Perl and Python that cannot evaluate to true must evaluate to false. In Ruby and RDF, the statement would return nil. This is because neither Ruby nor RDF draws any inferences (true OR false) that are unsupported by data. This is the so-called open world property of RDF and is fully supported by Ruby's Nil class.

Some of the current goals in biomedical informatics are as follows:

1. Organizing heterogeneous biomedical data, using RDF described by publicly available RDF schemas.
2. Developing software algorithms and implementations for collecting and analyze RDF data.

It seems compelling that if RDF is destined to play a large role in biomedical informatics, we should use a programming language that matches the RDF model. To the best of my knowledge, Ruby fits RDF better than any other language.

Appendix

1. Online Ruby Tutorials

   The first edition of *Programming Ruby: The Pragmatic Programmer's Guide* is available as a superb online tutorial. This tutorial and book are sometimes referred to as "the pickaxe," in reference to the pick-axe depicted on the book's cover. The tutorial includes descriptions of the built-in classes and methods in Ruby. This online site is an excellent resource for nubies who need to check method syntax.

   http://www.rubycentral.com/book/

   For a spiritual experience in Ruby programming, visit "Why's (poignant guide) to Ruby."

   http://poignantguide.net/ruby/
   and
   http://whytheluckystiff.net/

   A straightforward beginner's guide is available in Daniel Carrera's "Learning Ruby."

   http://www.math.umd.edu/~dcarrera/ruby/0.3/

   Other online tutorials are listed here:

   http://glasnost.itcarlow.ie/~barryp/ruby-tut.html
   http://www.troubleshooters.com/codecorn/ruby/basictutorial.htm
   http://www.rubyist.net/~slagell/ruby/

2. Ruby Quiz

   Ruby Quiz is a weekly online programming challenge, with an archive of responses from previous quizzes.

   http://rubyquiz.com/

3. Ruby-doc.Org

   This site contains RDoc documentation for all of the classes, modules, and instance methods in the current version of Ruby. For experienced Ruby programmers, this supports facile navigation through class hierarchies and methods and their calling syntax.

   http://ruby-doc.org/downloads

4. Ruby-lang.Org

   This site provides general Ruby news and information, including links to user groups, mailing lists, and upcoming Ruby conferences.

   http://www.ruby-lang.org/en/

5. Ruby Garden

   This is another Ruby language site.

   http://rubygarden.org/

   It includes an excellent Ruby FAQ (frequently asked questions).

   http://faq.rubygarden.org/

6. RubyForge

   RubyForge is a Website that supports multiple users who can work online to build new Ruby applications. It carries community-based applications comprising the core Ruby Language and the most popular Ruby add-ons.

   http://rubyforge.org/

7. Open Source BioPerl, BioPython, BioRuby

   Beginning with the venerable BioPerl organization, these language-specific bioinformatics efforts all provide open source environments supporting a range of bioinformatics tasks.

   http://www.bioperl.org/
   http://www.biojava.org/
   http://www.biopython.org/
   http://www.bioruby.org/

8. Open Source Compression and Archiving Utilities (Gzip, Gunzip, Tar, 7-zip, Bunzip)

   Gzip (short for GNU zip) is a GNU-licensed compression utility designed as a surrogate for "compress," a compression utility that uses a patented algorithm. Gzipped files are very popular among Linux users and are widely prevalent on Internet download sites.

   Gunzip is the decompression utility that operates on gzipped files.

Gzip and gunzip are available at no cost for many different operating systems, from *www.gzip.org*

TAR (originally Tape Archiver) has outlasted its original purpose. TAR works on multiple platforms to archive multiple files into a single file for easy storage and transport. TAR will decompress the files on command.

Many people will compress the TAR archive using gzip, and it is common to find files with a double suffix:

```
filename.tar.gz
```

When you consecutively decompress with gunzip and de-archive with TAR, you typically get a library of files distributed in a pre-named directory (and subdirectories).

http://www.gnu.org/software/tar/tar.html

7-zip is a compression/decompression and archiving/de-archiving utility. It will decompress files created with commercial software.

A download of this wonderful utility, distributed under a GNU LGPL license, is available at *http://www.7-zip.org/*

Bunzip is a free implementation of the clever Burrows-Wheeler transform. For certain types of data and with ample RAM memory, it can provide higher compression than many other algorithms.

Most users of the algorithms use the newer bunzip2 version.

http://www.bzip.org/

9. R Open Source Statistical Programming Language and Bioconductor

R is an open source programming language for statistics. A free, easy-to-install version for non-Linux users is available at

http://www.stats.bris.ac.uk/R/bin/windows/base/

A general R FAQ is available at

http://cran.r-project.org/doc/FAQ/R-FAQ.html

R is an example of a successful and sophisticated software project that was completed over several years by a group of dedicated experts scattered across the globe. The effort had virtually no funding.

Bioconductor is an open source software environment for computational biology and bioinformatics. It uses R extensively (34).

R methods are available in Ruby scripts through the RSRuby_gem (Linux users) or (D)COM (Windows users) (34).

10. Cygwin, Open Source Unix/Linux Emulator

Cygwin emulates many of the common Unix/Linux commands.

It can be downloaded by going to *http://www.cygwin.com/*

Download `setup.exe`. When the dialog box displays available components, expand the "`development tools`" box and check off all the `gcc` components. This will provide you with GNU's versions of C and C++.

11. GnuPG, Open Source Encryption Tool

    GnuPG, the GNU Privacy Guard, is a complete and free alternative to PGP.

    PGP (Pretty Good Privacy) has a colorful history. Phil Zimmermann, who labored to develop PGP as a freeware encryption program, was accused by the U.S. government as an exporter of munitions. PGP and other encryption software were considered a munition in the 1990s. Although this seems strange to many, it should be remembered that for decades, encryption algorithms were developed exclusively by mathematicians employed by the National Security Agency and possibly other intelligence agencies. The appearance and proliferation of innovative public encryption software were a shock to U.S. intelligence. The charges were eventually dropped. Today, PGP is a commercial software company.

    Those who prefer GNU's software may consider acquiring GnuPG. Because GnuPG does not include the patented IDEA algorithm, it can be used without any restrictions.

    GnuPG is a RFC2440 (OpenPGP) compliant application.

    http://www.faqs.org/rfcs/rfc2440.html

    GnuPG can be downloaded from *http://www.gnupg.org/download/*

    GnuPG is available for several popular operating systems.

    For those seeking simplicity, GnuPG can be used to produce a simple symmetric encryption of a file, using the -c command from the DOS command line, as shown:

    ```
    C:\gpgdos>gpg -c outline.txt
    ```

    Outline.txt is a sample file for encryption/decryption; gpgdos is simply a created subdirectory containing the GnuPG files.

    You will be prompted to create a password. The encrypted output file produced by gpg is `outline.txt.gpg`.

    The encrypted file can be decrypted with the -d decryption command and redirected to the output file named out.out:

    ```
    C:\gpgdos>gpg -d outline.txt.gpg >c:\gpgdos\out.out
    ```

    You will be prompted again for the same password used as the key for the encryption step.

12. Wget Website Mirroring Software

    Wget is a freely command-line utility that can be used to download Web pages or entire Websites.

Wget is the non-Linux version of the Linux utility `"get"`

Wget can be downloaded from

ftp://sunsite.dk/projects/wget/windows/

A tutorial on wget is located at

http://www.gnu.org/software/wget/wget.html

13. Emacs Open Source Text Editor

Emacs was developed as a text editor for Unix/Linux systems and is now available for the Windows operating system.

Information is available at

http://www.gnu.org/software/emacs/windows/faq2.html

Emacs is easy to install, but its user interface is somewhat strange, sometimes requiring the user to enter commands at the bottom of the screen. Emacs cannot be used with comfort without spending time and patience learning the operation procedures.

One of the optional features of Emacs is its specialized editing environment for scripting languages, including Ruby. A freely available Lisp file, `ruby-mode.el`, highlights the different syntactic structures in Ruby files, as they are composed in the Emacs environment. To acquire the Ruby editing environment in Emacs:

1. Obtain ruby-mode.el, available at *http://www.ruby-lang.org/cgi-bin/ cvsweb.cgi/ruby/misc/ruby-mode.el*
2. In Emacs, under options, select syntax highlighting.
3. At the bottom command pane, enter the command `alt-x`, followed by `load-file`. You will be prompted for the path and filename for `ruby-mode.el`.
4. Enter path/file, and Emacs should indicate that the file loaded successfully.
5. Now you should be able to load a Ruby script into Emacs and edit it in "pretty" mode.

14. Database Issue of Nucleic Acids Research

The most current database issue of Nucleic Acids Research

http://nar.oxfordjournals.org/content/vol33/suppl_1/index.dtl

This issue lists hundreds of biological and medical databases, and most of them are freely available to the public.

15. HL7—Health Level 7

HL7 is a specification for transporting certain types of data that are typically collected by hospitals. Collections of HL7 data are called messages and are used to encapsulate information such as:

Registration data—patient admissions, discharges, transfers

Results/observations—laboratory tests, diagnoses, clinical observations, operative notes, and large amounts of text

Orders—from pharmacy, laboratory, or nurse

Billing/charges

Virtually any kind of information can be packaged into an HL7 message. All HL7 messages have a similar structure.

The message begins with a header that contains a description of the message contents.

The message header is typically followed by a patient identification (PID) segment containing patient demographics.

This is followed by observations segments (OBR).

The segment is composed of individual observations (OBX) delimited by a vertical character " | ".

OBX segments typically specify the test identifier, description, value and code source, unit of measure, and observed value status for a test.

16. OBO (Open Biology Ontologies)

    OBO is an open source collection of biological ontologies.

    Currently, most of the ontologies are devoted to animals (other than human animals)

    http://obo.sourceforge.net/browse.html

17. MySQL

    MySQL is a popular, free, open-source database application. It can be used in conjunction with Ruby on Rails to develop database-backed Web applications.

    http://dev.mysql.com/downloads/mysql/5.0.html

    A 2010 page manual is available at *http://downloads.mysql.com/ docs/refman-5.0-en.pdf*

18. RMagick and ImageMagick

    RMagick is Ruby's interface to ImageMagick. ImageMagick can read, convert, and write images in over 90 image formats. It allows users to apply various effects to images. For the purposes of this book, ImageMagick's most important feature is that it permits programmers to examine information contained in image headers (the part of the image file that precedes the binary image and that may contain textual information describing the image).

    ImageMagick is free software, with a license similar to GNU's GPL license. Versions are available for most operating systems.

An important feature of ImageMagick is that many popular programming languages, including Ruby, provide interfaces to ImageMagick. Some of these program interfaces are

C => MagickWand

C++ => Magick++

Java => JMagick

Perl => PerlMagick

Python => PythonMagick

Ruby => RMagick

This means that you can easily write powerful Ruby scripts that manipulate images using methods provided in RMagick. Because all of the language interfaces rely on ImageMagick to execute the methods, imaging programs written with any of these interfaces should share common functionalities.

The ImageMagick Website is

http://www.imagemagick.com/

For Windows users, a good way to install RMagick is to go to the RubyForge site and download the combined RMagick and ImageMagick binaries, as follows:

1. Go to the RubyForge site:

   http://rubyforge.org/frs/?group_id=12&release_id=8170

   This page has a combined win32 binary package for RMagick and ImageMagick.

   Pick the binary that is appropriate for your version of Ruby.

   I use Ruby 1.8.4, and thus, I chose the following binary:

   rmagick-1.13.0-IM-6.2.9-0-win32.zip 12.39 MB

2. Download the binary (zip file) and expand it.

   This produces the subdirectory:

   rmagick-1.13.0-IM-6.2.9-0-win32

   The subdirectory contains a group of files:

   ImageMagick-6.2.9-0-Q8-windows-dll.exe

   README-RMAGICK.html

   README-RMAGICK.txt

   README.html 13,334 rmagick-1.13.0-win32.gem

3. Run the ImageMagick.exe file, and it will guide you through its installation.

4. After ImageMagick is installed, you can install the RMagick gem file by invoking Ruby's gem tool with an install command followed by the name of the gem file (add the full path to the gem file if you are not installing from its current subdirectory). For example:

```
c:\ftp>gem install rmagick-1.13.0-win32.gem
```

5. All of the information you need to start using RMagick from within your own Ruby Scripts is found at

   http://www.simplesystems.org/RMagick/doc/

6. Ruby scripts for displaying images are found at *http:www.julesberman. info/rubyhome.htm*

19. DICOM To JPEG Conversion—ezDicom and DCM2JPG and JPEG2DCM.

ezDICOM (Copyright 2002, Wolfgang Krug and Chris Rorden) is a medical viewer for DICOM images. It is distributed along with dcm2jpg, a command-line application that can convert DICOM images to standard bitmap file formats (jpeg, png, and bmp). In addition, it will convert a DICOM image to its textual header information.

The sample command line is

```
dcm2jpg -f p -o C:\TEMP -z 1.5 C:\DICOM\input1.dcm C:\input2.dcm
```

This command line may contain information for brightness, contrast, format of output, output target directory, input files, and so forth.

If you simply invoke

```
dcm2jpg <dicom filename and path if file is not in current directory>
```

The dicom file will be converted to a .jpg file in the directory that holds the dicom file.

The .exe file is

dcm2jpg.exe—converts to jpeg by default

If you wish, you can simply rename the .exe file to change the default conversion behavior.

dcm2bmp.exe—converts to bmp by default.

dcm2png.exe—converts to png by default

dcm2txt.exe—converts to text header by default

Any jpeg file can be converted to a DICOM file, with jpeg2dcm. This free software by CharruaSoft software can be downloaded from

http://www.charruasoft.com/downen.htm

It is a simple exe file (jpeg2dcm.exe 511,488 bytes) that can operate from a command line:

It will take an input file, such as gems.jpg and convert it to a DICOM file.

References (Commented)

1. REXML home, 3.3.6. http://www.germane-software.com/software/rexml/. Comment. REXML is a simple and powerful Ruby XML parser and processor.

2. Hayes B. The semicolon wars. *American Scientist,* July/August 2006, p. 299. Comment. This is an engaging essay on the linguistic diversity of programming languages. For historians of computer science, there is a diagram that classifies the major programming languages (imperative, functional, object oriented, and declarative) and provides the chronological relationship among languages and their intellectual ancestors.

3. Berman JJ. Tumor classification: molecular analysis meets Aristotle. *BMC Cancer* 4:10, 2004. http://www.biomedcentral.com/1471-2407/4/10. Comment. Neoplasms can be classified by their developmental lineage, much as living species can be classified by their evolutionary lineage.

4. RDOC—Ruby Documentation System. http://www.ruby-doc.org/stdlib/libdoc/rdoc/rdoc/index.html. Comment. RDoc is a tool that comes bundled in Ruby. It will create, for any Ruby script or class library, a set of HTML documents that list the files, classes, and methods included in the script. This site provides extensive documentation on the RDoc tool.

5. Unified Medical Language System (UMLS). http://www.nlm.nih.gov/research/umls/umlsmain.html. Comment. The UMLS is the largest curated medical vocabulary in existence. The UMLS metathesaurus is a composite of over 100 medical nomenclatures and is available at no cost from the U.S. National Library of Medicine.

6. Berman JJ. Modern classification of neoplasms: reconciling differences between morphologic and molecular approaches. *BMC Cancer* 5:100, 2005. http://www.biomedcentral.com/1471-2407/5/100. Comment. A new classification can sometimes resolve certain questions that arise in alternate classifications.

7. Berman JJ. Tumor taxonomy for the developmental lineage classification of neoplasms. *BMC Cancer* 4:88, 2004. http://www.biomedcentral.com/1471-2407/4/88. Comment. This taxonomy is the list of domain instances that fill a classification. This article describes the taxonomy for the Developmental Lineage Classification of Neoplasms.

8. Berman JJ. Automatic extraction of candidate nomenclature terms using the doublet method. *BMC Med Inform Decision Making* 5:35, 2005. Comment. This article describes a quick computer program that will scan a corpus of text (of any size) and extract potential new terms for any given nomenclature.

9. Association for Pathology Informatics Information Resources, 2006. http://www.pathologyinformatics.org/informatics_r.htm. Comment. This Website contains the latest versions of the Developmental Lineage Classification and Taxonomy of Neoplasms.

10. ISO/IEC 11179. http://en.wikipedia.org/wiki/ISO-11179. Comment. ISO 11179 is a "Specification and Standardization of Data Elements." It has been thought of as an unnecessary metadata standard and is often ignored in the XML community; however, ISO 11179 is a crucial and fundamental part of any informatics effort. It provides a formal mechanism for creating unique global identifiers for standard data elements and provides uniform guidance for identifying, developing, and describing data elements. If all metadata had formal descriptions conforming to ISO 11179, standardized data could be exchanged between different organizations, and the enormous redundancy of in-use data elements would be reduced or eliminated.

11. Zipf's law. http://en.wikipedia.org/wiki/Zipf. Comment. This is an excellent historical and technical discussion of the Zipf distribution.

12. Berman JJ. Confidentiality for medical data miners. *Artif Intell Med* 26:25–36, 2002. Comment. This article describes some of the innovative computational remedies that will permit researchers to conduct research and share their data without risk to patient or institution.

13. Department of Health and Human Services. 45 CFR (Code of Federal Regulations), Parts 160 through 164. Standards for Privacy of Individually Identifiable Health Information (Final Rule). *Federal Register*, Volume 65, Number 250, Pages 82461–82510, December 28, 2000. Comment. This is the much-feared HIPAA rule for protecting patient privacy.

14. Department of Health and Human Services. 45 CFR (Code of Federal Regulations), 46. Protection of Human Subjects (Common Rule). *Federal Register*, Volume 56, pp. 28003–28032, June 18, 1991. http://www.hhs.gov/ohrp/humansubjects/guidance/45cfr46.htm. Comment. Although HIPAA privacy regulations seem to get all the attention, the Common Rule sets the basic principles for protecting patients from research risks, mandating the activities of institutional review boards, and using human tissues in support of medical research. It is essential reading for anyone involved in human subject research.

15. Malin B, Sweeney L. How (not) to protect genomic data privacy in a distributed network: using trail re-identification to evaluate and design anonymity protection systems. *J Biomed Inform* 37:179–192, 2004. Comment. Latanya Sweeny was one of the first people to point out the difficulties in achieving deidentification of medical records. She has not published many articles, but each publication is worth reading.

16. Sweeney L. Guaranteeing anonymity when sharing medical data, the Datafly system. *Proc Am Med Informat Assoc* 51–55, 1997. Comment. Latanya Sweeney was one of the first researchers to show that personal data extracted from different databases can be connected to identify patients whose names were removed from clinical research datasets.

17. Sweeney L. Three computational systems for disclosing medical data in the year 1999. *Medinfo* 9(Pt 2):1124–1129, 1998. Comment. This is another contribution from Latanya Sweeney, who has pioneered computational methods for safely disclosing medical data without breaching patient confidentiality.

18. Berman JJ. Racing to share pathology data. *Am J Clin Pathol* 121:169–171, 2004. Comment. Patents are being sought on some of the basic methods for sharing biomedical data.

19. Berman JJ. Resources for comparing the speed and performance of medical autocoders. *BMC Med Inform Decision Making* 4:8, 2004. http://www.biomedcentral.com/1472-6947/4/8. Comment. The field of machine translation cannot proceed unless there is a way for developers and end-users to perform side-by-side comparisons between different translators. If each developer of autocoding software is reluctant to provide his or her software to his or her competitor, there should at least be some available baseline autocoder that can be used by everyone to express the relative speed and performance of their autocoder. This article provides a minimalist autocoder that can be used in benchmarking trials.

20. Grivell L. Mining the bibliome: searching for a needle in a haystack? *EMBO Rep* 3:200–203, 2002. Comment. Grivell describes a technique for creating a signature of text composed of a combination of terms

and concepts extracted from the text and serving as a metric against which other documents can be compared. Documents having similar signatures can be retrieved as a related group.

21. Heja G, Surjan G. Using n-gram method in the decomposition of compound medical diagnoses. *Int J Med Inf* 70:229–236, 2003. Comment. Some words appear frequently in combination with other words. The occurrence frequencies of two-word, three-word, n-word phrases can be used to make inferences about the intended meaning of text.

22. Orwant J, Hietaniemi J, Macdonald J. *Mastering Algorithms With Perl.* Sebastopol, California: O'Reilly 1999. Comment. This is an excellent book that clearly describes commonly used algorithms. Working Perl scripts are provided.

23. Schneier B. *Applied Cryptography: Protocols, Algorithms and Source Code in C.* New York: Wiley, 1994. Comment. Bruce Schneier is one of the most influential and creative thinkers in the field of cryptography and computer security. This book provides excellent discussion of the mathematical and technical aspects of the field.

24. Schneier B. *Secrets and Lies: Digital Security in a Networked World.* Indianapolis, IN: Wiley, 2000. Comment. This book delves into the social and human aspects of computer security. This is a very good companion to the same author's earlier book, *Applied Cryptography*.

25. Rivest R. Request for Comments: 1321, The MD5 Message-Digest Algorithm. http://rfc.net/rfc1321.html. Comment. This is also found at http://theory.lcs.mit.edu/~rivest/Rivest-MD5.txt. Message-Digest algorithms, also known as fingerprint algorithms or one-way hash algorithms, take a binary object, such as a file, and create a short, seemingly random string of characters (message digest) with the following properties: the same file will always produce the same message digest. If the file is changed in any way, the algorithm will produce a different message-digest, and it is impossible to compute the original file from any manipulation of the message digest. MD-5 is an open algorithm with easily obtained software implementations. It is used to authenticate data objects.

26. Secure Hash Algorithm (SHA-1), National Institute of Standards and Technology, NIST FIPS PUB 180-1, "Secure Hash Standard," U.S. Department of Commerce, April 1995. http://www.itl.nist.gov/fipspubs/fip180-1.htm. Comment. The Secure Hash Algorithm is a message digest algorithm that is approved by the U.S. Department of Commerce.

27. Berman JJ. Threshold protocol for the exchange of confidential medical data. *BMC Med Res Methodol* 2:12, 2002. http://www.biomedcentral.com/1471-2288/2/12. Comment. Threshold cryptographic protocols

divide messages into multiple pieces, with no single piece containing information that can reconstruct the original message. The article describes a novel threshold protocol that can be used to search, annotate, or transform confidential data without breaching patient confidentiality. The threshold algorithm produces two files (threshold pieces). In typical use, piece 2 is held by the data owner, and piece 1 is freely distributed. Piece 1 can be annotated and returned to the owner of the original data to enhance the complete dataset. Collections of piece 1 files can be merged and distributed without identifying patient records. Variations of the threshold protocol are described.

28. Fowler C. *Rails Recipes*. Lewisville, Texas: Pragmatic Bookshelf, 2006. Comment. These are techniques for implementing the features and support tools available to Rails developers.

29. Holzner S. *Beginning Ruby on Rails*. Hoboken, New Jersey: Wrox, 2006. Comment. This is an introductory book on Ruby on Rails by a gifted writer of many programming books.

30. Thomas D, Hansson DH, Schwarz A, Fuchs T, Breedt L, Clark M. *Agile Web Development with Rails: A Pragmatic Guide*. Lewisville, Texas: Pragmatic Bookshelf, 2005. Comment. The author list includes David Heinemeier Hansson, the creator of Ruby on Rails, and Dave Thomas, an author of the very popular *Programming Ruby: Programmatic Programmer's Guide*.

31. Hibbs C. Rolling with Ruby on Rails. http://www.onlamp.com/pub/a/onlamp/2005/01/20/rails.html. Comment. This is an excellent introduction to Ruby on Rails, using WEBrick to convert your own computer into a server.

32. Ahmed K, Ayers D, Birbeck M, Cousins J, Dodds D, Lubell J, Nic M, Rivers-Moore D, Watt A, Worden R, Wrightson A. *Professional XML Meta Data*. Birmingham, AL: Wrox Press, 2001. Comment. Metadata is the building block of XML, the semantic Web, ontologies, software agents, and just about every projected Web technology. Every informatician should have a deep understanding of metadata, and this book is an excellent resource.

33. OWL Web Ontology Language Reference, W3C Recommendation, 10 February 2004. http://www.w3.org/TR/owl-ref/. Comment. This is the official W3C reference for OWL, a formal specification for a set of RDF triples that provide logical inferencing structures for ontologies.

34. Gentleman RC, Carey VJ, Bates DM, Bolstad B, Dettling M, Dudoit S, Ellis B, Gautier L, Ge Y, Gentry J, Hornik K, Hothorn T, Huber W, Iacus S, Irizarry R, Leisch F, Li C, Maechler M, Rossini AJ, Sawitzki G, Smith C, Smyth G, Tierney L, Yang JY, Zhang J. Bioconductor: open software development for computational biology and bioinformatics.

Genome Biol 5:R8, 2004. http://genomebiology.com/2004/5/10/R80. Comment. The Bioconductor project is a collection of open-source software for computational biologists. It draws heavily on the statistics programming language R.

35. Dublin Core Metadata Initiative. http://dublincore.org/. Comment. The Dublin Core (see the Glossary) is a set of basic metadata that describe XML documents. The Dublin Core was developed by a forward-seeing group of library scientists who understood that every XML document needs to include self-describing metadata that will allow the document to be indexed and appropriately retrieved.

36. Dublin Core Metadata Element Set, Version 1.1: Reference Description http://dublincore.org/documents/1999/07/02/dces/. Comment. This is the Website for the Dublin Core elements.

37. Stallman R. Why "Free Software" is better than "Open Source." http://www.gnu.org/philosophy/free-software-for-freedom.html. Comment. In practice, there is very little difference between the free software movement and the open-source initiative. The essay by Richard Stallman, guru of the free-software movement, stresses philosophic differences between these two related projects.

38. What is copyleft? http://www.gnu.org/copyleft/. Comment. The GNU organization publishes two licenses, used for software produced by GNU and by anyone who would like to distribute their software under the terms of the GNU license. They are referred to as a copyleft license because they primarily serve the software users rather than the software creators. One of the GNU licenses, the General Public License, covers most software applications. The GNU Lesser General Public License, formerly known as the GNU Library General Public License, is intended for use with software libraries or unified collections of files comprising a complex application, language, or other body of work.

Glossary

$ (Ruby)—A "$" prepended to a variable name confers globality. Global variables can be used anywhere within a script and persist for the life of the script.

$/ (Ruby)—Ruby's built-in line-separator variable. The default value for $/ is a newline character, but the value of $/ can be changed within a script to accommodate any line delimiter. When the value of the line-separator variable is nil, a line read will port an entire file into a string variable. In DOS systems, it is sometimes useful to work in concert with the binmode method.

```
irb>File.size("walnut.jpg")                    => 229438
irb>f = File.open("walnut.jpg").binmode
irb>$/ = nil                                    => nil
irb>string_hold = f.gets
irb>string_hold.size                            => 229438
```

See binmode (see List 18.19.2).

$& (Ruby)—Ruby's built-in variable that represents the part of a string that successfully matches a regular expression.

```
irb>my_string = "adenocarcinoma of the prostate"
irb>my_string =~ /ca.+oma/ => 5
irb>$& => "carcinoma"
irb>$` => "adeno"
irb>$' => " of the prostate"
```

$` **(Ruby)**—Ruby's built-in variable that represents the part of a string that precedes $&.

```
irb>my_string = "adenocarcinoma of the prostate"]
irb>my_string =~ /ca.+oma/ => 5
irb>$& => "carcinoma"
irb>$` => "adeno"
irb>$' => " of the prostate"
```

$' **(Ruby)**—Ruby's built-in variable that represents the part of a string that follows $&.

```
irb>my_string = "adenocarcinoma of the prostate"
irb>my_string =~ /ca.+oma/ => 5
irb>$& => "carcinoma"
irb>$` => "adeno"
irb>$' => " of the prostate"
```

$SAFE—A Ruby global variable that determines how your script uses external objects. It is used primarily for scripts that share objects through a network (for example, CGI scripts). The default setting for $SAFE is 0, permitting the use of all externally supplied objects. The $SAFE value can be set within a script. A $SAFE level of 4 achieves the highest level of partitioning between a script and external objects.

<< **(Ruby Array#<<)**—An array operator that adds an array element to the end of an array list. For example,

```
irb>[1,2,3] << 64 => [1, 2, 3, 64]
```

! **(Ruby method suffix)**—A "!" is encountered at the end of the names of some Ruby methods. It usually implies that the method is destructive and modifies the object that receives the method. Many methods in Ruby have a nondestructive version (yielding an object distinct from the method's receiver object) and a destructive version (replacing the receiver object with the method result).

```
irb(main):001:0> string_object = "hello" => "hello"
irb(main):002:0> string_object.chop => "hell"
irb(main):003:0> string_object => "hello"
```

nondestructive method, chop, does not change string_object

```
irb(main):004:0> string_object.chop! => "hell"
irb(main):005:0> string_object => "hell"
```

destructive method, chop! changed string_object

```
irb(main):006:0> string_object.gsub(/e/,"eee") => "heeell"
irb(main):007:0> string_object => "hell"
```

nondestructive method, `gsub`, **does not change** `string_object`

```
irb(main):008:0> string_object.gsub!(/e/,"eee") => "heeell"
irb(main):009:0> string_object => "heeell"
```

destructive method, `gsub!`, changed `string_object`

% (Ruby String#%)—Specifies a format operation on an argument. It takes the form "string % argument" where string is a printf-type format specification and argument is the string to be formatted. It can take a form of multiple strings and multiple arguments with the number of format strings equaling the number of arguments. See printf.

%w (Ruby)—Operator eliminates need for commas and quotes around array elements separated by a space. For example,

```
alphabet = %w[alpha beta gamma delta epsilon]
```

instead of

```
alphabet = ["alpha", "beta", "gamma", "delta", "epsilon"]
```

@@ (Ruby)—In Ruby, a variable can be made accessible to every object and method in a class by appending "@@" to the name of the variable. Class variables, unlike global and instance variables, must be initialized, and this is typically done by assigning the class variable at the top level of the class. For example,

```
#!/usr/local/bin/ruby
class Person < String
  @@name = "EVERYONE"
  #Can be used in any Person class method
  def downcase
    puts "let's use lowercase characters"
    puts(@@name.downcase)
  end
end
me = Person.new
me.downcase
exit
```

Output:

```
C:\ftp\rb>ruby instance.rb
let's use lowercase characters
everyone
```

@ (Ruby)—In Ruby, a variable can be assigned to an object (that is, an instance of a class). This is done by appending an "@" to a variable name. Unlike regular variables that "disappear" outside of the method in which they appear, object variables will always be available to the object that has been assigned the variable. Each object variable "knows" the object that it is assigned, even when the identically named object variable is assigned to different objects. For example,

```
#!/usr/local/bin/ruby
class Person < String
  def name(param)
    @myname = param  #different objects are assigned
                          #the @myname variable
  end
  def getname
    return @myname
  end
end
me = Person.new
you = Person.new
me.name("Jules")
you.name("Henry")
puts me.getname
puts you.getname
exit

Output:
C:\ftp\rb>ruby instance.rb
Jules
Henry
```

Ruby knows which @myname value belongs to the correct object. See accessor methods.

__id__ (Ruby Object#__id__)—Same as the Object class's object_id method. See object_id.

 # (Ruby)—The pound sign in Ruby has several different meanings depending on the context in which it appears.

After a statement, it is a comment indicator. Everything appearing on the statement line after the pound sign is a comment that is ignored by the Ruby interpreter.

```
puts "Hello" #ignore this comment
```

Inside a quoted string, it tells Ruby to evaluate whatever is referenced by the contents in the curly braces. For example,

```
@myname = "Jules"
puts("#{@myname}")
```

This prints out the value referenced by the object variable @myname.

First character of a ruby script's shebang line appearing at top of script

```
#!/usr/local/bin/ruby
```

It is a simple pound character when escaped by a slash:

```
\#
```

Outside of a Ruby script, it is a separator between a class and a method name for the class

```
String#gsub
```

== (Ruby)—Equality test. It determines whether the object on the left is equal to the object on the right. It is polymorphous in the sense that the meaning of equality depends on the class of the object. It returns true or false. Examples are

```
irb>1 == 2/2 => true
irb>"A" == 65.chr => true
irb>nil == 0 => false
irb>nil.to_i == 0 => true
```

=== (Ruby)—Class-dependent equality test. Different classes in Ruby have their own === methods that test for equality based on conditions particular for the particular method. Returns are true or false. For example,

```
irb>Module === Comparable => true
```

The Module class has an === method that determines whether the object on the right (Comparable in this case) is a descendent of the Module class. Actually, all classes and all modules descend from the Module class, so the equality would hold for any existing Ruby Class or Module.

```
irb>Module === Module => true
irb>Module === Object => true
irb>Module === String => true
irb>Module === 54 => false
```

=~ **(Ruby)**—Pattern match method. The String class =~ method looks for the first occurrence of a pattern (right side) in a provided string (left side). For example,

```
irb>"xxxxxxHellozzzzz" =~ /Hello/ => 6
```

"H" is the sixth character in the string, beginning from the zeroth character on the left.

abandonware—Software that was once shown to serve some useful purpose but which is no longer used. Almost all of the useful software ever written is now abandonware. In many cases, software loses its value if it is not continually debugged, enhanced, and aggressively marketed. The term abandonware is often applied to software created by graduate students as part of a funded research effort. After the funding period ends and the students have moved to new pursuits, there is no support for marketing and distributing the software. Even when interest remains in the original software, it can be very difficult for a new programmer to understand the source code left by the original programmer. In addition, funding is typically rewarded for innovative ideas, and it is sometimes impossible to attract new funding to maintain a previously funded project.

abstraction—A technique that generalizes algorithms and methods to accommodate a variety of different parameters and input data. Through abstraction, methods can be reused under a wide variety of conditions. Abstraction is a technique that can be used in any programming language, but the class structure of objects (in Ruby) requires abstraction technique.

access control—Ruby has three levels of access for class methods: public (default access level), protected, and private. See public method, protected method, and private method.

accessor method—Accessor methods read and write data to variables. In Ruby, whenever you assign a data value to a class object, you are transparently calling an accessor method that assigns the same value to an instance variable (prefixed with an @ sign) defined as a method within the object's class definition. The instance variable persists for the life of the object. Similarly, when you use the value referred through an object, you are actually calling an accessor method to pull the referred data from the assigned instance variable defined within the class definition. The Ruby classes all have built-in accessor methods that work transparently whenever you use assignment commands in your Ruby scripts.

acronym—An acronym is a specialized form of abbreviation in which selected letters from a word phrase (usually the first character of each word in the phrase) are sequentially fused to form a new word. See backronym.

aggregation—Synonym for composition or layering. See composition.

algorithm—An algorithm is a logical sequence of steps that lead to a desired computational result. Algorithms serve the same function in the computer world as production processes serve in the manufacturing world. Fundamental algorithms can be linked or embedded to create new algorithms. Algorithms are the most important intellectual capital in informatics, and students of the field should master a set of basic algorithms.

`alias_method` **(Ruby Module#alias_method)**—In class Module, the private instance method, `alias_method`, creates a new object id for a method. The aliased method retains all of the features of the original method at the moment it is aliased. Subsequent changes to the original method do not change the copied method.

The syntax is `alias_method(aliased_name_id, original_name_id)`

American National Standards Institute—See ANSI.

American Standard Code for Information Interchange—See ASCII.

`ancestors` **(Ruby Module#ancestors)**—Provides a list of the ancestors of a class, including the names of modules included in the ancestor classes. Knowledge of an object's ancestors informs you of the methods available to the objects. For example,

```
irb>Bignum.ancestors
=> [Bignum, Integer, Precision, Numeric, Comparable,
    Object, Kernel]
```

annotation—In general terms, involves adding information to describe a data object (for example, annotating sequence data with names of contained genes). Often, the information is drawn from multiple databases. In XML documents, annotation often involves adding metadata/data pairs to add to data records or to better describe data objects.

ANSI (American National Standards Institute)—ANSI is a Standards Activities Organization. As such, ANSI does not itself develop standards. ANSI accredits standards developing organizations to create American National Standards (ANS). When something is described as an ANSI standard, it means that an ANSI-accredited standards development organization followed ANSI procedures and received accreditation from ANSI that all of the procedures were followed. ANSI works with over 270 ANSI-accredited standards developers. Groups of ANSI-accredited standards development organizations work together to develop voluntary national consensus standards and American National Standards (ANS). ANSI coordinates the effort to gain international standards certification from the ISO or IEC.

arguments (Ruby)—The objects passed to a receiver by a method.

`Array` **(Ruby)**—The class of arrays, ordered and indexed lists of items. The items in an array can be any data structure, including strings, numbers, hashes, or other arrays. Array objects begin with the zeroth element. For example,

```
irb>this_array = [43,22,18,190]  => [43, 22, 18, 190]
irb>this_array[1] => 22
```

artificial intelligence—Also called AI. It is impossible to discuss futuristic concepts found in this book without some mention of artificial intelligence and so-called thinking machines. In the opinion of some, formal knowledge specifications such as RDF, DAML, and OWL provide the ingredients for autonomous software agents to perform intelligently and to make complex decisions. I am of the opinion it will be awhile before we see powerful and complex software agents. Biomedical professionals will spend the next decade collecting, annotating, and merging large heterogeneous datasets in preparation for the exciting work that follows. In the next few years, biomedical software agents will be relegated to simple but important tasks, such as detecting errors in medication, laboratory reports, and physician orders. The field of artificial intelligence in biomedicine still requires a lot of groundwork.

ASCII editor—see text editor.

ASCII standard—ASCII is the American Standard Code for Information Interchange, ISO-14962-1997. The ASCII standard is a way of assigning specific 8-bit strings (a string of 0s and 1s of length 8) to the alphanumeric characters and punctuation. Uppercase letters are assigned a different string of 0s and 1s than their matching lowercase letters. There are 256 ways of combining 0s and 1s in strings of length 8, and this means there are 256 different ASCII characters. For some uses, the 256 ASCII character limit is too constraining. There are many languages in the world, with their own alphabets or with their own accented versions of the ASCII romanized alphabet. Consequently, a new character code (UNICODE) has been designed as an expansion of ASCII. To maintain facile software conversion (from ASCII to Unicode), ASCII code is embedded in the Unicode standard.

associative array (Ruby)—Synonym for Hash and Dictionary. A fundamental Ruby data structure composed of key/value pairs. In Ruby, associative arrays are members of class `Hash`. For example,

```
#!/usr/local/bin/ruby
my_hash = Hash.new
my_hash["C0000005"] = "(131)I-Macroaggregated Albumin"
my_hash["C0000039"] = "1,2-Dipalmitoylphosphatidylcholine"
my_hash.each {|key,value| STDOUT.print(key, " --- ", value,
    "\n")}
exit
```

```
C:\ftp\rb>ruby hash.rb
C0000005 —- (131)I-Macroaggregated Albumin
C0000039 —- 1,2-Dipalmitoylphosphatidylcholine
```

at_exit **(Ruby Kernel#at_exit)**—Receives a block of code for execution when the program exits.

```
#!/usr/local/bin/ruby
at_exit{puts "goodbye"}
exit
```

Output:

```
C:\ftp\rb>try.rb
goodbye
```

attribute (XML)—An XML attribute is a metadata/value data pair embedded within an XML tag. An equals sign separates the key from the value, and the value must occur within quotation marks. Typically, but not necessarily, a tag with embedded attributes has no included data and therefore includes a tag terminator "/" within the tag. For example,

```
<Person first_name="Fred" last_name="Smith" />
```

The two attribute key/value pairs are

```
first_name => Fred
last_name => Smith
```

autocoder—A software program capable of parsing large collections of medical records (for example, radiology reports, surgical pathology reports, autopsy reports, admission notes, discharge notes, operating room notes, medical administrative e-mails, memoranda, and manuscripts), capturing the medical concepts contained in t0he text and assigning them an identifying code from a nomenclature. See coding.

autopsy—A postmortem examination on a human, conducted by a pathologist. The pathologist reviews organs to determine the lesions in the patient at the time of death, as well as the cause of death. A postmortem examination performed on an animal is called a necropsy.

backronym—Opposite of acronym. In a backronym, a series of words, each beginning with a successive letter from an existing term, is assigned to a pre-existing abbreviation. A backronym for Perl is Practical Extraction Report Language.

BEGIN **block**—A block of code prefixed by the word "BEGIN" that executes before any other part of the script, regardless of its location in the script. See END block.

Benchmark **(Ruby)**—In the Ruby Standard Library, Benchmark allows you to determine the speed of scripts and code fragments.

binary data—Technically, all digital information is coded as binary data. Strings of 0s and 1s are the fundamental units of all electronic information; however, when people use the term "binary data," they most often are referring to digital information that is not intended to be machine-interpreted as alphanumeric characters (text). Images, sound files, and movie files are almost always binary data files. So-called plain-text files, HTML files, and XML files (consisting entirely of text characters) are distinguished from binary data files and referred to as plain-text or ASCII files. Confusion arises in files that represent text but which have their own proprietary format for representing text characters and text display instructions. Although these files are intended to display text, they are usually referred to as binary word-processing files.

binmode **(Ruby IO#binmode)**—In class IO, this an IO object (often, a file) in binary mode. The binmode method is only useful in MS-DOS, which has a different internal representation for the newline character than is used in Unix systems. It may be preferable, when using MS-DOS files and Unix files together, to treat all the files as binary objects, rather than trying to compensate for the differences in the way that the newline character is represented in either type of file.

biocurator—A person who collects and organizes biological information relevant to a particular biological field so that it can be effectively understood and used by experimental scientists who work in the field.

biomedical informatics—The scientific field that uses the data produced by research laboratories (sometimes called discovery data) and the data obtained from clinical repositories to obtain clinically useful results (for example, new discoveries, tests, therapies, services, or procedures). Because biomedical informatics translates basic science into clinical reality, it is typically regarded as a translational or applied science.

C prompt—In a DOS window, the C prompt lists the path to the current directory and awaits user input. An example of a C prompt:

```
C:\ftp\rb>
```

\ftp is a subdirectory of C: and \rb is a subdirectory of ftp:

callback—In most languages, a callback is a routine that is passed (usually as a reference in an argument list) to other routines. In Ruby, callbacks are built into the standard Ruby syntax, as all methods are allowed to accept optional code blocks (equivalent to subroutines) as passed parameters. See Proc object (Ruby).

CGI—Common Gateway Interface. CGI scripts reside on Internet servers, accept input from Web clients through the HTTP protocol, and return Web pages to the client.

clade—A group of objects (in a classification) that have a common ancestor and that include all of the descendants of that ancestor.

class—A Ruby class is an object that contains methods and variables and can make objects that are instances of the class. In Ruby, each class can inherit from one specified parent class.

class method (Ruby)—Class methods are methods that are sent directly to a class, not to instances of a class. The most common class method is new, which is sent to a class to create a new instance object of the class. For example:

```
Array.new
```

To define a class method, the name of the class followed by a dot followed by the name of the method must appear in the definition line. This is an example of a class method, name, for class Person.

```
class Person
  def Person.name
    "Jules"
  end
end
```

To define an instance method, simply list the method name, without preceding the name with the name of the class. An instance method can be received by any instance object of the class.

class#method **syntax (Ruby)**—In Ruby, different methods in different classes may have the same name. In fact, it is common programming practice to include methods in a subclass that override methods of the same name in a super (ancestor) class. Polymorphism can often be achieved by providing class methods that share a name with methods included in other classes. This means that in Ruby, when you want to discuss a particular method, you need to specify the class that defines the method. The standard shorthand for conveying the name of a method in descriptive text is to write the class name followed by a pound sign followed by the method name. For example,

```
Array#length (designates the class Array length method)
Hash#length (designates the class Hash length method)
```

class-oriented programming language—In an object-oriented programming language, the main job of a class is to create class objects (instances of the class). The classes contain object methods, and the programs operate by sending method operations to instances of the class. This is how Ruby works. Some object-oriented languages create only class methods. Methods are sent to a class receiver, along with the name of an instance object (included as a method parameter). Such languages are usually referred to as object-oriented languages, but they would more precisely be labeled class-oriented languages because all methods are class methods and all method calls are sent to the class, not the class instance object.

class variables—See @@.

classification—An organization of everything in a domain by hierarchical groups, according to features generalizable to the members of the groups.

`close` **(Ruby IO#close)**—Closes an IO object (usually a file) and returns `nil`. After closed, the IO object is not available for read or write operations (until reopened).

```
irb>text = File.open("ruby.txt", "r") => #<File:ruby.txt>
irb>text.close => nil
```

closure—Closures are software constructs that preserve the values of the variables created at the time of its construction, even when those variables have vanished from the block that created the closure. In Ruby, method blocks are always closures, preserving the value of local variables created when the block was called by the script.

cluster analysis—A mathematical method of grouping members of a population into clusters based on their similarity.

coding—The term "coding" has two very different meanings. For computer programmers, coding is the act of writing programs composed of statements that conform to a programming language (that is, the code). To informaticians, coding is the assignment of a code extracted from a medical nomenclature that maps to a concept that is represented within the text. A surgical pathology report may include this sentence: "Adenocarcinoma of prostate extends to the prostate capsule." A nomenclature may assign a code C4863000 that uniquely identifies the concept "Adenocarcinoma." Coding the report may involve annotating the sentence with "C4863000." See autocoder.

`collect` **(Ruby Array#collect)**—Ruby has built-in iterators (`each`, `find`, `collect`, `inject`) that invoke a block of code for each of the elements of an object to return an array consisting of the evaluated result of each iteration. For example,

```
irb>[1,2,3,4,5].collect{|element| element=0 unless element>3}
=> [0, 0, 0, nil, nil]
```

Common Gateway Interface—See CGI.

Common Rule—In the United States, the Common Rule (Title 45 Code of Federal Regulations, Part 46, Protection of Human Subjects) regulates protections for human subjects involved in medical research. The Common Rule specifies that research using medical records is a type of human subject research and falls under Common Rule protection. Under the Common Rule, medical records can be used freely for research purposes if records are made anonymous by removing any identifying links between the record and the patient.

composition—Composition is a technique used in object-oriented programming wherein objects in a class are bestowed with methods typically associated with objects of other classes. If a human were given the power of flight, this would be an example of composition. In Ruby, composition is typically achieved with the use of modules mixed into a class. Synonyms for composition are layering and aggregation.

concordance—A complete listing of all the words in a text, along with the locations in the text where they occur.

`constants` **(Ruby Module#constants)**—Class method in class Module that yields the constants defined for a class. For example,

```
irb>Math.constants => ["PI", "E"]
irb>Math::PI => 3.14159265358979
```

copying objects (Ruby)—Ruby provides a variety of methods for copying objects (Object#clone, Object#dup, and Module#alias_method).

curator—The word "curator" derives from the Latin, *curatus*, the same root for "curative" and signifies that curators "take care of" things. The curator must ensure that nomenclatures are comprehensive for their knowledge domain, and this can be quite difficult when the knowledge domain is growing rapidly. The modern curator must also ensure that the nomenclature is formatted and annotated in a manner that permits interoperability with other databases. See biocurator.

DAML (DARPA Agent Markup Language)—Shortly after RDF was invented, it was obvious that it contained no descriptors for data types (that is, formal restrictions on the type of data that can be contained in a data object) and for describing some of the the logical relationships between RDF domains. DAML is an RDF extension written in RDF. DAML is easy to understand and implement within RDF documents (*http://www.daml.org/about.html*).

DARPA (Defense Advanced Research Projects Agency)—DARPA is run by the U.S. Department of Defense and is intended to develop technologies of military value. Surprisingly, many DARPA efforts have yielded enormous benefit to society. In particular, DARPA has contributed to the design and implementation of the Internet. DARPA's DAML project adds utility to RDF, the key ingredient of the so-called semantic Web.

DARPA Agent Markup Language—See DAML. See DARPA.

data annotation—Data annotation is the act of supplementing existing data with descriptive data (metadata) and related data from external information sources (for example, clinical or pathological details) for the purpose of enhancing the utility of the data. Today, data annotation is usually accomplished with the help of XML (eXtensible Markup Language).

data integration—Occurs when information is gathered from multiple datasets, relating diverse data extracted from different data sources. Data integration is particularly important to biomedical researchers because data obtained from experiments on human tissue specimens have little applied value unless they can be combined with medical data (that is, pathological and clinical information). In the past, research data were correlated with medical data by manually retrieving, reading, assembling, and abstracting patient charts, pathology reports, radiology reports, and the results of special tests and procedures. Manual annotation of research data is not feasible when experiments involve hundreds or thousands of tissue specimens, and thus, the development of automatic methods for data annotation is a very important area of research.

data-intensive biomedicine—Modern biomedical science is data intensive. Gene, protein, and tissue microarrays allow us to look at changes in thousands of variables all at once. Vast amounts of data are generated from single experiments. Likewise, large hospital information systems routinely collect and store terabytes of patient-related data. A human biopsy sample used in a high throughput array experiment is likely to have a wealth of clinical information stored in one or more hospital databases. Each biopsy has a surgical pathology report describing the specimen and listing pathologic findings. The surgical pathology report may contain an archived image of the lesion and a variety of special ancillary tests, including immunohistochemistry and cytogenetics. The biopsy used in the array experiment may be one of many different biopsies excised from the same patient, and any of these biopsies may contain information pertinent to the experimental study. The patient's entire medical record, with demographic information (age, ethnicity, gender), history, physical examination, treatment, and outcome may reside in one or more hospital databases. The connected informational resources for an experiment can easily involve terabytes of data, and this explains why biomedicine is now considered a data-intensive field.

data mining—A special kind of data searching in which a valued class of data is sought from within one or more data sets. The role of the biomedical data miner is to confer sense on an otherwise inchoate data collection.

data object—In the simpler past, it was easy to think of data as a number or as a collection of numbers. Today, almost all information can be represented digitally, and any type of information can be annotated with other information. For instance, an electrocardiogram (ECG) trace can be represented by a binary image, and the binary image can be annotated with information related to the format of the image, the ECG pattern of the image, the diagnosis rendered, a patient identifier, an ECG identifier, and so forth. The data related to the ECG can be attached to the patient's EMR (Electronic Medical Record) in whole or in part and can also be attached to other reports generated in the hospital (for example, billing records). Rather than thinking of the ECG as a record, it may be advantageous to think of the ECG as a data object, with a set of possible data elements belonging to the object, as well as a set of methods (software routines) that can be called on to port sets of these data elements to other objects and a set of general properties (list of methods) that are shared with other designated data objects. See also object-oriented programming.

data sharing—Data sharing involves one entity allowing data (whole datasets, specific records, or specific items from one or more records) to be accessed by another entity. This process may permit no-charge open access to the public, or it can be performed on a fee basis, through contracts and other business arrangements. It may be performed to comply with administrative or regulatory requirements, or it may be performed under the duress of a subpoena, or it may be performed as an altruistic gesture. In all cases, medical data sharing transactions must protect patients from harm (that is, in particular, a loss of privacy or breach of confidentiality).

Defense Advanced Research Projects Agency—See DARPA.

deidentification—Removal of personal identifiers from text. Closely related to anonymization but differs in one aspect: Deidentification can be reversible. A deidentified document may permit identifiers to be restored under carefully specified conditions approved by an Institutional Review Board. An anonymized document is prepared so that identifying information is irreversibly unlinked to individuals.

destructive method—See imperative programming.

Developmental Lineage Classification and Taxonomy of Neoplasms—The shortened name is the Neoplasm Classification. This is a free nomenclature that consists of classified names of human neoplasms. Over 130,000 names of neoplasms organized under about 6,000 concepts are included in the 2007 version of the Neoplasm Classification. The neoplasms are classified by their developmental lineage. Several versions of the classification files are available (XML version, simple ASCII list of neoplasms, and a flat-file list of lineage ancestries for each term). See the Appendix.

DICOM (Digital Imaging and Communications in Medicine)—A standard format and network protocol for medical images. DICOM is used almost exclusively by Radiology departments and by the manufacturers of radiology equipment (for example, MRIs and CT scanners) to pass image data to PACS systems. See PACS.

dictionary (Ruby)—A synonym for associative array or hash. See associative array.

dictionary—A vocabulary or a nomenclature with definitions for each entry.

differentiated software—Software developers sometimes speak of undifferentiated software and of differentiated software. Differentiated software is developed for a specific use and is often commissioned by a specific user. An example would be a hospital information system designed to meet the needs of a specific facility and to interface with the equipment held at the facility. Undifferentiated software are code fragments, code modules, or utilities designed to implement basic, general, and well-known computer algorithms or that solve very common computational tasks. Virtually all of the Ruby code included in this book could be called undifferentiated software.

`Digest`—Module for producing one-way hashes for strings using MD5, SHA, or RIPEMD methods.

Digital Imaging and Communications in Medicine—See DICOM.

`Dir` **(Ruby)**—`Dir` is Ruby's directory and filesystem class. For example,

```
#!/usr/local/bin/ruby
print((Dir.glob("*")).join("\n"))
exit
```

In this example, the `Dir` class method `glob` pulls all of the files and subdirectories from the current directory.

discovery—In programming, discovery is a technique in which a computer program dynamically finds information (often about an aspect of a client or server's configuration) that determines actions (often the choice of routines, arguments, or interchange protocol) necessary to execute the program successfully. Discovery is closely related to reflection. See reflection.

discrimination (statistics)—Finding features that separate members of a group according to expected variations in group behavior. Examples of discrimination in medicine are "grading and staging." Grading and staging involve reporting additional morphologic features (grading) or clinical behavior (staging) that place a tumor into a group with a predictable clinical course or response to therapy.

DOS command line—Although DOS (Disk Operating System) is seldom used as a computer operating system, all versions of Windows come with a DOS application that can be found by searching your desktop for All Programs>Accessories>Command Prompt. Clicking on the DOS program icon results in a black DOS window featuring a C prompt (see the top line of Figure 1.2.1). The DOS window is the easiest way to launch command-line applications (such as Ruby Scripts). For example,

```
C:\ftp\rb>ruby interest.rb
```

This command-line would launch the Ruby script, `interest.rb`.

downcase **(Ruby String#downcase)**—Converts string to lowercase characters. For example,

```
irb>"HELLO WORLD".downcase => "hello world"
```

Dublin Core Metadata—There is a fundamental difference between creating a document for oneself and creating a document for others. If you have created a document for yourself, you do not need to include the name of the person who made the document or the date that the document was created or the purpose of the document or restrictions of the use of the document, and so forth. If you have made a document that can be obtained and used by anyone, however, you have got to include all of this information and more. Librarians understand the importance of having a set of information attached to every document that can be used to index documents for retrieval and that establish the terms under which the document can be distributed and used. The Dublin Core is a set of metadata elements (XML tags) that were developed by a group of librarians who met in Dublin, Ohio. Every XML document should contain the standard set of annotations for the Dublin Core Metadata Element set (35, 36).

each **(Ruby Array#each)**—The class `Array` `each` method iterates over every element of the array and passes the array element to a block.

each **(Ruby Hash#each)**—The class `Hash` `each` method calls a block once for each key,value pair in a hash and passes the key,value pair to the block. See `each_key`. See `each_value`.

each **(Ruby IO#each)**—The class `IO` `each` iterator is extremely useful. It parses a file of any size one line at a time. An example is shown with some pseudocode:

```
corpus_file = File.open("pubmed.txt")
corpus_file.each do
    |line|
    <something here>
    <something here>
    end
```

each_index **(Ruby Array#each_index)**—Iterates through an array, passing the index number of the array element (instead of the array element itself) to the block for each iteration.

```
irb(main):001:0> [45,21,99,156,72].each_index{|x|puts x}
0
1
2
3
4
```

each_key **(Ruby Hash#each_key)**—Iterates over each key of a hash.

each_line **(Ruby IO#each_line)**—Same IO#each.

each_value **(Ruby Hash#each_value)**—Iterates over each key of a hash, passing the value (of the key/value pair) to the block.

EHR (electronic health record)—Synonymous with EMR.

Electronic medical record—See EMR.

EMR (electronic medical record)—A computerized version of the venerable patient chart. EMR hospital record systems attach all records and data for a patient to his or her EMR data object. Non-EMR hospital information systems tended to allow patient records to reside unconnected in different software modules and applications throughout the medical system. For instance, a patient's dermatology records might have been saved in the dermatology clinic's software package, and this may have had no connection to the radiologic records kept in the radiology department's PACS system. In theory, an EMR-based system allows a complete set of medical records for a patient to be exchanged between medical centers.

encapsulation—Objects contain (encapsulate) attributes (properties and data), identity (information that distinguishes the object from other objects), and behavior (methods). Most object-oriented languages are characterized by encapsulation, polymorphism, inheritance, and composition.

END **block (Ruby)**—A block of code prefixed by the word "END" that executes before and after other parts of the script, regardless of its location in the script. See BEGIN block.

Entrez—The National Library of Medicine's text-based search and retrieval service that includes PubMed, Nucleotide and Protein Sequences, Protein Structures, Complete Genomes, Taxonomy, and other NCBI databases. An Entrez tutorial is available at

*http://www.ncbi.nlm.nih.gov/entrez/query/static/help/
entrez_tutorial_BIB.pdf*

Enumerable **(Ruby)**—Module Enumerable provides a variety of methods that work particularly well within blocks to perform operations on iterated values. Classes `Range`, `Array`, and `Hash` all mix in module `Enumerable`. Some of the useful methods in module `Enumerable` are `collect`, `detect`, `find`, `grep`, `inject`, `map`, `reject`, `select`, and `sort_by`.

`eof` **(Ruby IO#eof)**—Returns true if the `IO` object (typically, a file) is at its end.

`exit` **(Ruby Kernel#exit)**—Initiates the termination of a script. See `at_exit`.

`extend` **(Ruby Object#extend)**—Provides an instance object with the instance methods contained in the module provided as the argument for the `extend` method. Syntax:

```
object.extend(ModuleName)
```

extending Ruby—The Ruby language can be extended by creating new classes and modules in Ruby. Ruby can also be extended by writing calls from Ruby to external C functions. In general parlance, writing Ruby extensions is taken to mean that you are writing Ruby scripts that call external C functions.

eXtensible Markup Language—see XML.

`false` **(Ruby)**—In Ruby, a statement can be `false`, `nil`, or `true`. If a statement is neither true nor nil, it must be false. Neither zero nor the empty set nor zero-length strings are considered false in Ruby (unlike Perl). In Ruby, everything is an object, including false, as demonstrated by sending the class method to the false object.

```
irb>false.class => FalseClass
```

See `true`. See `nil`.

`fetch` **(Ruby Hash#fetch)**—In class `Hash`, the `fetch` method returns the value associated with a provided key. Options for `fetch` include a default parameter and a default code block (when the hash does not contain the provided key).

For example,

```
#!/usr/local/bin/ruby
concepts = {"first" => "inheritance", "second" =>
    "encapsulation",
  "third" => "polymorphism"}
puts concepts.fetch("second")
puts concepts.fetch("fourth","composition")
puts concepts.fetch("fourth"){|idea|"The #{idea} concept
    is composition"}
exit
```

Output:

```
C:\ftp\rb>ruby try.rb
encapsulation
composition
The fourth concept is composition
```

File **(Ruby)**—The class of file objects. Class File is a subclass of IO, and many of the methods one might generally associate with file operations are found in the parent class, IO.

File transfer protocol—See FTP.

find **(Ruby Enumerable#find)**—Ruby has built-in iterators (each, find, collect, inject) that invoke a block of code for each of the elements of an object to yield some output determined by the iterator. The find iterator yields the first iterated element that yields a true value for an expression contained in the block. For example,

```
irb>[1,2,3,4,5].find{|x| x > 4}   => 5
irb>[1,2,3,4,5,6].find{|x| x > 4} => 5
```

Find **(Ruby Library)**—Contains methods that traverse file paths.

first **(Array#first)**—Operates on instance objects of Class Array to return the zeroth element of the array.

```
irb>myarray = %w[6 9 4 100] => ["6", "9", "4", "100"]
irb>myarray.first => "6"
```

flat file—A file consisting of data records, where each record is either a separate line of the file or is separated from adjacent records by a defined record delimiter. The elements of each record are arranged in a specified order and separated by a delimiter. Flat files are typically plain text.

foreach **(Ruby Dir#foreach)**—Foreach is an iterator method that appears in several classes. In the Dir class, foreach is a class method that calls a block for each filename in a directory. For example,

```
Dir.foreach("."){|file| puts(file)}
```
Prints the files in the current directory, one filename per line.

foreach **(Ruby IO#foreach)**—In the IO class foreach executes a block for every iterated line in the IO object (usually a file).

FOSS (free and open-source software)—This term encompasses both free software and open-source software and can be used to placate sticklers who distinguish between the two related movements. Another term sometimes encountered is FLOSS (Free Libre Open-Source Software), which holds international appeal.

Free and open-source software—See FOSS.

Free software—The concept of free software, as popularized by the Free Software Foundation, refers to software that can be used freely, without restriction, and does not necessarily relate to the actual cost of the software. The generally acknowledged father of the free software movement is Richard Stallman, an MIT visionary who has led an energetic and unwavering campaign to create and freely distribute some of the most valued software applications in use today. The free software movement is similar to the open-source software movement, but some of the features of free software (ability to modify and redistribute software in a prescribed manner as discussed in the software license) are not always guaranteed in open-source software.

Free software license—Virtually all free software is distributed under a license that assigns copyright to the software creator and protects the creator from damages that might result from using the software. Software sponsored by the Free Software Foundation and much of the software described as either free software or open-source software are distributed under one of the GNU software licenses.

Free software movement versus open-source initiative—Beyond trivial semantics, the difference between free software and open-source software relates to the essential feature necessary of "open-source" software (that is, access to the source code) and to the different distribution licenses of free software and open-source software. Most informaticians use the two monikers interchangeably and do not seem to suffer for the oversight. The most important feature common to free and open-source software is that they are nonproprietary. Richard Stallman has written an essay that summarizes the two different approaches to creating free software and open-source software (37).

`ftools` **(Ruby)**—A library of methods, including `move` and `copy`, for class `File`.

FTP (file transfer protocol)—An Internet protocol for transferring files between different networked computers. Files can be uploaded or downloaded using FTP.

functional programming—Uses so-called nondestructive methods that act on an object or variable to yield a return value but that do not actually change the value of the object that receives the method. Most Ruby methods are functional methods. The exceptions are those methods whose names end in an exclamation point. Nondestructive methods can be chained together, one of the more appealing features of Ruby programming. See imperative programming.

gene expression array—Also known as gene chips, DNA microarrays, or DNA chips. These consist of thousands of small samples of DNA arrayed onto a support material (usually a glass slide). Each sample of DNA is prepared by copying molecules of RNA of known sequence onto fluor-tagged sequences of complementary DNA, which are carefully placed on the array. When the array is incubated with cell samples, hybridization will occur between molecules on the array and single-stranded complementary (that is, identically sequenced) molecules present in the cell sample. The greater the concentration of complementary molecules in the cell sample, the greater the number of fluor-tagged hybridized molecules in the array. A specialized instrument prepares an image of the array and quantifies the fluorescence in each array spot. The greater the amount of fluorescence for each array spot, the greater the concentration of the molecule in the cell sample. The dataset comprised by the fluorescent intensity of each posthybridization array spot produces a gene expression profile characteristic of the cell sample. By comparing individual gene expression levels in normal cells and diseased cells, researchers may discover candidate genes that may play a causal role in disease processes. By comparing whole profiles of different tissue samples, researchers may identify subsets of genes representing cellular pathways that distinguish one cell condition from another.

gets **(Ruby IO#gets)**—The class IO gets method reads the next line from the designated IO stream. When the IO stream is STDIN (standard input device, or keyboard), Ruby collects the keyboarded input and assigns it a string object. The last character key entered is the return key. The return key sends a newline character to the input. It is customary to remove the newline character from the input line with class String's chomp! command. The chomp! command removes the newline character (or any designated line separator) if it is present at the end of a line and returns the shortened line.

```
#!/usr/bin/ruby
puts "Enter anything and press the return key"
input = STDIN.gets.chomp!
puts "You just entered \"#{input}\""
exit
Output and interaction
C:\ftp\rb>ruby get.rb
Enter anything and press the return key
hello world
You just entered "hello world"
```

glob **(Ruby Dir#glob)**—In the Dir class, glob returns the filenames provided in the glob pattern. The glob pattern corresponds roughly to DOS's file shorthand, and does not use Regex. For example,

```
#!/usr/local/bin/ruby
print((Dir.glob("*")).join("\n"))
exit
```

In this example, the `Dir` class method `glob` pulls all of the files and sub-directories from the current directory in alphabetic order.

GNU software licenses—The GNU organization publishes two licenses used for software produced by GNU and by anyone who would like to distribute their software under the terms of the GNU license. They are referred to a copyleft license because they primarily serve the software users rather than the software creators. One of the GNU licenses, the General Public License covers most software applications. The GNU Lesser General Public License, formerly known as the GNU Library General Public License, is intended for use with software libraries or unified collections of files comprising a complex application, language, or other body of work (38).

GRID computing—A method for providing Web services by brokering client requests through a network of participating servers. In the most advanced grid computing architecture, requests can be broken into computational tasks that are processed in parallel on multiple computers and transparently (from the client's perspective) assembled and returned.

`gsub` **(Ruby String#gsub)**—Substitutes a substring within a string at every location where a matching pattern is found. The `sub` method works like `gsub` but only makes one substitution at the first match. For example,

```
irb>"Rabies is great".sub(/a/,'u').gsub(/ies/,'y')
=> "Ruby is great"
```

`Hash` **(Ruby)**—An object of class `Hash` is an unordered list of key/value pairs. Associative array and dictionary are synonyms for hashes. The `Hash` class provides a wide variety of methods for `Hash` objects.

hashed message authentication codes—See HMAC.

heterogeneous data—A pathology report and a histopathology image are very different types of data. One is a narrative text containing diagnostic terms along with clinical, demographic, and administrative information. The other is a binary file relating color and position to pixels. These are examples of heterogeneous data that are tied by a medical relationship. A digital representation of a bone x-ray may have a relationship to an operative note, a bill for hospital services, or an accident report. In these instances, the data are likely to have very different types of representations and formats and may have relationships that were not anticipated by the persons who created the data formats for each type of collected information.

HIPAA Standards for Privacy of Individually Identifiable Health Information, Final Rule—Usually referred to under the broader act, the Health Insurance Portability and Accountability Act. Researchers who wish to use confidential medical records must fully comply with this set of regulations. HIPAA permits the use of pre-existing records for human subject research, without acquiring patient consent, when the records are rendered harmless through deidentification.

HIS (Hospital Information System)—The database of all information collected in a hospital, along with the input and output technology for real-time multiuser entry and retrieval of data throughout the hospital.

HL7 (Health Level 7)—HL7 is an international data exchange specification for medical record data. The term "HL7" applies both to the data-exchange specification and the international group of health standards experts who work on the specification. The HL7 specification provides interoperability between the different devices and record types within a hospital and between different hospitals. For example, it may be used to share records between a laboratory information system (with blood test data) and the hospital's billing system. The latest version of HL7, version 3, permits data to be exchanged through XML, using an HL7 metadata vocabulary.

HMAC (hashed message authentication codes)—The one-way hash of a message. The one-way hash value is said to authenticate the message in the restricted sense that if the message that is associated with the provided one-way hash is altered, a new one-way hash computed on the message will yield a different value than the original one-way hash.

hospital information system—See HIS.

HTTP (hyper text transfer protocol)—The familiar Web protocol that permits Web pages to be exchanged over the Internet. Enhancements of server and client functionality (through CGI scripts on the server side and HTML-embedded programs on the client side) empower users to distribute computational tasks using the HTTP protocol.

identifier—Some symbol or thing that uniquely characterizes an object and distinguishes the object from all other objects. In Ruby, every object is unique, and every object is assigned a unique identifier integer. See `object_id`.

imperative methods—Uses so-called destructive methods that act on an object or variable and changes the object or variable. In Ruby, the methods that have an exclamation point in their name, usually as a suffix, are imperative methods. For example,

```
inputline.chop!
```

Replaces the value of inputline with the value returned by the chomp! method (that is, inputline has its last character removed). See functional programming.

include **(Ruby)**—The include statement is sometimes confused with the require statement. The include statement is almost always used with modules. For a class or a module to include another module, the include statement is used to bind the namespace of the module (including module constants and module methods) into the namespace of the object that is importing the module. Of course, in order for a module to be included in an object, the source code for the module must be available to the script, and this is done with the require statement. Typically, modules are mixed into a class by first requiring the Ruby script that contains the source code for the module (assuming the module code is in an external file) and then including the module.

information technology (IT)—All of the software and hardware and intellectual property involved in handling electronic data.

inheritance—In object-oriented programming languages, each class inherits the methods of its ancestors. In Ruby, when a class is defined, you can declare just one ancestor for the class. For example,

```
class Person_name < String
```
String is the superclass of Person_name. See superclass method.

inheritance polymorphism—Polymorphism determined by an object's class hierarchy. When you send a method to an object, the method may not be included in the method definitions of the object's class. When this happens, Ruby searches through the ancestor classes of the object and will dispatch the first method it finds in an ancestor class that has the same name as the sender method, assuming that the arguments for the method are consistent with the arguments required by the ancestor method. The method is polymorphic for the methods that happen to appear in the class definitions of the ancestors of a class. See polymorphism. See interface polymorphism.

initialize **(Ruby)**—A private method called from the "new" method to set up a new instance's state. This usually involves providing newly created objects with a set of instance variables.

inject **(Ruby)**—Ruby has built-in iterators (each, find, collect, inject) that invoke a block of code for each of the elements of an object to yield some output determined by the iterator. The inject iterator accrues a value across all the members of a collection. Examples are as follows:

```
irb>[-1,0,1,2,3].inject(0) {|total, x| total + x} => 5
irb>[-1,0,1,2,3].inject(0) {|total, x| total * x} => 0
```

```
irb>[-1,0,1,2,3].inject(1) {|total, x| total * x} => 0
irb>[-1,1,2,3].inject(1) {|total, x| total * x} => -6
irb>[1,2,3,4].inject({}) {|start,x| start.merge({x*2=>x})}
=> {6=>3, 2=>1, 8=>4, 4=>2}
irb>[1,2,3,4].inject({80=>90}) {|start,x| start.merge ({x*2=>x})}
=> {6=>3, 2=>1, 8=>4, 80=>90, 4=>2}
```

The inject method operates over ranges as well as arrays.

```
irb>(1..30).inject(0){|accum,x|accum + x} => 465
```

instance_methods **(Ruby Module#instance_methods)**—Returns an array listing the public instance methods available to the module or to the class. For example,

```
irb>(Fixnum.instance_methods - Numeric.instance_methods).
join(" ")=> "% to_r << rdiv > prec_f & size to_bn * next +
gcd rpower - id2name / denominator | ~ downto to_sym ^ lcm
upto prec ** power! times numerator succ to_i gcdlcm prec_i
chr [] to_f"
```

See reflection.

Instance methods—Instance methods are the methods that can be sent to receivers that are instance objects of a class. See class methods.

Instiki—A free, Ruby-based, wiki platform. It is maintained at *www.instiki.org.* See Wiki.

Institutional review board—See IRB.

intellectual property—Ideas, methods, algorithms, or processes protected by license, contract, copyright, or patent.

interface polymorphism—When a method of a given name occurs in multiple unrelated class hierarchies (for example, new, each, ==), the method will operate on the receiver regardless of the class of the receiver object, but the result will be class dependent. Interface polymorphism is not used in any of the examples in this book. See inheritance polymorphism. See polymorphism.

introspection—See reflection.

IRB (institutional review boards)—Committees created under the Common Rule by hospitals and research organizations to ensure that human subject research is performed in a manner that protects human subjects. The most important activities of these committees in the realm of data sharing involves ensuring the confidentiality and privacy of patients.

`irb` **(interactive Ruby)**—An interactive interface for Ruby that evaluates individual lines of Ruby code as you build a script. Simply invoke `irb` from the command-line prompt:

```
C:\ftp\rb>irb
```

This will result in an irb prompt that will evaluate any line of Ruby code.

```
irb>"hello".class => String
```

ISO—International Standards Organization.

ISO/IEC 11179 (ISO-11179)—XML data are flanked by metadata tags that describe the data (for instance, <date>October 1, 2005</date>). The metadata in this example is "date," but how do we know what the metadata "date" actually means? How do we know that it is referring to a day of the year and not a type of dried fruit? Even metadata needs to be defined, and the ISO/IEC-11179 sets a standard for describing metadata. Well-defined metadata should be defined in an accessible document that includes the following defining information for the metadata tag: name, the label assigned to the tag; identifier, the unique identifier assigned to the tag; version, the version of the tag; registration authority, the entity authorized to register the tag; language, the language in which the tag is specified; definition, a statement that clearly represents the concept and essential nature of the tag; obligation, indicates whether the tag is required to always or sometimes be present (contain a value); data type, indicates the type of data that can be represented in the value of the tag; maximum occurrence, indicates any limit to the repeatability of the tag; and comment, a remark concerning the application of the tag.

ISO-8601—An international standard for expressing date and time.

iterator (Ruby)—Iterators are one of the most convenient shortcuts in Ruby. Basically, if an object can be enumerated and the object class (or any of its ancestors) supports an iterator method, the elements of the object can be passed to a block that assigns a variable to the object element and performs a block of code. Using iterators, you can achieve more with one line of Ruby than most other languages can achieve with a dozen lines of code.

`join` **(Ruby Array#join)**—In the `Array` class, `join` concatenates each element of an array, separated by the provided parameter. For example,

```
#!/usr/local/bin/ruby
print((Dir.glob("*")).join("\n"))
exit
```

The output would consist of a list of the files and subdirectories in the current directory, with each element of the list separated by a newline character.

jpeg (Joint Photographic Experts Group)—A widely used image format and lossy image compression method. It is by far the most popular format for images found on the Web. It is sometimes referred to as jpg, as .jpg is the suffix used for jpeg file names.

keys **(Hash#keys)**—Returns the array of keys in a Hash object. For example,

```
#!/usr/local/bin/ruby
freq = Hash.new(0)
my_string = "A man, a plan, a canal, Panama"
my_string.downcase.scan(/\w+/){|word| freq[word] = freq[word]+1}
freq.keys.sort.each {|k| print k, " - ", freq[k], "\n"}
exit
```

layering—Synonym for composition or for aggregation. See composition.

lineno **(Ruby IO#lineno)**—In an IO instance object (typically a file), lineno returns the current line location (the line number) in the file.

load **(Ruby)**—The load statement is much like Ruby's require statement. The key difference is that load imports only Ruby scripts (not binary files), and it needs to be provided with the full script file name (including the .rb extension). See require. See include.

local variables—A local variable is a variable that only exists for the duration of its containing code block. At the end of code block, it ceases to exist. A local variable of the same name can be used in several different code blocks without confusion. The evanescence of variables in Ruby simplifies the design of Ruby scripts. In Ruby, all variables are, by default, local, unless they are specifically designated to be instance variables, class variables, or global variables. In practice, Ruby scripts seldom attach nonlocal designations to variables. This is because object methods are designed to do this automatically. In particular, the initialize method typically assigns instance variables to newly created objects. An object's accessor methods will update the value of instance variables encapsulated by the object.

machine translation—Usually refers to programs that transform free-text from one language into another. In the realm of biomedical informatics, the term machine translation is sometimes expanded to include autocoding (extracting terms from free text that match a coded vocabulary, such as UMLS or MESH).

medical subject headings (MESH)—See the Appendix.

medical vocabulary—see vocabulary.

memoization—A method that reduces the performance decline inherent in repeating subroutines. Memoization stores results of calculations from a repeating subroutine in a `Hash` object (or some other data structure). When the repeating subroutine is called, the memoization subroutine "looks" in the `Hash` object to see if the repeating calculation has been previously stored. If so, the stored value substitutes for the repeating calculation.

`merge` **(Ruby Hash#merge)**—The `Hash` class `merge` method combines the members of two hashes. In the following examples, notice that when hashes are merged, strange things can occur if the two hashes contain the same key, with a different associated value in either hash. A block added to the merge can specify how the `merge` method should handle key/value clashes.

Examples are as follows:

```
irb>hash1 = {6=>3, 2=>1, 8=>4, 80=>90, 4=>2}
=> {6=>3, 2=>1, 8=>4, 80=>90, 4=>2}
irb>hash2 = {6=>2, 12=>4, 80=>90, 3=>1, 9=>3}
=> {6=>2, 12=>4, 3=>1, 80=>90, 9=>3}
irb>hash1.merge(hash2)
=> {6=>2, 12=>4, 2=>1, 8=>4, 3=>1, 80=>90, 9=>3, 4=>2}
irb>hash1.merge(hash2){|key,v1,v2| v1+v2}
=> {6=>5, 12=>4, 2=>1, 8=>4, 3=>1, 80=>180, 9=>3, 4=>2}
irb>h1 = {"a"=>"b","c"=>"d"}
=> {"a"=>"b", "c"=>"d"}
```

For strings, a hash merge can preserve all the values in the case of duplicate keys.

```
irb>h1 = {"a"=>"b","c"=>"d"} => {"a"=>"b", "c"=>"d"}
irb>h2 = {"a"=>"y","c"=>"z"} => {"a"=>"y", "c"=>"z"}
irb>h1.merge(h2) => {"a"=>"y", "c"=>"z"}
irb>h1.merge(h2){|key,v1,v2| v1 = v1, v2}
=> {"a"=>["b", "y"], "c"=>["d", "z"]}
```

metaprogram—A program that creates or changes other programs or itself. Metaprogramming is a feature of languages that are modifiable at runtime. Ruby is a metaprogramming language. Ruby most often implements metaprogramming through reflection or discovery techniques. See reflection and discovery.

metasyntactic variables—Variable names that import no specific meaning, such as `x`, `n`, `foo`. These are often used as temporary variables in iterating loops. Good form dictates that metasyntactic variables should be used only sparingly.

method (Ruby)—In Ruby, a method is a subroutine available to a class, class instance, or module. In Ruby, instance methods are declared with a "def" declaration followed by the name of the method in lowercase. Example of an instance method, hello, for the Salutation class:

```
class Salutation
  def hello
      puts "hello there"
  end
end
```

See class method.

middleware—An ill-defined realm of software development curiously described by middleware guru Ken Klingenstein as the "intersection of the stuff that network engineers don't want to do with the stuff that applications developers don't want to do." In more practical terms, middleware is software that operates over a network and supports interoperation between two different software applications. Closely related terms are mediators, wrappers, and agents. All these software tools function to merge, explain or intelligently process diverse types of data spread through a network.

mixins—A technique for including modules within a class to extend the functionality of the class.

mode strings (Ruby)—Assigned characters that designate the mode in which a file may be opened or created. The most frequently used mode strings are r, read only; w, write only; a, write append by starting at the end of a file; and b, binary file mode (applies only to DOS/Windows). See open.

module (Ruby)—In Ruby, a module is a section of invoked code that contains methods and constants assigned to a namespace (the declared module name). For example,

```
module Modulename
  def say hello
    puts "hello"
  end
end
```

Despite this deceptively simple definition, modules are the heart of compositional object orientation and provide a way for classes to acquire methods that enhance the functionality of the class without changing the identity and the purpose of the class. Many of the built-in Ruby classes contain modules that are common to other Ruby classes. One of the most important differences between modules and classes is that modules do not create object instances of themselves. See composition.

MRCON—Pronounced Mr. Con, MRCON is the file containing every term in the UMLS metathesaurus. Each term is assigned a CUI code (concept unique identifier). The most recent UMLS metathesaurus has replaced the MRCON file with the MRCONSO file. See Appendix.

natural language processing (NLP)—Involves parsing through free text (also called narrative text, written text, prose and unstructured data) to produce a particular organization, transformation, or annotation that corresponds, in whole or in part, to the intended meaning of the original text. Machine translation is the prototypical example of an NLP task. The input text is parsed and converted to an output text in another human language. Autocoding is another task that can be performed with NLP. The parsed text is tokenized into parts of speech, recombined, and normalized to conform to the typical organization of parts of speech found in a preferred nomenclature, and mapped to the identical or equivalent terms found in the nomenclature. As an editorial comment of no promised merit, the author believes that NLP-based implementations are always slow and inaccurate. NLP processing should be avoided when free text can be computationally analyzed by some other method.

Neoplasm Classification—See Developmental Lineage Classification and Taxonomy of Neoplasms.

nested class—In Ruby, you can actually nest one class inside the source code of another class.

`new` **method (Ruby)**—The most important purpose of a class is to create class instances. This is done through the `new` method. Some classes have their own `new` method. Other classes have no `new` method of their own and depend on the existence of an ancestral `new`. Examples are as follows:

```
some_array = Array.new
some_hash = Hash.new
text = File.open("filename.txt", "r")
```

In the case of the `File.open` statement, the `open` method in the File class calls the `new` method without being explicitly invoked.

newbie—A novice or newcomer. Usually refers to someone who is just beginning to use a programming language or an intricate technology. Newbies are expected to confess their newbie status when they communicate in public forums with more experienced programmers. See nuby.

`nil` **(Ruby NilClass)**—In Ruby, `nil` is the singleton object that is neither true nor false. It typically appears in Ruby scripts as the returned value for an unsuccessful method call. Although the `nil` object represents emptiness, it is not equivalent to the empty objects of classes (for example, `zero` or `""` or `[]` or `{}`), none of which evaluate to `nil` or to `false` (in Ruby). The `nil` object inherits the `NilClass` class method `nil?`, which returns `true` for `nil` and otherwise returns `false`. Examples are as follows:

```
irb>nil.class => NilClass
irb>nil.nil? => true
irb>5.nil? => false
irb>!5.nil? => true
irb>nil => nil
irb>true => true
irb>false => false
irb>nil => nil
irb>0.nil? => false
irb>nil.nil? => true
irb>"".nil? => false
irb>[].nil? => false
irb>"hello" =~ /a/ => nil
irb>"hello" =~ /ell/ => 1
irb>"hello" =~ /ell/.nil? => false
irb>("hello" == "hello") => true
irb>("hello" == "world").nil? => false
irb>nil.to_s => ""
irb>nil.to_a => []
irb>nil.to_i => 0
irb>nil.to_f => 0.0
```

NLP—See natural language processing.

nomenclature—Comprehensive collection of the words contained in a specific knowledge domain. An example of a fine, open-access biomedical nomenclature is MESH (*http://www.nlm.nih.gov/mesh/*).

Notation 3—Also called n3. A shorthand syntax for RDF providing a cleaner, less verbose format.

nuby—A Ruby newbie. See newbie.

`object_id` **(Ruby Object#object_id)**—Ruby assigns every unique object an object identifier that can be accessed through the `Object` class `object_id` method. Examples are as follows:

```
irb>5.object_id => 11
irb>6.object_id => 13
irb>"hello".object_id => 23120130
irb>"hello".object_id => 23116710
```

```
irb>hello_object = String.new("hello") => "hello"
irb>hello_object.object_id => 23111210
irb>hello_double = hello_object => "hello"
irb>hello_double.object_id => 23111210
```

The "hello" object has two different identifiers even though the string is the same in both cases. This is because an object is simply a reference that points to a location where the string is stored. Each invocation of "hello" results in the creation of a new and temporary object reference with a new object identifier; however, when a new object is created and that object is assigned another name, the object does not change, and the object's identifier is unchanged.

ObjectSpace **(Ruby Module)**—Module ObjectSpace provides a method (each_object) to iterate over the permanent objects (for example, constants, environment variables) available to a class or module. Ruby allows you to extract every object in its object space. For example,

```
irb>ObjectSpace.each_object(Numeric){|object|puts object}
2.71828182845905
3.14159265358979
2.22044604925031e-016
1.79769313486232e+308
2.2250738585072e-308
100.0
=> 6
```

For the Numeric class, the objects are constants, such as the values of PI and e. The each_object method returns the total number of objects (six in this case). If you substitute Kernel for Numeric in this example, you will see about 14,000 internal objects flash on your monitor!

OMIM—Online Mendelian Inheritance in Man. See the Appendix.

one-way hash—A one-way hash is an algorithm that transforms a string into another string in such a way that the original string cannot be calculated by operations on the output value (hence the term one-way hash). These popular algorithms are discussed in HIPAA, where they are referred to as HMACs (Hashed Message Authentication Codes). Examples of public domain one-way hash algorithms are MD5 (25) and SHA, the Secure Hash Algorithm (26). These differ from encryption protocols that produce an output that can be decrypted by a second computation on the encrypted string. Synonyms are message digests and HMACs.

Online Mendelian Inheritance in Man—OMIM. See the Appendix.

ontology—An ontology is a rule-based grouping of members of a knowledge domain. Ontologies support queries and logical inferences pertaining to the (ontologic) group members. They can be used to test data for logical consistency and can be designed to discover relationships between different classes of data.

open (**Ruby IO#open**)—The class IO open method prepares an IO object (usually a file) for reading or writing. If the file does not exist, it calls the new method and creates a file.

```
text = File.open("anatomy.txt", "r")
```
Opens file anatomy.txt for reading

```
outf = File.open("objects.txt", "w")
```
Opens file anatomy.txt for writing

See mode strings.

open access—Open access applies to documents in the same manner as open source applies to software. A formal definition of open access is available at *http://www.biomedcentral.com/openaccess/bethesda/*.

open source—The open-source software movement is an offspring of the free software movement. The reason that the open-source movement was created was in part to placate developers who wanted to sell software and felt the term "free," as in "free software movement," would be misconstrued by prospective customers to mean that the developer requires no remuneration. Although a good deal of free software is no-cost software, the intended meaning of the term "free" is that the software can be used without restrictions. The term "open source" obviates the need to draw this distinction.

open standard—How could a standard not be "open?" Sadly, there are no prohibitions against imposing use and distribution restrictions on standards. Many standards are available only as copyrighted documents sold by the organizations that developed the standard. Some standards have restrictions on the distribution of the standard that may extend to all materials annotated with elements of the standard.

or **(Ruby)**—Boolean operation. Returns true if either of two assertions are true.

overriding methods—In Ruby, any method can be rewritten to change its functionality. To override a method in Ruby, you merely redefine the method in your script or in your class library. You do not need to go to the original method to make a change. In Ruby, when a method call is sent to an object, Ruby initiates a search for the method, ascending through the class hierarchy of the object receiving the method call. It will use the first method (of the called name) that it encounters. For example, here is the file certain.rb, in which we define class Certain and method announce.

```
#!/usr/local/bin/ruby
class Certain
  def announce
    puts "I am certain."
  end
end
```

Here is the ruby script, `override.rb`, in which we require class `Certain`, create an object of class `Certain`, call the announce method, override the announce method, and call the announce method again.

```
#!/usr/local/bin/ruby
require 'certain'
assertion = Certain.new
assertion.announce
class Certain
  def announce
    puts "I have changed my mind"
  end
end
assertion.announce
exit
```

Here is the output of Ruby script `override.rb`:

```
C:\ftp\rb>ruby override.rb
I am certain.
I have changed my mind
```

P2P (peer-to-peer or peer-2-peer)—A protocol for distributing messages (queries and responses) through a network of peers. See peer-to-peer network.

PACS (Picture ArChiving System)—Used by radiology departments to archive and manage their images (for example, MRIs, CT scan and x-rays).

parsing—Moving sequentially through a file, separating the contents according to a chosen intent (for example, parsing words, numbers, lines, and sentences).

peer-to-peer network—Sometimes data do not reside on a single server. To an ever-increasing extent, the data needed by scientist and healthcare workers reside on many different servers distributed over a wide geographic area and organized in a variety of data formats. When a group of data holders need to share their data without moving their data to a central repository, they may choose to create an Internet-based network of peer servers that can all respond to the same requests. The responses from the different peers can be collected into a single document and sent back to the requesting client. As far as the client is concerned, the request for information and the reply document might have been created by a single Website (even though dozens of sites contributed to the reply). The peer-to-peer network is a strategy for data sharing that permits entities to maintain custody and control over their own data.

persistence—The ability to preserve script variables (that is, data structures) after the script has finished executing. Persistence also includes the ability to resurrect these variables when the program is reactivated. Ruby provides a variety of approaches to achieve data persistence. Three persistence methods are marshalling (also called serializing), porting to a database application, and tying to a database manager (such as SDBM).

picture archiving system—See PACS.

pos **(Ruby IO#pos)**—Returns the current location of an IO object (usually a file) as the number of bytes offset from the beginning of the IO object.

print **(Ruby IO#print)**—Prints objects. For example,

```
out.print(value, "\n")
```

prints to the out object (usually a file object)

```
my_hash.each {|key,value| STDOUT.print(key, "--- ", value, "\n")}
```

For each key,value pair in the hash, prints to the computer monitor the key followed by a space and three hyphens and another space, followed by the value followed by the newline character.

printf **(Ruby IO#printf)**—The printf method in Ruby has the same functionality as printf in other languages (C, perl, and so on). Like Regex, printf can be approached as a microlanguage, with its own syntactic conventions. Although you may never need to use printf, you will find that mastering the printf syntax will provide you with a way of instantly formatting your output into presentable columns and rows. To use printf, you assign a field specifier for each of the elements you plan to display, followed by the list of the actual elements that will be formatted into the designated fields. Each field specifier consists of a percent sign, followed by an integer that dictates the size of the column, followed by a dot, followed by an integer that dictates the maximum size of the element to be placed in the field, followed by a letter indicating the type of element (for example, string and decimal integer). Following the list of specifiers (enclosed by quotations) is the list of variables in the same order as their specifiers. In this example, an array is integrated through a block that assigns consecutive elements of the array to a specifier that assigns a column length of 10 and a maximum element size of 6 to a string variable.

```
irb>%w[I am spaced out today].each{|word| printf "%10.6s",word}
```

Output:

```
I       am      spaced      out      today
```

Here is a list of `printf` field specifiers:

```
%%    a percent sign
%c    a character with the given number
%s    a string
%d    a signed integer, in decimal
%u    an unsigned integer, in decimal
%o    an unsigned integer, in octal
%x    an unsigned integer, in hexadecimal
%e    a floating-point number, in scientific notation
%f    a floating-point number, in fixed decimal notation
%g    a floating-point number, in %e or %f notation
```

`private` **(Ruby Module#private)**—In Ruby, private methods are only available to the current object. No object can access a private method that serves another object. A method (and all subsequently occurring methods in a class description) can be made private by invoking the `private` method. For example,

```
#!/usr/local/bin/ruby
class Greetings
    def first
        puts "hello"
    end
    private
    def second
        puts " world"
    end
end
say = Greetings.new
say.first
say.second
exit
```

Output:

```
C:\ftp\rb>ruby private.rb
hello
t.rb:13: private method `second' called
for #<Greetings:0x27edacc> (NoMethodError)
```

By privatizing a method, other objects (including other objects of the same class) cannot change the internal state of an object. In Ruby, the `initialize` method is always private. In general, privatizing methods is an excellent way of reducing the complexity of software. To privatize a single method, use the syntax:

```
private:method_name_here
```

See `public`. See `protected`.

`Proc` **(Ruby)**—In Ruby, everything is an object, including code. Class `Proc` binds code to an object, allowing the code to be recalled anywhere in a script. Class `Proc` also provides a set of class and instance methods that would not otherwise be available to code blocks. `Proc` objects can be invoked with the `Proc call` method. For example,

```
irb(main):003:0> my_code = Proc.new{|x| puts x} =>
#<Proc:0x02c14d6c@(irb):3>
irb(main):004:0> my_code.call(%w[hello world])
hello
world
=> nil
```

`protected` **(Ruby Module#protected)**—Protected methods are methods that are available to objects of a class but are unavailable to objects outside the class. To protect a method (and all subsequent methods in a class description), simply invoke the method `protected` one time above the first applicable method. For example,

```
#!/usr/local/bin/ruby
class Interest
    protected
    def return_number(number)
        return(number)
    end
end
me = Numeric.new
me = Interest.new.return_number(1000)
STDOUT.print(me.to_s)
exit
```

Output:

```
C:\ftp\rb>ruby protected.rb
protected.rb:9: protected method `return_number' called for
#<Interest:0x27edb6c> (NoMethodError)
```

In this example, Ruby protected the method return_number and returned a `NoMethodError`. To protect individual methods, you may use the alternate syntax,

```
protected :method_name_here
```

See `public`. See `private`.

public (Ruby)—In Ruby, all methods (except initialize) are public by default. This means that objects of a class (or a subclass of the class) can access the method. See `protected`. See `private`.

public domain—Works in the public domain are not copyrighted, and anyone can use, copy, and distribute such works freely. Most data produced by the U.S. government cannot be copyrighted and fall into the public domain. Copyrighted materials that have exceeded the term limits of copyright also fall into the public domain. Some people simply waive copyright on published materials, sending their works directly to the public domain. Data, documents, and books that are not owned by anyone fall into the public domain. Sometimes people forget to provide proper citation to authors of public domain material. Public domain material must be cited just like any other original information source. To take false credit for another person's effort is plagiarism, even when the material is public domain. Authors who wish their works to be freely copied and distributed but who wish to retain some sense of attachment to their works might consider establishing copyright under the GNU free-documentation license. The GNU documentation license is designed for manuscripts and books (*http://www.gnu.org/copyleft/fdl.html*).

PubMed—The National Library of Medicine's public database of medical journal articles. It provides easy search access to millions of journal abstracts (*http://www.pubmed.org*).

`puts` **(Ruby Kernel#puts)**—Useful alternative to `print`. Automatically adds a newline character to an object and prints to the standard output by default. See `print`.

`rand` **(Ruby Kernel#rand)**—Returns a pseudorandom floating point number between 0 and a provided integer or between 0 and 1 if 0 is provided as an argument. For example,

```
irb>rand(0) => 0.432647535748461
```

`Range` **(Ruby)**—Class `Range` represents intervals. `Range` has an `each` method that iterates over the members of the range and `Range` mixes in the Enumerable Module, which contains block methods that operate on iterated values. The `Range` syntax is `(first..last)` to indicate all values between and including the first and last values and `(first...last)` to indicate all values between and including the first value but excluding the last value. For example,

```
irb>(1..5).each{|x|puts x}
1
2
3
4
5
```

RDF (Resource Description Framework)—A special syntax within XML that constrains content to assertions that consist of a declaration of a specified object followed by a metadata/data pair that pertains to the object. These assertion triples (specified object, metadata, data) are necessary and sufficient to create statements of meaning. These statements of meaning can be aggregated with other statements from the same dataset or from other datasets, as long as they pertain to the same specified object. A simple syntactical ploy, such as RDF, is the foundation for the semantic Web, in which logical inferences can be drawn from meaningful assertions (RDF triples) distributed throughout the Internet.

RDF ontology—Although ontologists may find this definition lacking in rigor, an RDF ontology is simply an RDF schema (i.e., a dictionary in RDF format) that consists exclusively of classes (that is, no properties).

RDF schema—A formal dictionary of the classes and properties related to a data domain and prepared in a special RDF syntax. RDF documents use RDF schemas when they create new instances of classes contained in the RDF schema and when they use metadata corresponding properties described in the RDF schema. An RDF document can refer to zero, one, or many RDF schemas.

read **(Ruby IO#read class method)**—The read class method enters an IO object (usually a file) and returns a string of a provided length beginning from a provided offset byte in the file. Without length and offset parameters, the read method will return the entire file as a string. Syntax:

```
read(filename,length_of_string,file_offset)
```
Example prints file named `anatomy.rb` to the computer screen.

```
irb(main):011:0> print(IO.read("anatomy.rb"))
```
Should not be confused with class IO instance method of the same name (that is, read).

readline **(Ruby IO#readlines)**—Reads a single line from the IO object and passes it to a string.

readlines **(Ruby IO#readlines)**—Reads all of the lines from an IO object (typically a file) and puts them into an array.

receiver—In Ruby, commands consist of a message (actually a call for a Ruby method) sent to a receiver (an object). The syntax is as follows: `object.method(parameters){block}`. Parameters and block are optional components of the message. Sometimes, when the object receiving the message has a Ruby default value or when it has an implied value of `"self,"` the name of the object is omitted.

recursive method—A method that calls itself.

reflection—A term borrowed from Java to express a set of available methods that provide information about objects appearing in the programming environment. It is synonymous with introspection. Reflection methods can be used to learn about a class system, and they can be incorporated within scripts to dynamically change the behavior of a program. Some reflection methods are `inspect`, `instance_of?`, `instance_variables`, `instance_variable_get`, `is_a?`, `instance_of?`, `class`, `superclass`, `methods`, `ancestors`, `instance_methods`, `constants`, `class_variables`, `object_id`, `private_methods`, `protect_methods`, `public_methods`, `singleton_methods`, `kind_of?`.

Regex—A shortened form for regular expression. It is a formal syntax for describing string patterns. The syntax, once mastered, permits programmers to write remarkably clever and useful pattern matching routines. Many different programming languages and markup languages use the same Regex syntax. An example of Regex is `"b[na]+"`, which represents a string pattern that begins with the letter "b" and is followed by any one of the letters "n," or "a," with at least one occurrence. Thus, "banana" would match the regular expression, as would "baaaaaa," signifying that the regular expression could be useful to computer programmers, monkeys, or sheep.

remote procedure call—See RPC.

`require` **(Ruby)**—When the Ruby interpreter encounters a require statement followed by the name of a Ruby script file (you can omit the `.rb` extension from the file name), it pulls in and evaluates the code from the external file. Use path information in the file name to ensure that Ruby can find the required file and that Ruby does not open another file (of the same name) when it looks through its list of searchable directories and subdirectories (stored in the global variable, $:). Ruby will raise a `LoadError` exception if it cannot fine the required file. The `require` method will try to pull in extension files other than Ruby scripts, including some types of binary files. If you are only interested in requiring Ruby scripts, you may choose to use the `"load"` statement. See `load`.

Resource Description Framework—See RDF.

RPC (remote procedure call)—A protocol that permits a calling program running on a client computer to invoke a computational method and call another networked computer to execute the method, returning the result as a variable that is used in the calling program. This is all done without interrupting the flow of the calling program. RPCs are perhaps the easiest form of networked computation.

Safe Level—See $SAFE.

scan **(Ruby String#scan)**—Repeatedly matches a string against a pattern and returns, as an array, the matching substrings. For example, freq.rb extracts from MESH all words and their frequencies:

```
#!/usr/local/bin/ruby
freq = Hash.new(0)
file1 = File.open("c\:\\entrez\\d2007.bin")   #substitute
    #your filepath here
file1.read.downcase.scan(/[a-z]+/){|word| freq[word] =
    freq[word]+1}
freq.keys.sort.each {|k| printf "%-20.20 s%8.06d\n", k,
    freq[k]}
exit
```

Sample of output:

```
c:\ftp>ruby freq.rb
zyme                   000002
zymofren               000001
zymogen                000013
zymogenic              000006
zymogens               000002
zymolase               000001
zymomonas              000002
zymosan                000003
zymosans               000001
zyntabac               000001
zyrtec                 000001
zz                     000001
```

See downcase. See printf. See keys. See sort.

scope operator—A class can create a new constant. Constants are never declared within methods because the scope of a class constant extends to all the methods of the class. Different classes can declare constants that have the same name. Ruby provides the scope operator (::) to reach into classes and pull out constants specific for the class. The scope operator is also used to call module methods without an `include` statement for the module. Examples are as follows:

```
irb>Math.constants => ["PI", "E"] #See Constants
irb>Math::PI => 3.14159265358979
irb> Math::E => 2.71828182845905
irb>Math::sqrt(4) => 2.0
```

scrubbing—The process of removing objectionable words, private information, and personal identifiers from confidential medical reports.

`seek` **(Ruby IO#seek)**—The seek method moves to a particular byte location in a file or `IO` object. The byte location is determined by a starting position in the file, offset by a preferred number of bytes. The syntax is `fileobject.seek(offset,from_location)`. The offset is an integer that should not exceed the number of bytes in the file. There are three allowed values for `from_location`.

`IO::SEEK_CUR`
Begins from whatever byte location the file happens to occupy when the method is called.

`IO::SEEK_END`
Begins from the end of the file and expects a negative number for the offset to indicate the number of bytes from the end of the file.

`IO::SEEK_SET`
Begins from the beginning byte in the file.

semantics—The study of meaning (Greek root, *semantikos*, significant meaning). Data can be structured and meaningless. Consider this assertion: Sam is tired. This is an adequately structured sentence with a subject verb and object. What is the meaning of the sentence? There are a lot of people named Sam. Which Sam is being referred to in this sentence? What does it mean to say that Sam is tired? Is "tiredness" a constitutive property of Sam, or does it only apply to specific moments? If so, for what moment in time is the assertion "Sam is tired" actually true? To a computer, meaning comes from assertions that have a specific, identified subject associated with some sensible piece of fully described data (metadata coupled with the data they describe). As you may suspect, most data contained in databases are not strictly "meaningful."

semantic Web—A vision of the Internet in which distributed information is organized as meaningful data triples (as described for RDF) that can be used to merge, interrogate, and retrieve heterogeneous information, to classify the subjects of triples into ontologies and to draw logical inferences about the subjects of triples through the use of software agents.

shebang (Ruby)—Ruby scripts always start with a shebang, a pound character, "#" (known by the musically inclined as a sharp character), followed by an exclamation sign, "!" (connoting a surprise or a bang).

simple object access protocol—See SOAP.

singleton class—In object-oriented programming languages, a singleton class is a class that can have only one instance object.

singleton method—In object-oriented programming languages, a singleton method is a method that only operates for a single instance object.

`size` **(Ruby Array#size)**—Returns the number of elements in an array. For example,

```
irb> ["l","e","y","l","b"].size => 5
```

`slice` **(Ruby Array#slice)**—Returns a subset of an array. For example,

```
irb>["l","e","y","l","b"].slice(0..2) => ["l", "e", "y"]
```

SOAP (simple object access protocol)—An XML protocol for expressing Web Service requests and for encapsulating Web Service replies, using a syntax that is operating system and programming language independent.

Socket (Ruby Library)—A software device that allows you to make connections to servers through the Internet. The Ruby Socket Library is a standard library distributed with Ruby. It provides a group of classes that support socket-level communication over the Internet.

software agent—A computer program that can operate in a somewhat autonomous fashion: collecting data, making logical inferences, and proceeding based on automated decisions. Although the definition of a software agent varies, most definitions convey the idea that software agents can interact with other software agents. This requires each software agent to contain instructions to describe itself using a standard data format that is understood by other agents. A special breed of software agent, the autonomous agent, proceeds through multiple interactions without human supervision.

software interoperability—It is not realistic to expect everyone to use the same operating system, the same programming language, and the same software applications. It is nonetheless often necessary to have software that can operate with other software regardless of differences in operating systems and programming language. There are a wide variety of methods by which this can be achieved. The topic of software interoperability has become complex, but it remains a fundamental issue for all attempts to share analytic methods.

`sort` **(Ruby Array#sort)**—Sorts an array in alphabetic order. For example,

```
irb>["l","e","y","l","b"].sort.join => "belly"
```

specification—A specification is a standard way of describing something using well-defined descriptors and well-defined units of measurement and organizing the descriptive data in a manner than can be unambiguously understood.

speed of execution—object-oriented languages, including Ruby, are slow. When I write a Ruby script, I assume that it will run at about half the speed of a nonobjectified Perl script.

`split` **(Ruby String#split)**—Class String's `split` method is used in virtually every script that parses strings of words. The split method breaks a string at locations in the string that match a provided pattern and returns an array. The syntax is `my_string.split(regexpattern, number_of_returned_elements)`.

If no arguments are provided, split divides a string on the space character. If the number of returned elements is not provided, split matches every pattern in the string. Examples are as follows:

```
irb>my_string = String.new("calcifying epithelioma of Malherbe")
=> "calcifying epithelioma of Malherbe"
irb>my_string.split
=> ["calcifying", "epithelioma", "of", "Malherbe"]
irb>my_string.split(/e/)
=> ["calcifying ", "pith", "lioma of Malh", "rb"]
irb>my_string.split(/e/,2)
=> ["calcifying ", "pithelioma of Malherbe"]
irb>my_string.split(/l.+e/)
=> ["ca"]
irb>my_string.split(/l.+e?/)
=> ["ca"]
irb>my_string.split(//)
=> ["c", "a", "l", "c", "i", "f", "y", "i", "n", "g", " ",
"e", "p", "i", "t", "h", "e", "l", "i", "o", "m", "a", " ",
"o", "f", " ", "M", "a", "l", "h", "e", "r", "b", "e"]
```

`sprintf` **(Ruby Kernel#sprintf)**—Much like `printf`, but returns a string (rather than a print operation). See `printf`.

standards development organization—Hundreds and perhaps thousands of organizations develop biomedical standards. Standards development organizations may become members of a standards activities organization, such as the American National Standards Institute, so that their efforts will yield a national or international standard.

standards organizations—Only a few organizations certify new standards, and in the field of biomedical informatics, the two most important are ISO (International Organization for Standardization) and IEC (International Electrochemical Commission).

`stat` **(Ruby IO#stat)**—Operates on IO objects (usually files) and returns a set of data describing the object. An example returns `stat` elements for the `LL_TMPL` file.

```
irb>this_file = File.new("c\:\\entrez\\ll_tmpl")
=> #<File:c:\entrez\ll_tmpl>
irb(main):002:0> this_file.stat.to_a
(irb):2: warning: default `to_a' will be obsolete
=> [#<File::Stat dev=0x0, ino=0, mode=0100666, nlink=1,
   uid=0, gid=0,
rdev=0x0, size=245045067, blksize=nil, blocks=nil,
atime=Sun Nov 26 09:16:14 Eastern Standard Time 2006,
mtime=Sun Oct 15 11:25:32 Eastern Standard Time 2006,
ctime=Mon Oct 16 16:03:35 Eastern Standard Time 2006>
```

`STDIN` **(standard input)**—The default input device, usually your keyboard. Ruby accepts keyboarded input from your computer screen with the `gets` method. See `gets`.

`STDOUT` **(standard output)**—The default output device, usually the computer monitor.

stop words—High-frequency words such as "the," "and," "an," "but," and "if" that tend to delineate phrases or terms in text. They are used in machine translation projects and are also called barrier words.

string—In computer parlance, a string generally refers to a sequence of ASCII characters (that is, a character string). All words are strings. All phrases are strings.

`sub` **(Ruby String#sub)**—Substitutes a substring within a string at the first location where a matching pattern is found. The `gsub` method works like `sub`, but makes a substitution at every match. For example,

```
irb>"Rabies is great".sub(/a/,'u').gsub(/ies/,'y')
=>Ruby is great
```

subclass—A subclass is a class that inherits from a designated parent class. Ruby does not enforce sense on subclasses. In Ruby, you can create a class named `Proteins` and declare it to be a subclass of `Laboratories`. Good programming technique would dictate that a subclass must have an `"is a"` relation to its superclass. In other words, the objects in a subclass should qualify logically as members of the superclass. A `Proteins` class may qualify as a subclass of `Biological_macromolecules`, but it probably should not be created as a subclass of `Laboratories` (because proteins are not laboratories). In Ruby, a subclass may have only one named superclass. Because this condition also holds for the superclass, every subclass has a single ancestral line.

`super` **(Ruby)**—Calls the parent class's version of the method of the same name as the calling method's name. The `super` method provides a way to access methods of a parent class that may have been overridden in the child class. Super is a fundamental feature of the Ruby language (like the syntax for sending a message to an object or an if expression).

```
class Person < String
  def downcase
    puts "Calling Person.superclass method"
    super  #calls String class's downcase method
  end
end
```

`superclass` **(Ruby Class#superclass)**—A method of class Class that returns the ancestor class of a class. Examples are as follows:

```
irb>Array.superclass => Object
irb>Hash.superclass => Object
irb>Object.superclass => nil
irb>Class.superclass => Module
```

See reflection.

`taint` **(Ruby Object#taint)**—Ruby permits you to mark objects as tainted. The syntax is `object.taint`. After an object is tainted, the tainted state may restrict the manner in which the object is used in a script, based on the Safe Level assigned to the script. `taint` is used as a security measure and is usually applied to object received from an external source (for example, the Internet). See list 15.3.1. See `untaint`. See Safe Level.

taxonomy—The list of all the instances in a classification or ontology.

taxonomy.dat—Public file listing the organisms used in genetics research and classified by their evolutionary relationships (available at *ftp://ftp.ebi.ac.uk/pub/databases/taxonomy/*).

`tell` **(Ruby IO#tell)**—Same as IO#pos. See `pos`.

telnet—A network protocol for establishing command-line sessions on remote host computers.

terminology—See nomenclature.

text editor—Also called ASCII editor. It is a software program that is designed to display simple unformatted text files. ASCII editors differ from word-processing software applications that produce files with formatting information embedded within the file. Text editors use the ASCII standard code that converts 8-bit binary sequences into

alphanumeric characters. Text editors have certain important quali-
ties that are lacking in word-processor applications. Text editors are
much faster than word processors because they display the contents
of files without having to interpret and execute formatting instructions. They can typically open files of enormous size, with ease. Most
word-processing files choke on files that are hundreds of megabytes
in length. Examples of free and open-source text editors are Emacs
(see the Appendix) and vi.

thesaurus—A vocabulary that groups together synonymous terms.

threshold protocols—Cryptographic protocols that divide messages into
multiple pieces, with no single piece containing information that can
reconstruct the original message.

Time **(Ruby)**—Ruby class that provides the time in a standard format.
For example,

```
irb>Time.new => Fri Dec 29 18:07:46 Eastern Standard Time 2006
```

times **(Ruby Integer#times)**—Iterates a block of code for a specified
number of times. Syntax:

```
provided_integer.times{|iterating_integer| code_block}
```

For example:

```
irb(main):002:0> 3.times{|iterator_integer|puts
    iterator_integer}
0
1
2
```

time stamp—There are many occasions when it is important to know
when a document was produced. Simply typing in a time and date does
not suffice. You could be purposefully wrong, or you could provide
wrong information inadvertently. The file systems of virtually all computer operating systems automatically add time and date information to
every created file. Unfortunately, falsely setting the computer's time is
a simple matter. In fact, the time and date for any file can be easily
altered. Hospital Information Systems must have a dependable way of
time stamping patient transactions (for example, when specimen was
received, when report was generated, when physician was notified,
when doctor orders were entered, when doctor orders were completed,
when blood was received and when blood was typed and matched).
This sometimes involves regular checks of the computer clock against
an external standard clock and saving time-stamped transaction data on
an external medium that cannot be altered. In some instances, the use
of a time-stamp service may be required.

to_a **(Ruby Time#to_a)**—Ruby has many useful array methods. Unfortunately, these methods only operate on arrays. For this reason, many different classes have their own to_a method that will convert objects of their own class to objects of the array class. For example,

```
irb>Time.now.to_a
=> [25, 12, 14, 27, 10, 2006, 5, 300, true, "Eastern
    Standard Time"]
```

to_i **(Ruby String#to_i)**—Converts an object to an integer. Several Ruby classes have a to_i method, but the most commonly used method is probably the class String to_i, which converts a character string composed of numbers to an integer.

to_s **(Ruby Array#to_s)**—Ruby has many useful String methods; however, class String methods only work on class String objects. For this reason, many different classes have their own to_s method that will convert an object of one class to an object of the String class (so that the object can receive String methods). Example of the class Array to_s method is as follows:

```
irb(main):001:0> [1,2,3].to_s => "123"
```

tr **(Ruby String#tr)**—tr (translate) is a String method that replaces every occurrence of a specific type of character in a string with a specified alternate character. Examples are as follows:

```
irb>my_string = "t-cell lymphoma" => "t-cell lymphoma"
irb>my_string.tr("-"," ") => "t cell lymphoma"
irb>my_string.tr("t","T") => "T-cell lymphoma"
irb>my_string.tr("a-z","A-Z") => "T-CELL LYMPHOMA"
```

translational research—This term includes all biomedical research that attempts to find new therapies, devices, techniques, or tests that can be used in a clinical setting. Much of translational research is aimed at deriving benefit from the many advances in basic biomedical research achieved in the past decade. Data sharing methods would be a type of translational research.

triples—The essence of RDF is that all assertions are composed of three things: a subject, a piece of data (about the subject) and a metadata element (that describes the data). All RDF documents can be deconstructed as collections of triples.

true **(Ruby TrueClass#true)**—In Ruby, all expressions are true unless they are false or nil. Like everything in Ruby, true is an object and belongs to a class TrueClass, as shown by sending the class method to the true object.

```
irb>true.class => TrueClass
```

See false. See nil.

`type` **(Ruby Object#type)**—The "`type`" method returns the object's class. The "`type`" method is deprecated in favor of the object's "class" method.

```
irb>this_array = Array.new([45,16]) => [45, 16]
    irb>this_array.type
(irb):2: warning: Object#type]
is deprecated; use Object#class => Array
irb>this_array.class => Array
```

UML (unified modeling language)—A standard method, developed by the OMG (object management group), for specifying how a complex software application works. Properly specifying software using UML notation (or using UML diagramming techniques) requires significant expertise. For simple software scripts (the kind discussed in this book), UML is not necessary.

UMLS (Unified Medical Language System)—See the Appendix.

UMLS metathesaurus—The UMLS files that contain the terminologies used by the software components of UMLS.

undifferentiated software—Software developers sometimes speak of undifferentiated software and of differentiated software. Undifferentiated software comprises the basic algorithms that everyone uses and reuses in the process of developing new software applications. All software developers have reasons to keep undifferentiated software free because nobody knows who developed the algorithms originally and nobody wants to devote his or her career to prosecuting or defending tenuous legal claims over the ownership of the fundamental building blocks of computer science.

Unified Medical Language System (UMLS)—See the Appendix.

Unified Modeling Language—See UML.

Uniform Resource Locator—See URL.

`uniq` **(Ruby Array#uniq)**—Removes replicate occurrences of array elements.

```
irb>[4,2,2,2,2,3,5,6,4,5].uniq  => [4, 2, 3, 5, 6]
```

unique identifier—An elusive concept. A unique identifier serves to identify an object in a manner that distinguishes the object from all other objects. Three conditions should hold: (1) the unique identifier for an object can serve as the name of the object, (2) if two objects have the same unique identifier, they must be equivalent (that is, interchangeable) objects. In most instances (such as identifiers for people), two objects cannot have the same identifier. (3) If an object has more than one unique identifier (for example, an LSID identifier and a DICOM identifier), the object itself must contain, in an accessible form, all of the unique identifiers that apply. The third feature needs some explanation. If an object does not contain all of its different unique identifiers, an object can be distinguished from itself. In the case of LSID and DICOM identifiers, the LSID identifier could (erroneously) distinguish the object from itself, identified by the DICOM identifier. There needs to be a way of knowing that the LSID identifier and the DICOM identifier both represent the same object. The only reliable way of accomplishing this is to have both pieces of data encapsulated by the object. Of course, the best approach is to forbid subsequent identifiers after the first identifier has been assigned.

unique object—Objects that have immutable features that make the object different from all other objects. Every person is a unique object. Every moment in time is a unique object. The original Eiffel tower in Paris is a unique object. The class of "architectural towers" may not qualify as a unique object, but it can be a fully specified object and can be assigned a unique identifier.

unless **(Ruby Expression)**—Same as if not.

```
unless(expression)
```

equivalent to

```
if !(expression)
```

untaint **(Ruby Object#untaint)**—Removes the taint from an object. See List 15.3.1. See taint. See Safe Level.

URL (uniform resource locator)—The Internet address of a net resource, such as a Web page or an ftp file.

user input—Ruby accepts a line of input from the computer screen using the gets method. See gets.

validation—One of the best uses of biomedical data is to validate assertions using existing data sources. You validate an assertion (which may appear in the form of a hypothesis or a statement about the value of a new laboratory test or a therapeutic protocol) by showing that you draw the same conclusion repeatedly whenever you analyze relevant datasets. It may be useful to compare reproducibility and validation. Reproducibility is when you get the same result (for example, a diagnostic test result or an observed experimental value) over and over when you perform the test. Validation is when you draw the same conclusion over and over. Biomedical datasets may contain millions of test observations, often annotated with clinical outcome data and epidemiologic data. Many people believe that a wide range of clinically important validation efforts could be performed quickly and cheaply if the data collected in hospitals were made available to researchers.

variable—In most computer languages, a variable can be thought of as a container that holds an assigned value. In Perl, x = 5 is an assignment of the number 5 to the variable x. In Ruby, everything is an object, and x = 5 means that the number 5 is assigned to the object x.

vocabulary—A comprehensive collection of the words used in a general area of knowledge. A vocabulary can be less focused than a nomenclature.

Web services—Resident server functionalities that accept client-initiated requests through an interface described by WSDL (Web services descriptive language).

WEBrick—An HTTP server application written in Ruby and bundled in Ruby distributions.

Wiki—A Web page that can be edited from client computers. See Instiki.

WSDL (Web Services Description Language)—An XML language used to describe a Web service's functionalities.

XML (eXtensible Markup Language)—An informatics technology that allows any data element (for example, a gene sequence, the weight of a patient or a biopsy diagnosis) to be bound to other data that describes the data element (metadata). Surprisingly, this simple relationship between data and the data that describe data is the most powerful innovation in data organization since the invention of the book.

XML-RPC—An RPC (remote procedure call) rendered in XML syntax. XML-RPC is the forerunner of SOAP.

XML-RPC **(Ruby)**—Ruby's Standard Library for remote procedure calling using the XML-RPC protocol.

yield **(Ruby)**—In a method that receives a block of code passed as a parameter, the yield method evaluates the block and returns its value.

Zipf distribution—Zipf's law asserts that in a text corpus the frequency of any word is roughly inversely proportional to its rank in the frequency table (11). A Zipf distribution is a listing of the different words in a text, in the descending order of their occurrences. For example,

```ruby
#!/usr/local/bin/ruby
freq = Hash.new(0)
file1 = File.open("c\:\\ftp\\OMIM")    #substitute your
   #filepath here
file1.read.downcase.scan(/\w+/){|word| freq[word] =
   freq[word]+1}
freq.keys.sort.each {|k| print k, " - ", freq[k], "\n"}
exit
```

List of Lists

ALL 58 SCRIPTS IN RUBY PROGRAMMING FOR BIOLOGY AND MEDICINE

Index